BETTER BORN LUCKY
THAN RICH

In this 'Diary of an Ordinary Airman', Flt. Lt. Lovejoy tells of his entry into the RAF before the Second World War. First trained as a pilot, he found his niche when he became a navigator, completing two tours during his war service.

Following demobilization he rejoined the service and, before his final retirement from the RAF in 1965, fulfilled his ambition by navigating across both the Sahara Desert and the Atlantic Ocean.

Lucky, indeed, as one needed to be on bombing raids during the war, one also needed a marked degree of professionalism and dedication — qualities which have always been to the forefront during the author's career.

GW00646582

BETTER BORN LUCKY THAN RICH
THE DIARY OF AN ORDINARY AIRMAN

Flt. Lt., E. W. (Eddie) Lovejoy DFC
RAF(Retd.)

MERLIN BOOKS LTD.
Braunton   Devon

ISBN 0 86303 322-9
Printed in England by Maslands Ltd., Tiverton, Devon

CONTENTS

ILLUSTRATIONS

PROLOGUE
Spring and Summer of 1939

So this was it! This was the end product of years of lapping up facts about aeroplanes, pilots and flying — this now was what it actually felt like to be airborne. After this first flight on 13th April, the world would never seem quite the same to me.

I had applied for entry into the Royal Air Force Volunteer Reserve late in 1938 when, amidst a spate of trench digging, gas mask drills and air raid instructions, it had finally dawned upon us that war was no longer an older man's recollections but a very real prospect. It had enabled me to enter the RAF through the back door, so to speak. My father, like most of his generation, regarded the Services as the last resort of the dead beats and had very promptly vetoed my application to join the regular Air Force via Halton on leaving school. It took time to undergo the aptitude tests and the medical examinations — which were truly very strict because even though time was pressing as never before, the Air Force would not relax any of its very high standards for aircrew although we were only part-time volunteers. However all things come to fruition in the end and so it was that on arrival home from work one evening, there was the so often looked for official envelope, and I was in. After the induction and the taking of the oath at our town headquarters in Store Street, just off Tottenham Court Road, came my assignment to No. 15 Elementary and Reserve Flying Training (ERFTS) at Redhill in Surrey, close to the edge of the North Downs, and that really is how I came to be 2,000 feet up in the calm air of a spring evening, and it really was the start of a kind of Odyssey.

The organizer of air exercises for budding pilots must have known his subjects well since exercise number one was simply entitled 'Air Experience'. This is what it was — fifteen minutes of flight to get the wonder and awe out of the way so that on our next flight instead of goggling at the sights above, below and around, one would actually listen to the instructor and look inside the cockpit at the controls.

Eight more flights totalling 4¼ hours of instruction went by and suddenly it was May and my selected period of fifteen days' continuous training had arrived and it was so much more exciting than the holiday I had given up for it. (The next time I would be on holiday was to be the summer of 1947 and many things had changed for me by then.) On the first Sunday of that dream fortnight I was taken aloft and shown the dreaded spin for the first time. It was a little

7

frightening (it was after all the 13th of the month) both in actuality and somewhat from the Magister's 1938 reputation when some had failed to recover very easily from spins, as it was believed that the elevators were set a trifle too low and thereby shielded the rudder, which made recovery difficult if not impossible. The mechanics of entering a spin entail stalling first and then flicking on rudder at the point of stall. To start a stall, which is nothing more or less than the loss of flying speed, the throttle is closed and the nose pulled up high in the air and, in the ensuing silence of the engineless world, it seems to take an age for the nose to drop from its position 60 degrees upwards in the air in front of you. Recovery from a spin is relatively simple merely requiring sufficient height. Rudder bars are centralized and the steep nose-dive attitude maintained until the rotation of the wings stops. Then a gentle pull back on the stick is required to level off, not forgetting to open the throttle at the same time. I have described this manoeuvre fully because it had some significance in the not too distant future and it was in any case an essential piece of knowledge to have, as badly performed aerobatics often ended in a spin.

Eleven fine spring days later, the really big day arrived — the day of the first solo. I had spent 13¾ hours in the air and it was perhaps about two hours more than the average, but on a lovely May morning I was tested by the Assistant Chief Flying Instructor as my own instructor was still not really confident of my flying ability to go it alone. After 35 minutes of circuits and landings (bumps), out stepped the Assistant CFI and pointing to the sky said, "One circuit and landing and I will sit here and watch." I had the feeling that he really meant, "I will sit here and pray."

There is nothing in an airman's career like that first solo. You have butterflies in the stomach and there is no voice coming through the Gosport tubes from the seat in front — in fact there is no one in the seat in front at all. No one to criticize your take-off, circuit pattern or landing — it was unbelievable but that time was here and now. A rather tentative piece of taxiing ensued, back to the take-off point and then round with the nose into wind, and with a roar the lightened Magister was off into the bright blue May morning. Ten minutes later it was all over with a reasonable landing and a suddenly happier Assistant CFI to say, "That was OK."

The following day my instructor took me off on Exercise No. 14, Low Flying. It was very obviously an excuse for him to have an enjoyable 'beat up' but as we sped over the fields of Surrey and Sussex at a height of 20 feet, I discovered that 90 m.p.h. is a lot of speed. Low flying is something else again and although it must be one of the skills in the possession of RAF pilots, it is dangerous and really should only be indulged in for operational reasons — but my word, it is exhilarating! So the 15 days' training period closed with a total of 23½ flying hours under my belt, 7 hours of which were all my own, solo hours.

By 8th June all the solo I had acquired was flying tied to the airfield circuit, practising take-off and landing, and at this stage a check by the Chief Flying Instructor was deemed necessary to ensure that I had picked up no bad habits.

Our CFI was a regular officer, a Flight Lieutenant of some seniority and of a size which filled the front cockpit of the Magister to overflowing, and the possessor of one of the best RAF moustaches I had then encountered. It was rumoured that he was a man of iron nerve and was indeed one of those strange characters who jumped out of aeroplanes when there was no emergency, a parachutist of some experience. We climbed aboard the 'Maggie' and the circuit and landing which followed were acceptable enough to bring forth no comment from the great man. We now proceeded to climb for altitude and at between 4,000 and 5,000 feet, the CFI snapped, "Spin to the left," so I gingerly raised the nose preparatory to stalling. The action was too slow for the CFI and with a firm jerk backwards on the stick, he had the nose of the aeroplane in a very steep upwards attitude indeed. The stall was consequently rather sudden for me and having yanked the stick to the left before actually stalling, we flipped over into a really fast spin. This seemed to take the man in front somewhat by surprise for he uttered no word as we went on spinning violently downwards. I knew that he was in charge, but at 2,000 feet or so I really thought that he ought to call a halt. As he had not, I then used up all my initiative in one go, centralized controls, stopped the spin and pulled the nose up before it struck the ground but forgetting to put the throttle forward and bring on engine power. The result was a rather nice glide at 75 m.p.h. — losing some 300 feet a minute. All further initiative having been drained from me, we continued in this happy state for some little time. Then through the Gosport tubes came a rumbling roar:

"Sergeant Lovejoy!"

"Sir?"

"It is very quiet up here isn't it?"

"Er — yes Sir."

"Might almost be in our graves don't you think?"

"Er — yes I suppose so Sir."

"And we bloody well will be if you don't open that throttle immediately."

This exchange brought me out of the miasma of inaction surrounding me and so the throttle came on and the test duly continued. After a full 40 minutes in the air, we landed and I awaited the wrath to come. The sky was temporarily blotted out as the bulky officer rose and stepped out of the front cockpit and his only words to me were, "It will take more than the likes of you to kill me laddie," which I gathered was some sort of pass mark.

June slipped away into July and finally on the 9th of that month, with my solo hours now totalling 12, I was allowed to leave the circuit at last and practise 'Air Navigation'. Under this rather grand title, I flew compass courses and learned to read a map simultaneously and as there were no such things in those days as control zones and air corridors, I flew happily over the suburbs of South London to see what my home town looked like from 2,000 feet. It was in fact amazing how much of London could be seen on a beautifully fine day like this with no haze to lower the visibility. Four days later I repeated the exercise but the normal town haze was back again on this occasion and it was very much more comfortable to head towards the South Downs, passing over the small and very inactive field at Gatwick Airport!

By the end of the month I had been taught to do steep turns and side-slipping manoeuvres which I felt might be leading up to aerobatics. Then suddenly in August my instructor and I seemed to be spending an awful lot of time together practising forced landings. This exercise was quite fun since I was doing all the flying and would suddenly hear through the Gosports — "Try and land in that field there," and following the pointing finger would come total engine failure as my instructor firmly closed the throttles. On nearly every occasion the approach was too high or too low and certainly it was slab-sided. So we nearly always roared open the throttle and soared up in the air again without actually touching down.

I had suffered the indignity of a self-inflicted 'near one' on a recent fine Sunday morning when once again on circuits and landings. After take-off, I circled Redhill airfield and came in for a landing then saw for the first time that a white T-shaped signal was in the signal square in front of the Watch Office. Now here is where a fatal flaw in our training was exposed. We flew regularly one evening a week and every weekend. However, our ground syllabus, which was very extensive, was taught on only two nights in the week. As there are a multiplicity of subjects to learn, armament, engines, airframes, airmanship, signalling and the like, we only got a piece of information per subject each week. I had therefore not progressed far enough in airmanship to know what the white T-shaped signal stood for. Hence, once again initiative had to be used and unfortunately, I made the wrong diagnosis. I assumed that as the wind was very light, they had told me in which direction the wind was blowing and therefore proceeded to land from the opposite direction. It was only later I found out that when this signal is displayed together with the flying of a black ball from the signal mast, you are required to land compulsorily in the direction of the Tee. I now landed in exactly the opposite direction to the one I should have taken and of course had what wind there was behind me instead of in front, where it was required to help slow the landing speed. The result was very nearly disastrous, the wheels simply would not stay put on the grass and the tail would not come down. As I could not lose flying speed, the only thing left to do was to go round again. The only trouble was that the decision had been left a trifle late and in roaring off into the blue yonder, I ploughed through the green near by — the tops of the trees dotted round the boundary. Nothing daunted and nothing learnt, in I came again in exactly the same direction with the same result. This time I had at least appreciated that an earlier overshoot was required and accordingly leapt off once again. It is true that third time is lucky — on my arrival this time in the same direction as before the wind must have dropped completely away and I managed to stay put on the ground. Minor damage had occurred to the undercart and the CFI was not best pleased, but he did appreciate my explanation and the point was pushed forward to HQ that airmanship must take some priority over other subjects.

On a later Sunday, all we student pilots acquired a salutory lesson from a sombre experience, Redhill's first and only peacetime fatality. The pilot of a Hawker Hart had taken off and at 50 feet or so his engine had failed. He then made the cardinal error of turning back towards the airfield and with only 50 feet of space beneath him, the inevitable happened — the turn lost him his flying speed and he nose-dived into a brand new Fairey Battle, just received, on the tarmac. As the CFI said to all of us afterwards, "Never turn back after take-off at a low height, go straight ahead and make a *controlled* crash landing."

On the last Sunday I flew in peacetime (although of course, we did not realize this was it) I managed two good forced landings, touching down in really small fields. Before my next visit to the airfield, Hitler had invaded Poland and I returned from work at about 5.30 on Friday, 1st September, to find my father waiting at the gate for me. (This was somewhat of a switch as on my early visits to Redhill for flying lessons, I always found Mother waiting at the gate, fearing the worst from this dreadful flying lark.) It appeared that the BBC was broadcasting almost continually that all reservists should report immediately to their places of joining. Having packed my kitbag with probably more than I needed, I set off to Store Street, only on arrival to be confronted with a milling crowd of hundreds of acting Sergeant Pilots all trying to join the war. I was one among many sent off to report again the following morning, the organization just was not geared to the instant mobilization of the 5,000.

I thought that this would be an excellent chance to see, before the unknown events to come took over, that lovely lady who later became my wife. My memories of that evening are very chaotic — as I recall London was in an uproar and travelling was difficult because many of the bridges over the Thames were closed and some form of child evacuation was beginning. I found my lady after a struggle because she too had disappeared from civilian life, as a peacetime Auxiliary Firewoman she had also been mobilized. We met in a Remand Home at Shepherd's Bush now a Fire Service Station, but had very little to say to each other. As I could not reach home that night, I stayed north of the river in my cousin's house in Shepherd's Bush and reported in to Store Street bright and early. Mobilization was then completed and for the first and last time in my life, I refused an advance of pay — my last civilian pay day had been that Friday.

I retained one sharp memory from that peacetime flying period and it is still sharp today. I was on the last circuit of a beautiful May evening at about 8.30, I was solo, relaxed, wildly happy and enjoying the fine weather. Looking below I spied an old man leaning on a fence looking southwards over the vale of Surrey and Sussex. My attention had been caught by his act of lighting a pipe and the flare of the match in the deepening gloom had caught my eye. All of peacetime England was in that scene and here was I very happy doing something I had dreamed about for years — the combination of things made a magic memory that one never forgets. And so to war . . . .

Our concert party, St. Leonards, October 1939. The late (and great) Len Harvey, former Heavyweight Boxing Champion is third from left. The author is top left.

CHAPTER ONE
Training and Other Events

We left Store Street in a very military way, in squadrons of 100 men, four ranks in those days, and marched all the way down Tottenham Court Road, Charing Cross Road and Trafalgar Square to Charing Cross Station. Our destination was a hotel in St. Leonards, but the huge crowds we passed on the way were of course not aware of this but probably thought we were a part of the British Expeditionary Force on the way to France — at least that is my impression by the way they cheered us. I thought it seemed rather like the modern equivalent of going to the Crusades!

Hastings and St. Leonards was a weird interlude lasting for three of the war's first four weeks. I suspect that we were sent there for two reasons, firstly to receive a dose of the Service indoctrination in obeying orders immediately and unquestioningly; and secondly with our usual unpreparedness at the start of the war, we simply had not got enough flying training schools in existence to cope with the massive influx of reservists.

There is no better method of Service indoctrination than time on the square. Ours was the sea front marine parade of St. Leonards and our barracks were a former hotel which had been sequestered, which had a rounded end rather like the bows of a ship. Within a week of our arrival the general disgust with the food we were given was expressed by some wag painting 'HMS Outrageous' on the 'bows' of the barracks.

Our day started early and finished late and was entirely devoted to making us fit enough to push a cliff over. Out before breakfast, we were marched to the pier head where a stiff half an hour of Swedish drill took place. At 8.30 after breakfast, foot and arms drill filled the entire morning whilst afternoons were devoted to football, water polo, boxing and six mile route marches. I became very interested in boxing because our particular Physical Training Instructor (PTI) was none other than the peerless Len Harvey, British and Empire Heavyweight Champion. He was a great sportsman and a gentleman in every sense and we even got him to agree to appear in our concert party.

I mentioned that it was a weird interlude because, believe it or not, we performed our sea front evolutions under the interested gaze of hundreds of holidaymakers making an unadvertised addition to the list of entertainments to be found in St. Leonards that year. It did somehow seem off-key; here we were taking our first steps towards preparing for war whilst half of London seemed to be down here on holiday. The other weird event was the solemn mounting of the guard over the barracks and our Link Trainer, which was located under the marine parade and just at the edge of the beach. I stood several nights, unarmed, outside that trainer gazing out to the dark sea and wondering when a submarine would surface, send out a boarding party and capture our trainer and probably me as well.

One fairly amusing incident happened whilst I was on sentry go round our barracks one evening soon after arrival. One of the more eccentric characters in the same flight as myself arrived back at base, well after lights out, not so clean and bright but slightly oiled. There was no way that he was going to be able to edge past the brightly lit guardroom at the entrance, so obligingly I proceeded to give him a leg up over the wall to an open window. He was half-way there when a stern voice said, "What is going on here then?" and of course there we were caught red-handed by the Station Warrant Officer (SWO). There seemed to be no suitable explanation I could offer, so I stayed silent. Not so my drunken friend.

"Who wants to know?" was his slurred contribution to the gaiety of nations.

Our SWO growled, "I do, and I am the Station Warrant Officer."

To which the drunken reply was, "Prove it." Out came a small shielded torch which was directed on to the SWO's right sleeve there illuminating a massive royal coat of arms sewn on to it. My friend found the throw-away line that ensured CB, and Guard Duty for both of us for the next week — "The only place I have seen that is on a tin of Tate and Lyle Golden Syrup."

Our SWO was a character in his own right, a man transferred from the Army to the newly formed RAF in 1918 and very much travelled between the wars to such delightful RAF stations as Shaiba on the Gulf and various places in India on the North West Frontier. He was known to us as 'Two Fingers' because of the habit he had of stressing his authority to raw trainees by jabbing two fingers at the coat of arms on his sleeve, announcing at the same time that the badge made him a Warrant Officer and therefore far above us in position and usefulness.

On Pay Parade on one occasion I heard him say to one member of our flight — "'Ere, you lad, what's your name?"

"Phillips, Sir," was the reply.

He was told in no uncertain terms, "Then get fell in with the 'F's."

On 5th November we bade our Sussex seaside station farewell, but not before we had the unnerving experience of hearing Lord Haw-Haw announce over the German airwaves that he knew we were all gathered together at Hastings, St. Leonards and Bexhill and we had better watch out. Whether this warning had any influence on the Air Ministry's thinking I know not but certainly soon enough thereafter, the schools were all removed to Cornwall and South Wales.

Throughout Guy Fawkes day we travelled; first to London and then across to King's Cross and on to an LNER train for the first time in my life and all the way up to Brough on the north bank of the Humber, near Hull, to No. 4 EFTS (Elementary Flying Training School). For a lad who had never been further than the Isle of Wight from a London home, the journey was an adventure in itself.

No time was lost now as we recommenced flying training all over again only this time on a biplane, the old Blackburn B2, which resembled the famous Tiger Moth. It had one vital difference however, the cockpit was wide enough for two pilots to sit side by side and this meant that one was now on the end of the instructor's glare when mistakes were made instead of being behind him and safely out of his sight. On the second morning after our arrival No. 1 War Course was airborne and in the next three weeks I had acquired a further 28 flying hours and reflown all the exercises I had soldiered through between April and August of that year. Then on 30th November I was instructed in aerobatics for the first time, and after one hour's instruction was given 45 minutes to practise my own too-slow slow rolls and too-flat loops. Putting the aeroplane in these strange attitudes never really came naturally to me and I suppose that accounted for my anything but smooth flying in aerobatics — I used to think that if I was to spend so much time seeing the world upside down, I might as well have been born a sloth.

During December I was allowed to leave the circuit and explore South Yorkshire, Nottinghamshire and Lincolnshire, an area of England I was to get to know a lot better later on. This was the part of the syllabus I liked best and even at this elementary stage, navigation was enjoyable. We flew busily and attended ground school meticulously right through to Christmas when we did get a short break, but afterwards ploughed on until 20th January. On that evening snow started falling and it did not stop for a month — it was in fact 23rd February before we got airborne again.

To keep us occupied during this enforced period of grounding the Chief Instructor had devised sports programmes which included his favourite sport, cross country running. At this point I must diverge to talk about the car I and three friends had purchased. It was a very old Morris 8 and it had cost £1.10.0 that is 7/6d. (37½p) each and after some garage time it ran quite well. True, somebody had to perch on the front wing and keep tickling the carburettor to keep it going but it had taken us into Hull and back several times using this method. On the day of our cross country run the car was paying one of its fairly frequent visits to the garage at Elloughton.

The Chief Instructor duly started the 31 runners on the course at the camp gates and off we trotted in the direction of Elloughton. As we approached the village we thought that we might as well check on the progress of the car and on entering the garage, lo and behold, it was ready to roll and this time without the benefit of carburettor tickling. Jack Goodman and Ted Kilsby thought that we might as well collect it as we were here, so the four of us piled in and drove off towards North Cave where the rest of the course were wearily plodding their way along the route. As we progressed so we acquired more 'runners' — on the wings, on the bonnet, the running boards, the roof and even on the spare wheel at the back. Of course with such a weight aboard the speed was not very great, about 10 m.p.h. I should say. We drove through South Cave passing the keen types running as if their lives depended upon it, and at the road running up the side of No. 1 hangar — which was out of sight of the main gate — we parked, dismounted our athletes and rounding the corner of the hangar, trotted up to the main gate three hundred yards away in a close bunch of about twelve or so. Here we came unstuck — at the gate stood the CI, stop watch in hand, with his sandy eyebrows raised in sheer disbelief. There then followed a pause of some minutes before the real runners appeared. The old man got his own back though, the speedy twelve were entered for the South Yorkshire Harriers championship cross country some days later and as this was for real, I regret to report that we did not perform too well.

Towards the end of February we witnessed an extraordinary happening. A pilot and gunner had travelled all the way from Lee on Solent to pick up a new Blackburn Skua from the factory on the other side of the field. The Skua was a very heavy single-engined monster and had a gliding angle with no engine power like the proverbial brick-built convenience. Consequently, when this one took off over the Humber and suffered an immediate engine failure, I suppose it was no real surprise that it entered the river at once. Both pilot and gunner surfaced in their Mae Wests (life saving jackets) and were safely brought ashore — of the Skua there was never another sign. I have never seen anybody as pale as that aircraftman gunner sipping hot tea in our Mess. The only time his expression relaxed was when the adjutant gave him his rail warrant for the return trip to Lee. I felt quite glad that I was in the RAF and not the Fleet Air Arm at this point.

On 1st March we did our last day's flying at Brough and incidentally my last solo acrobatics. Two days later we joined a train to York and then changed on to another heading for the frozen north. I left Brough the proud possessor of a flying gimmick — a trick that could only be achieved with a B2 or a Tiger Moth, because the landing speeds of these aircraft were in the region of 45-50 m.p.h. On a day when high wind speeds approach the landing speed, it was perfectly possible to arrive over the near hedge at a height of 1,000 feet and then by a stall and a side-slip, lose all that height directly above the hedge. Then with engine on and nose down, one could slip over the hedge and lose the remaining flying speed, settling neatly inside the boundary. In excessively windy conditions of course one never flew these light aircraft at all, but occasionally having started a flight in reasonable albeit windy conditions, a return to the circuit could find that the wind had perked up during the absence from the field. When the wind had risen to near gale proportions you allowed plenty of space inside the field before landing in case you got blown backwards.

The journey from York to Aberdeen was interesting because it was the first penetration of Scotland by this particular Sassenach and as we steamed further north so the snow got progressively deeper. It had obviously been an even harder winter here than in Yorkshire, where it had been quite severe. With two hours between trains in Aberdeen, we spent a very cold hour looking round the Granite City and then in self-defence, an hour in the bar of the large railway owned hotel, warming up again. Finally, we boarded the train for the scheduled three hours' journey to Kinloss on the Moray Firth. The carriages were all but completely iced over, the water in the lavatories and wash-basins was frozen rock solid, and the heaters were not working. As we slowly moved through the frozen mountains of the Highland countryside it was difficult to decide whether it was colder outside or inside. Through Keith and Inch and many more little villages, each looking more frozen up than the last, we finally reached Elgin where a stop of sufficient length occurred to allow us to visit the Refreshment Room for a much needed hot drink. The remainder of the journey was mercifully brief and after de-training at the tiny Kinloss station, we were whisked off to the RAF airfield where, in our wooden hut, we defrosted in front of the old-fashioned pot-bellied iron stove whose roaring fire had turned the lid a dull red in colour.

Early next morning we paraded on the station square and I could not take my eyes off the sight — real mountains, snow covered on nearly all sides. South were the Grampians, north across the Moray Firth were those of Ross and Cromarty and west hills stretching into the vast distances of Argyll. The air was so extraordinarily clear that mountains 50 miles away were perfectly visible and the beautiful vistas seen from this small piece of flat coastal plain fascinated me throughout my short stay here. I have been back many times since and it is still as rugged and beautiful.

On 8th March I made my acquaintance with the Airspeed Oxford. With my instructor I spent over an hour climbing, gliding, turning and stalling and then over the next four days practised landings, low-flying, one-engined flying and action in the event of a fire — all the necessary preliminaries to going solo again. This time it was even easier, I was off solo after only four hours dual including the test flight before the solo. On the 12th I was off on my own in a box-framed stubby-winged twin-engined aeroplane which had a very high sloping profile when doing a three-point landing and which, with its relatively high wing loading, stalled quite viciously. Nevertheless I was happy, I sat inside my aeroplane in a cabin fully protected from the outside elements, I had two engines at my command and I did not have to perform any more aerobatics.

Once having mastered circuits, approaches and landings, all sorts of fascinating exercises were undertaken. I remember being taken on a height test which consisted in flying round and round in expanding circuits climbing all the time to 12,000 feet. Five days later I did it by myself and reached the incredible (to me at least) height of 15,000 feet. As there was no oxygen fitted one tended to be rather breathless and a little light-headed at this altitude. The descent is always much faster and soon brought us back to full alertness. Quite a lot of time was spent with one or the other engine feathered but as the Oxford glided like a brick-built lavatory it was advisable never to knock two feathering buttons off at the same time.

Air navigation now began to feature largely in the programme and I made the acquaintance of the mountainous country surrounding us. We ventured across the Firth to Evanton and I made my first ever landing away from a base. Finally came the day for my solo exercise which involved flying to Aberdeen and back. I set out boldly enough but after leaving the coast of the Firth heading ESE the cloud began to thicken quite quickly. I was at 4,000 feet heading towards Kinnairds Head with the ground rising up towards me and the cloud coming down. I decided discretion was the better part of valour, turned round and returned, heaving a hearty sigh of relief when the ground became visible once more. I suppose I was always a cautious airman but I never did see the point of getting killed in training by flying into a 'stuffed' cloud.

At about this time a rather nerve racking experience proved the value of the one engined flying time I had put in. I took off one clear cold morning and rounding the circuit flew over Findhorn to the north of the airfield. Just over the village there was a loud bang followed by terrible vibrations from the starboard engine. Not knowing the reason for this, I quickly went through the drill for closing down and feathering the engine. I then proceeded to complete the circuit on one engine and made quite a decent single engine landing. At the end of the landing run the aeroplane swung to the left and then for the first time I had the opportunity to lean across the cockpit and look out of the starboard window. I was somewhat horrified to see that the top half circle of the engine cowling was missing and this of course caused the vibration as the airflow had broken up around all the engine protuberances. I discovered later that my cowling had fallen into the main street of Findhorn just outside the front door of The Crown. Fortunately it was before opening time and no one was about.

Our time in the north of Scotland was drawing to a close although we were not then aware of it. This was the period when the Nazis invaded Norway and there then became requirements for bases within range of Norway. Consequently in early April a Wellington bomber squadron appeared to share the base with us. Several times they disappeared eastwards and each time returned in slightly less numbers and somewhat shot up. Finally one day a Flight Sergeant captain whom we had got to know in the Sergeants' Mess returned in a bad state. Great chunks of fabric were stripped from the 'Wimpey' bomber, holes were all over the aircraft, and severe shell damage was apparent around the cockpit. One dead crew member was removed and the Flight Sergeant, who was severely wounded in the chest and shoulder, was extricated with difficulty. At this point it came home to us what we were really training for. True the flying was all fun and pleasure but this day's sights underlined that all fun must sooner or later be paid for.

When Kinloss became a bomber station it ceased to be a flying training unit and thus we were posted out to Cranfield near Bedford. Columns of transport carried kit and equipment, the rest of us travelled by train except those favoured and talented few selected to fly the unit's Oxfords and Harvards to our new base. Over the next couple of days aircraft landed all over the north of England but rising to the occasion, they eventually all made it to Cranfield.

We started flying on the course again on 2nd May and whilst we progressed through our exercises that month, the fronts crumbled and finally Dunkirk happened. In consequence our air navigation exercises were routed to the west so that we were kept well clear of London to the south of us which now seemed to stand alone in the whole of Europe as the only unconquered western capital. On the 9th I completed a successful cross-country flight to South Cerney in Gloucestershire where a reasonable landing, refuelling and take-off was made within the hour, followed by a successful return to Cranfield. After this we began to practise formation flying because of course it was still envisaged that bombers would attack in formation. Of all the tactical flying exercises I found formation flying to be the most tiring and it certainly demands terrific concentration — we all used to return from an hour's formation flying tired out. Like most things, practice makes more perfect and after some hours we began to get the hang of things and sense our position in relation to each other instead of having constantly swivelling eyes.

Then came 16th May and the ill-fated cross-country to Hullavington and back — well not actually back. The whole affair was messy from the outset as it had been decided that I would do the exercise that day but no aircraft was available that morning. Consequently after lunch a set of tracks and distances with courses all worked out were thrust into my hands and an urgent order given to get airborne as soon as possible. Ten minutes later I was roaring off into the air heading south-west and steering the first course listed in the flight plan I had been given. From the map I could see that I was drifting to the south, so I brought the nose ten degrees to the northwards. Fifteen minutes later the same manoeuvre was necessary and again shortly after that. Although I could not work it out then and there, what had obviously happened was that the flight plan had been worked out that morning and with the three hours or so delay, the wind had changed more than somewhat. Whilst I was flying over ground with plenty of well marked features it was a comparatively easy matter to correct the heading and fly over the landmarks in the direction in which I wished to go. However, having reached Hullavington I now turned on the heading for the next relatively short leg to Old Sarum and immediately started flying over the comparatively featureless Salisbury Plain. Just over fifteen years later I could map read across places like the Sahara and the Arabian deserts, but at this juncture a place like Salisbury Plain was as bad as the trackless jungle as far as I was concerned.

With the incorrect course set it was inevitable that on ETA (expected time of arrival) Old Sarum was nowhere to be seen. I held on for another five minutes until ahead of me in the far distance I could see the glint of the English Channel so obviously I was too far south and therefore turned north-east, but as I was now off the edge of my map none of the towns and railway lines I could see fitted with anything on it. A further anxiety obtruded, fuel was getting on the low side and it was time to find somewhere to land. There were numerous airfields all over Britain but as luck would have it I could not find one. In desperation, by now completely lost with fuel running out and the afternoon ebbing away, I searched for any reasonable landing area and there ahead of me was a very large open space in the now thickening populated area I was flying over.

As I arrived over the top I discovered it was a racecourse and with the happy thought that there must be sufficient room to bring the Oxford in between the ends of the course, I circled and approached. With the flaps and wheels down, I zoomed over the nearer set of racecourse railings and just as I had flared out for a three pointer, discovered a ditch dug right across the course. I suppose it was there to prevent Germans doing what I was about to attempt, but it compelled me to give the Oxford a full burst of throttle to lift it over the ditch and of course this completed my undoing. Throttles were immediately snapped back but the aircraft had far too much speed to be lost in the distance remaining before reaching the far set of race rails. In the event, I slammed on right rudder and brake and succeeded in snapping off the port wing on the railings. The railings themselves collapsed for about fifty yards in each direction.

Switching everything off, I gave a sigh, relaxed and then slowly climbed out of the now silent wreck. Almost immediately six of the largest soldiers I had ever seen surrounded me and despite protests, marched me off to the guardroom situated under the main stand. There I was held infuriatedly incommunicado for some little time until a lieutenant appeared on the scene. My trouble was that firstly we never carried identity papers of any sort when flying (a practice which was happily reversed later on in the war for non-operational flights). Secondly it was a very warm May day (the start of that fabulous 1940 summer) and I was flying only in shirt sleeves under my Sidcot flying suit. Eventually my heated requests to be put in touch with the police were acceded to and a squad car with an inspector and two constables arrived to collect me, my parachute and my elementary navigational instruments. I was allowed to use the telephone to contact Cranfield and I only found out on arrival at the police station that I was in Esher and had just damaged the racecourse railings at Sandown Park.

The person I contacted at Cranfield was our laconic Scots Engineer Officer, Jock Thompson a Warrant Officer, later commissioned and rapidly promoted, who was very experienced and much travelled. I explained my predicament to him to be greeted with, "What can I do about it laddie? You got there, you get back." Eight telephone calls later, I had found an RAF station ready to assist. Northolt sent out two men with a pup tent to mount guard on the aeroplane overnight and gave me and my gear a lift back to Northolt. After a night in a strange barrack block, I visited SHQ to obtain a railway warrant from the Adjutant and proceed on my undignified return to Cranfield. A seat type parachute is an extremely bulky and weighty object to carry very far, and as it is also an expensive item of equipment, you do not let it out of your sight. This combination of circumstances ensured a hot, sweaty and hostile journey back. I boarded a tube train at Ruislip Gardens and travelled right through the heart of London to St. Pancras. I was in a flying suit carrying a flying helmet and parachute. The war was going badly in France and there were all sorts of rumours about German parachutists landing here, there and everywhere, some dressed as nuns and some with bicycles, and if rumour had been only half right, we would have been knee deep in the German army. However, quite a few people believed these stories and there were many mutters and pointed stares on that train and no doubt reports spread to others as people left the train and others got on to be confronted with the unusual sight of an airman and parachute standing just inside. I eventually dragged my weary way back to Cranfield and spent the next day writing reports on the whole affair and finally getting into the air again in the afternoon but this time tied to the circuit practising landings and take-offs. Then it was night flying, something I had been looking forward to and yet dreading at the same time.

To start night flying in 1940 was a far more daunting prospect than in the happy days before the war. Black-out restrictions for England at this time were total and the outcome on a cloudy night was absolute blackness — not the velvety blackness of a tropical or Mediterranean night, but the total absence of any form of light or any plane of reference. Thus to lift an aeroplane into the air in this thick darkness one had to rely entirely on the instruments, and this I had found extremely difficult both in the Link Trainer and under the hood in the air. We were in fact bombarded with the idea that 'seat of the pants' flying was definitely dangerous at night and the instruments were to be one's sole guide. Thus I approached the night of 17th May with no little trepidation.

My recollection of the weather that night is that it was practically windless, cloudy and very very dark. The use of a small torch was mandatory to illuminate the non-phosphorous painted instruments during pre-flight checks and the desire to see the instruments conflicted with the fear that the torchlight would destroy the painfully acquired night vision. Eventually we reached the Chance Light at the end of the runway and here I must explain a little of the ground organization. Goose-neck flares were lit every hundred yards or so down the sides of the runway and the Chance Light was positioned at the beginning of the runway and so placed to light up the first few hundred yards of it to landing aircraft. As soon as their wheels were safely on the ground out went the light. Somewhere within a couple of miles or so of the airfield a red beacon emitting two Morse code letters would enable one to identify the airfield because of course you were also given the bearing and distance of the airfield from the beacon. When ready for take-off a green shuttered Aldis lamp was shone at you and if for any reason the ground controller did not want you to land the red light was pointed at you on the approach and round again you had to go. Should, of course, there be an air raid every light went out and you then had to maintain timed runs round and round until the all clear — *sauve qui peut*!

TMPFU at taxi-post at the end of the runway — **T**hrottle set, **M**ixture in rich, **P**itch of propellers in fully fine, **F**laps down 10° for take-off assistance, and **U**ndercarriage firmly down and locked. Forward fully with the throttles and bouncing and jouncing down the concrete we went, eyes on stalks checking for take-off speed and, on its arrival, gingerly lifting off. I swear I held my breath for the entire period of the time straight ahead to 800 feet. Then a careful turn to the left and on to the downwind leg, trying desperately hard to pick up those fitful pinpricks of lights down the side of the runway. Having got them in sight there was a reluctance to lose them as they slid behind your head and this often led to a truncated downwind leg which meant that you were too high on the approach. Eventually I got it right and then it was wheels down and lock, three masked green lights showing, tap out one's code letters on the downward shining light in the belly of the aircraft, receive a green from the ground and turn on to the final approach. Then one set the flaps down and held speed and rate of descent steady, concentrating on those sickly little flares beside the runway surrounded by total blackness. Finally at about fifty feet or so and with the runway roughly 100 yards ahead, on would come the Chance Light and there was the ground. The hard white light shining down the runway made touchdown judgement very difficult indeed and many a kangaroo leap was made that night.

One hour and forty minutes later my instructor and I had made no less than ten assorted landings and at that point out he climbed saying, "Now do two by yourself." Those two circuits and landings took half an hour of some of the most concentrated flying I had ever done. Eventually at about 1 a.m. I touched down for the last time that night and an hour afterwards hit the hay, utterly exhausted.

This night marked our translation into senior course as the earlier course sewed on their wings and disappeared to various operational training units (OTU). The rest of May saw our introduction to bombing, high and low level, and formation flying. Both demanded considerable concentration which resulted in my sleeping very well at nights. My rating at this half-way stage of the course was 'below the average' and this was certainly true of the night flying — I just could not relax during it and with every muscle nerve and sinew wound up tight I found it totally exhausting. My confidence in this connection was not boosted by the happenings of the night of 14th June. I had just made one circuit and arrival and was taxiing back to the take-off point watching one of my three friends on the course lining up at the end of the runway, as it fortunately turned out with his instructor aboard. I watched them take off and to my horror the aircraft began to veer sharply left when half-way down the runway. Somehow they got the Oxford airborne but still turning to the left and well off its take-off line. Then, just when it seemed they had finally got control and were levelling out, there was a hell of a bang and a flash and then silence until a tiny spark of flame started. The fire engine driver, to his eternal credit, was there in minutes and the small fire was never allowed to grow. The aircraft had literally flown straight into the thatched roof of a two storey house in the village. Both Dennis and his instructor were sitting in the aircraft with the nose sheared off, both suffering only minor injuries and their big problem was how to get down from the roof. Night flying for the rest of us was cancelled and it was a very shaky pilot who tried again four nights later.

Later in June I was navigator over two cross-countries, one through the Midlands to Yorkshire and back, the other to Herefordshire and down to Dorset and back, both flown by a safety pilot. I enjoyed both exercises and completed them very successfully, which should have told me something about myself. The course ran on until 11th July with more bombing practices, real live air-to-ground gunnery shoots and some formation flying, all of which was riveting stuff and very enjoyable in the fine summer weather. I left Cranfield with my wings up and an assessment 'improved to average'.

One day later I had arrived at St. Athan in South Wales for a course on navigation which lasted for six weeks and provided some very enjoyable flying and one or two interesting experiences. It was here that I received my first real grounding in air navigation, and let me say at once that even in 1940 it had become considerably more sophisticated than following a railway line on a map. Not that I had not benefited from that form of navigation — only a few weeks earlier, whilst not exactly lost but temporarily uncertain of my position, I had followed a railway line into a large station and by descending to fifty feet or so had deciphered the station name and discovered that I was actually over Northampton. But as I say, here things were going to be rather more sophisticated — for a start we were issued with sextants. The sextant is of marvellous assistance to a navigator but it does need a cloudless sky which I did not find too often during wartime. However this summer of 1940 was one of our rare ones and we spent hours sitting outside our billets 'shooting' the sun and later the moon and the more easily recognizable stars. In our early attempts St. Athan seemed to move east, west, north and south with every shot.

In the classroom we got a thorough grounding in the mysteries of maintaining an accurate dead reckoning plot.

At this stage of the war, one measured off course (heading) and travelled down it at the air speed flown at and when altering course plotted in the next heading at a distance equal to the number of minutes on the previous course at the air speed flown. When one definitely identified the landmark a line was drawn from there to one's position on the air plot which represented the direction and force of the wind affecting heading, thus making a track. The distance from the landmark to the last plotted ground position was calculated against the time it had taken to fly that distance, which produced ground speed.

Having mastered this technique we took it into the air and proceeded to fly out to sea where there were no landmarks. Instead you estimated your drift through a drift sight (that is the angle between your heading and your tracks) and by taking this drift angle on three headings 60° apart you could find a wind speed and direction. I found sea navigation fascinating and as we were flying in what was then to us a very large aircraft, the Avro Anson, we had a fair sized

24

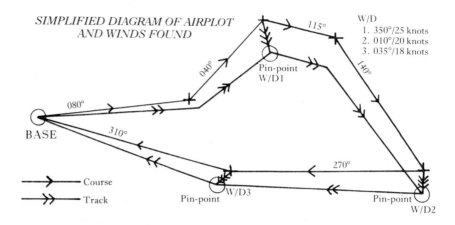

SIMPLIFIED DIAGRAM OF AIRPLOT AND WINDS FOUND

W/D
1. 350°/25 knots
2. 010°/20 knots
3. 035°/18 knots

115°

040°

140°

Pin-point W/D1

080°

BASE

310°

270°

Course
Track

Pin-point
W/D3

Pin-point
W/D2

navigational table to work on and I got fairly good results.

One odd incident happened when flying one day early in August. On the way out of St. Athan, down the Bristol Channel to start yet again another dead reckoning exercise, I saw what I thought was a periscope off Barry Island but my co-navigator (we flew in pairs on the course) equally an innocent abroad, pooh-poohed such an idea. What German submarine would dare to come up the Bristol Channel? I supposed that he was right but felt that it would be equally odd for a British submarine to be there in a submerged state. Anyway we said nothing further until after we had landed back at base some two hours later. When it was then mentioned all hell broke loose — the duty bomber set out to scour the Channel and we got a tongue lashing for being so simple minded. Our pilot was somewhat aggrieved too because we always carried a live anti-submarine bomb in the bomb bay and he simply would have loved to have had a go.

Entertainment in the area around St. Athan was somewhat sparse but there was a cinema in a little town called Llantwit Major which also contained a fish and chip bar which sold excellent fish and chips quite cheaply. The combination proved irresistible on Saturday evenings and we spent most of ours there. We had come out of the cinema at about eight o'clock on Saturday the 10th (they closed places of entertainment early then) and made our way to the fish and chip bar, which was crowded wall to wall with hungry servicemen from all three Services. Suddenly there came the shrill whine of diving aircraft and with one accord we all tried to get down at once. We never made it of course, there were too many of us, and so it was that as the bombs crashed down terribly close we saw the rents and holes appear in the roof and walls. Mercifully no one was any more than bruised but a lot of packets of good fish and chips were ruined. As we struggled to a fully upright position again, still hemmed in by the surrounding bodies, I recognized my large neighbour — a commando. He and I had worked in the same West End office a year or so before.

The course drew to its close on 25th August and I had now spent 275 hours in the air, 106 of them solo, and we were now getting close to operational flying. The next step was to convert to the bomber one was to fly at Operational Training Unit and I had been assigned to the Handley Page Hampden at 14 OTU at RAF Cottesmore in the hunting country of tiny Rutland. Before leaving the Anson though, I would like to mention what a thoroughbred she was — if ever there was a vice-less aeroplane it was the old 'Annie' and this first experience of her was the first in the span of twenty-five years. There was a report that an Anson returning from one of our dead reckoning exercises was attacked by a German Messerschmitt ME 110. The Anson armed only with one gun in the midships turret and constructed largely of wood and fabric could not fight the powerful all metal fighter, so the pilot put down wheels and flaps and each time the 110 made a pass at him, turned very very slowly and as tight as possible. The 110 was far too fast and flashed past the Anson each time without getting his guns to bear. Fortunately for the Anson pilot, the German was at extreme range and had little fuel left for combat time so after several passes he broke off and headed south-east for his home base, leaving the Anson unscathed.

I reported in at Cottesmore on 25th August — a day of high summer in this apparently endless one of 1940. Oakham was the nearest railway station and the little county town of Rutland was destined to be seen many times in the next two years. We were collected by an RAF tender and driven the four miles or so to the RAF station, passing through the pretty village of Cottesmore, and incidentally passed the churchyard to the north of the village containing a few tombstones relating to the victims of the few accidents that had occurred in Hampdens up to this point in time. The following day saw the commencement of our OTU course which involved ground training in such a multiplicity of subjects that we never even got close to an aircraft for over two weeks after our arrival. Even then we spent a further two weeks learning to fly the Anson on which I soloed after two hours and twenty minutes dual. Thereafter we spent most of our flying time on navigation, wireless training and instrument flying. On the 24th September I was introduced to the Hampden and a hate relationship between me and that aircraft began to develop. I think it fair to say that from late September flying ceased to be fun and became a struggle for survival.

My 'flying for fun' days had been somewhat clouded over the previous week when I had set out as second pilot to a staff pilot to do a night navigation exercise which was being used for a practical purpose — to check whether light was escaping from blast furnaces in the Melton Mowbray-Gainsborough-Corby area. We had been airborne for one hour and forty minutes and were 800 feet above Corby circling round the vast furnaces there and making notes of any pin-points of light escaping into the night sky, when the Captain called for tanks to be changed over. In the Anson this was done by pulling two large knobs downwards and pushing two other large knobs upwards and having duly performed this exercise I had just reported change-over complete when both engines cut out. I needed no exhortation to change quickly back to our original tanks when both engines caught again. Within a minute or so the starboard engine had stopped and not surprisingly either, since the fuel gauges showed EMPTY! I once again changed tanks and again both engines cut out and again it was not really surprising as the gauges still showed empty, so very obviously the inboard tanks had not been refuelled after the last flight. By this time we were gliding down from about 600 feet into pitch darkness and my pilot really had no idea what was at the end of the glide but kept it going to prevent a stall and hoped for the best. From my seat on the starboard side, I saw a church spire whistle perilously close past the starboard wing-tip and shouted a warning to everybody to brace for impact. A second or so later there came a jolt from below, followed by a hearty bang and then the squeal of tortured wood and metal, followed by what seemed a prolonged silence.

Some time later (it seemed) the Captain said — "We're down lads, everyone get out," and this order sounded rather low keyed as we were really quite anxious to leave. We assembled at the front of the wreck and checked on our injuries. There were none really — I had banged my left elbow and suffered from the after paralysis of a heavy blow on the humerus (funny bone), the gunner had been backing out of the turret at the moment of impact and the gun breech had come down and slapped him smartly across the head, giving him a fair sized cut, and the wireless operator had knocked his knees rather sharply under the WT table. It was very dark and there was a deathly hush, nothing seemed to be moving at all. By common consent the others moved off to obtain some sort of help and I was left to mount guard on the wreck.

I dare say I was probably suffering from shock and I did feel cold, but ten minutes after the others had left I suddenly got a real shock and my temperature leapt as did I when someone nudged into my back. When my heart had gone back down my throat and my feet firmly on the ground again, I peered behind me into the gloom to see about twenty cows making their stately way towards me. It was their leader who had nudged me and I devoutly hoped there was no bull amongst them. It was well into the early hours of the morning now and I began to wonder whether I would ever see a human again but eventually noises off heralded the arrival of help. These lovely people took me off with them explaining that it had taken a long time to find me as the crew had had no idea of the exact position either. Two aircraftmen being left to guard the shattered Anson, I was taken to the local pub, which turned out to be in the village of

Raunds, where I joined the others, and that was easily the best part of that particular flying exercise.

However, back to the Hampden. This was a mid-wing monoplane bomber powered by two Bristol Pegasus 17s air cooled engines. The airframe design was diabolical for a crew, we were all out of sight of each other and once in position could only move with the greatest possible difficulty and only knew the others were with us by listening to their sepulchral voices on the somewhat rudimentary intercom system. The aircraft could be flown by one pilot only, and although mid-air seat changing was practised (in readiness for the possible wounding of the pilot in operations) it was difficult and dangerous. To start with you had to let down a 20lb armoured seat back behind the pilot and then somehow hold the stick with one hand while he wriggled back past you, and as two could not pass side by side, he usually crept back underneath you whilst you were bent double beneath the top escape hatch. I hated the drill and so did most of the other chaps on the course but there it was, it had to be done.

The biggest draw back of all to me was that there could be no dual flying instruction. I had three flights with three different pilots totalling 1 hour 50 minutes, in which I spent the time crouched behind them trying to spot what they did with their hands whilst peering over one shoulder. Then it was up and off on my own. The first take-off was a nightmare. The aircraft wanted to swing left forcing me to trim rudder and exert pressure on the right rudder bar to keep straight. Having successfully left the ground, I was so busy trimming aircraft, bringing in flaps, easing back throttles, and pulling the hood over my head, that I had reached 1,500 feet before I could look round. By then of course I was quite some way from the airfield and commenced a turn to the left to try and find it again. Unlike the Anson, the Hampden would permit no liberties to be taken and for that reason alone I reckon that the only men who enjoyed flying them were the good natural pilots — I now knew that I was not one of them.

Through the rest of September, October and early November I flew sometimes in Ansons, sometimes in Hampdens, a good deal of it under the hood sweating at instrumental flying. We spent time practising formation flying in Hampdens and in soloing in the Anson at night. There were many bombing runs made with practice bombs across our local bombing range at Grimsthorpe, a couple of thousand yards across and set among the farms of rural Lincolnshire. We practised air firing sometimes firing at and sometimes towing a large drogue. This was rather like a wind sock in shape and was reeled out behind the aircraft — some little way behind to give the amateur gunners plenty of margin for error. It was whilst a pair of us flying Hampdens were engaged thus one afternoon that we were challenged by a Spitfire on a fighting pass; we both banked away and thereby displayed the RAF roundels on the wings and were grateful to see the Spit fly off. The silhouette of the Hampden was alarmingly like that of the Dornier 111, so much so that the ground fire from ships out in the North Sea was almost commonplace. So with high level and low level bombing exercises, cross-countries and instrument approaches, the course wore on towards the approach of night flying exercises for us in the Hampden.

The 26th November was my date for the trial! The usual routine was to take off a little before the light started to fade from the sky and get a couple of circuits and landings before complete blackness set in. I was preparing for my first landing in the grey late afternoon when a red Very signal shot up from the flare-path below and I was forced to go round again. Peering down I could see a stationary Hampden at the end of the flare-path — we had no runways at Cottesmore, the flares were laid across the grass airfield at its widest part with due regard for wind direction. I learnt afterwards that the aircraft below had burst a tyre immediately on starting its take-off run. It took the devil of a time to get it jacked up and change the wheel so that by the time I lined up for my first landing it had been pitch dark for some time. It probably was not a really bad landing but it was certainly a wheeler with too much speed which resulted in a 'balloon', a gigantic kangaroo leap. As I sailed up into the darkness minor panic set in — I thought I must get off again — we'll stall in from this height. Suiting action to thought I rapped the pitch into fully fine and hurtled the throttles fully forward. But, as I said previously, you cannot take liberties with Hampden bombers and the old girl refused to come unstuck again after a bone shattering return to earth. We were now rushing forward into utter blackness, past the last flare, with me making desperate efforts to unstick the aeroplane from the ground. At last it became airborne and immediately afterwards there was a rattling jar right through the aircraft and all indication of height and airspeed disappeared as the Pitot head crumpled under the impact of the far hedge.

I really was in a sweat now, having to keep the aircraft level on the turn and bank indicator, climb fearfully slowly so as not to lose too much speed and stall, and at the same time not lose contact with those precious flickering lights on the ground. I wound up and up into the wintry sky, until I judged there was sufficient air below and ordered the crew to jump. With one accord they said "Piss off" and refused. I explained that although I was going to try and bring it in to land there were a host of difficulties ahead which made a safe landing an odds against chance. However they were not about to jump, so it was a case of best endeavours. A long slow descent, a slow circuit and then we were finally lined up with the flares and at this point, still flying without airspeed and height indication, I thought that perhaps I was a mite too high. I could see the flare-path only now about half a mile away or less and so I eased off a tickle of throttle.

The next event was notable only for its rapidity — I cannot to this day sort out the sequence. It seems the wheels touched the tops of a line of tall elms and literally threw the aircraft over on to its back and straight down on to the ground with the most colossal bang. After that there was a brooding silence broken only by the drip of fuel from broken lines and the hiss of oil on hot engines. This percolated through to my brain and said DANGER in large capitals and the next action was fairly automatic. I released the Sutton harness securing me to the pilot's seat and, upside down as I was, promptly fell on to my head, ricking my neck. I wriggled out of the opening by the hood and joined the other three fleeing figures. Having reached the edge of the field, we sat down to catch our breath and await the inevitable explosion. It never came and after five minutes or so I asked the crew whether anybody felt anything worse than bruises. Nobody admitted to being hurt, so I detailed Nobby, the rear gunner, to walk the five hundred yards across country to the airfield to give them the glad news.

About twenty minutes later a car arrived in the adjoining lane and out stepped my old acquaintance, the Engineering Officer from Cranfield, now an acting Flight Lieutenant and an Engineer at Cottesmore. He walked over to the wreck and was intent on removing the IFF coder (Identification Friend or Foe) in the tail of the aircraft. This was a tricky operation because the machines contained a small charge which could be exploded so that they would not fall into enemy hands. There were two things against the poor chap, firstly we had descended into a very deeply ploughed field and secondly on our entry we had burst through a four strand barbed wire fence which, like a taut violin string breaking, had hurled itself all over the field. Poor old Jock staggered out cuddling the black box, tripped over barbed wire and did several *pas de deux* across the ploughed ridges, disappearing into the night in a stream of strong Scottish oaths.

We were taken back to the station and reported in to the officer in charge of night flying in the watch tower and as I entered the brightly lit room I gasped. Nobby was there all right but there was blood all over his face and hands. I said to him, "Why did you not tell me you were hurt, I'd have sent someone else?"

He replied, "Oh, I was all right when I left you, I walked into a broken barbed wire fence on my way back." A court of enquiry was held two days later and the accident was put down to pilot error due to inexperience, which I thought was a very just verdict.

Four days afterwards I flew a Hampden for an hour and a half on daylight bombing exercises over Grimethorpe Range and a week after that, in fear and trembling, faced my next night flying in the beast.

The 7th December 1940 was once again a dark night, the sky covered in the heavy grey stratus cloud of winter, and when I stepped into Hampden No. 1276, the last shards of light were disappearing. My aircraft had come out from the hangars after a major service only an hour or so before, and it had been flown for fifteen minutes on an acceptance test, found serviceable and accepted back into 'A' Flight. I settled in, checked around the crew, went through the check list and started up both engines. On the run up the port engine spluttered a little but came back to a steady roar and so, trying hard to control the shakes, off we taxied down to the end of the flare-path. Having turned on, steadied, opened up and roared off without a trace of a swing, my spirits lifted with the aircraft. Climbing straight ahead into the black sky everything seemed normal when suddenly without any warning the port engine blew up with an enormous bang. At 900 feet in a climbing turn to port I was I suppose in the worst possible flying configuration for an inside engine to cut. It was a fact that the Hampden had a very poor asymetric (one engine) flying performance. At that time only one pilot at Cottesmore had successfully flown on and landed after an engine cut on take-off and not unnaturally he had been christened 'Lucky'. He was a well above average pilot and, let's face it, I was if anything a below average one.

Be that as it may, this situation was far beyond my limited skills and the immediate result of the loss of an inside of a turn engine in the dark was a stall turn and the start of a spin to the left. I struggled hard to right the aircraft, prayed a bit, swore a lot and sweated with fear — an ugly combination, it must be agreed.

I wrestled with stick and rudder bars with the startled yells of the crew in my earphones — Nobby was groaning, "Oh no, not again." Finally at an extremely low height I had stopped the rotation and began to pull back on the stick, which meant that I didn't stick in the ground like a dart, thus killing us all. No, I struck the very large two foot thick pole carrying the power lines to the camp. Amidst a shower of electric blue sparks the pole snapped and wires crashed the ground. The aircraft caroomed off the stump in a slightly upwards position and now minus the nose and thin twin booms in the tail, still doing close to 120 m.p.h. I never understood this — still don't. My feet had been in the rudder bars when we struck and the rudder bars disappeared with the nose, yet I still had my feet and they were only bruised.

The remaining 30 feet of aeroplane now entirely uncontrolled and indeed uncontrollable, continued through the air some ten feet up and sailed through the canvas tilt of a three ton army lorry parked at the edge of the Married Quarters, now used as barrack houses for we NCO aircrew on the courses. This lost us the wings and over 600 hundred gallons of fuel cascaded high into the air and on the surrounding houses. The remaining piece of fuselage containing all of us crew slid in between two houses in the Married Quarters and came to rest at last. The rest of the evening then turned into pure farce. I was in a state of shock and had only one thought in my head — 'I must get out of this wreck before it catches fire!' and having pulled the pin from my Sutton harness, promptly fell on my face from the pilot's seat, still some three or four feet above ground level. Still the thought persisted and with cracking pains in both legs I was unable to stand up and so proceeded to scuttle away on all fours. As it happened the starboard side of the fuselage had buckled back and the metal had bitten into my right leg below the knee. Having pulled myself away on all fours, there was quite a bit of blood about and naturally the medical attendant assumed I was a fit case for the insertion of pain killing morphia. He was therefore chasing me with an ampoule at the ready and finally overpowering me, inserted it into my arm. I went very drowsy and only came to in the crash room at Sick Quarters.

By this time I had been treated for shock and concussion and the doctor was now about to stitch up my right leg. Remember I had cut the power to the camp, and emergency lighting was the order of the day. Thus, there we were in the crash room with its brilliant white walls and a Tilley lamp for illumination on the same table top on which I was lying. The position of the doctor between the Tilley lamp and the wall was ideal for the projection of a shadowgraph. Thus he took up the needle — a foot long on the wall — threaded the catgut — the size of rope on the wall — and lifting my right leg — the size of a young tree trunk on the wall — proceeded to put half a dozen stitches into the huge cut. I laughed out loud at the pantomime projected on to the wall and faded into a black-out.

It was next morning before I was *compos mentis* again and then it was aches all over, plus fierce pain in both very swollen wrists — which were then found to be broken. So that was the full bill, for very luckily none of my crew were hurt. I spent two weeks in the Sick Quarters emerging as good as new one fine day to pass my rear gunner, Nobby, being carried in on a stretcher. It really was quite unbelievable — he had bumped his knee in our crash and it had taken two weeks for sinovitis (water on the knee!) to develop and cripple him — fortunately only temporarily.

My friend, Ken Letford, always insisted that I owed him a pint. It seems that he put his newly tasted pint down on the bar of the Sergeants' Mess just when I struck the power line pylon and plunged the entire camp into darkness. When the emergency lighting came on some minutes later, all he had in front of him was an empty glass — you will always find opportunists about in any situation.

In the time I was *hors de combat*, another dismal winter had come. Heavy snow had caused fantastic drifts to form and the camp was temporarily cut off from the outside world, thus causing a bit of a drop in the standard of meals for a while, after all there are only so many things you can do with bully beef and hard biscuit.

Because of the bitter weather, there was always intense competition for one of the chairs in a tight ring around the front of our large Mess log fire. Our station Flight Sergeant Armourer 'Mad Cassidy' had a sure-fire if unorthodox method of securing a chair. He appeared behind the circle, casually threw a handful of cordite, shredded from .303 bullets, into the fire and in the ensuing pandemonium as chairs were hastily pushed back and vacated, he would grab the recently vacated centre chair. This ploy succeeded many times but eventually the resident squatters became hardened to the banging and snapping from the fire and sat grimly tight, until the night the nose cone of a 40lb bomb appeared from the chimney above the fire. It had taken some organization on the flat roof of the Mess but 'Mad' got his chair.

On another occasion during my grounded convalescence, I was sitting in the Sergeants' Mess ante-room reading on one cold dark and gloomy January afternoon. The only other occupants of the room were four Australian aircrew sergeants playing poker, and very concentrated they were on the game. I was quite startled when the door opened and the Station Commander appeared with Group Captain HRH The Duke of Kent. I stood up but the four

Australians still concentrated on their poker game. The Duke walked over and stood behind them and enquired what game they were playing. In that unmistakable Australian twang a voice replied, "Poker mate, wanna hand?" The Duke with a broad smile gracefully declined whilst the Station Commander balefully noted the identities of the players. They both walked out again without the Aussies even noticing and when I tried to tell them who had spoken to them they refused to believe it until finally one said, "Well if it was him, I'd have liked his autograph."

Kinloss Station, May 1940. The author (with gas mask and cape) is seen with Sgt. McNair and, in background, Sgt. Parton.

CHAPTER TWO
Limbo

It was mid-January 1941 before I took to the air again. I was given half an hour's testing in an Anson in circuits and bumps and then sent solo for the same amount of time. Two weeks of appalling weather followed, heavy drifting snow, lowering grey skies and chill east winds. At the beginning of February it began to clear again and I found myself in a kind of suspended state of career. I had been posted to 'B' Flight at Cottesmore to act as a staff pilot flying course crews out on their navigational and training exercises in the Anson. This aircraft was the Mark I which had a handle down on the right side of the pilot's seat and to raise the undercarriage one held the stick with the left hand, bent down, thus losing one's views through the cockpit's windows, and twirled mightily at the handle, the size and shape of a large car starting-handle. Forty or fifty turns later the wheels tucked up into their nacelles and then when approaching to land one went into the whole process in reverse. You could always single out Anson pilots who had flown a lot of solo time, they all had mighty muscles in their right arms. Fortunately for me I nearly always had a crew with me and someone in the second pilot's seat to do the manual labour.

Six months went by, more or less peacefully, but the sense of not being in my rightful place — a front line bomber squadron — grew strong. Nevertheless I was in the grip of a giant organization and one simply did not, indeed could not, arrange what was to happen. So I ploughed on, flying all over England with numerous different crews in bad weather and good and acquired another 170 flying hours. But I was still dreading the onset of further night flying and/or a return to the flying coffin, the Hampden.

Finally in August, I made the return to the dreaded night flying and after nearly three hours of dual instruction I was once again off on my own. This time it was a lot better but circumstances were different; I was flying a pretty vice-less aeroplane, it was fine autumn weather in September and there seemed to be less pressure on me. So at the beginning of October, for the first time in my life, I left the relative safety of the airfield circuit and set out for a three hour night cross-country with a pair of navigators and wireless operators, all under training. The night was a fine one and since during the course of the exercise we approached the coast of Lincolnshire twice, I was able to obtain a visual fix on our position and ease my mind of the possibility of getting lost. We were back by midnight and there really was a sense of achievement as I set the wheels down on the grass at Cottesmore after having left it three hours earlier.

So life pursued its even way for the moment, lots of cross-country flights, some at night, a mildish winter by comparison with the last two years and only two really hairy incidents — both of course at night. On one occasion I arrived back to find no airfield lights in sight. I knew I was not lost as I could see the red occulting beacon beating out Cottesmore's code letters for the night. I knew the bearing and distance of the airfield from the beacon so turned on to course over it and flew down the bearing. There was nothing underneath to break the all-pervading blackness and with fuel beginning to run low, the edges of panic curled at my mind. On the second run attempting to locate the airfield I saw flashes of lights like dotted lines off to my left and realized to my horror that this was cannon tracer from an aircraft. We had a JU 88 in our circuit for company and as I estimated that we were in our circuit, I still had my navigation lights on. I quickly threw the switches to reduce us to the same invisibility as my fellow pilots flying around the blacked out airfield. Of course by now everyone's eyes were on stalks and heads were swivelling all over the place. Worse still the wireless operator/air gunner under training had taken his place in the turret, cocked the Vickers machine-guns and was looking for something to shoot at. I had a feeling that this might be more lethal than an attack from the JU. To everyone's great relief he sheered away, probably as worried about his fuel position as I was about mine. Twinkling flares began to appear on the airfield and suddenly as everyone switched on the flying lights again I felt part of an uncomfortably crowded piece of air. I am most happy to say that we all landed without further incident.

The second 'hairy' took place whilst carrying out a night cross-country which involved flying around a one and a half hour's triangular route twice with the navigators under training changing over to navigate one triangle each. On my first return to Cottesmore at the completion of the first triangle I thought that the flares below were looking somewhat dimmer than usual but tucking that thought to the back of my mind, off I set on the second exercise. The thought came back to the front of things with a bang when, having arrived at our dead reckoning position, on the coast, the usual line between land and sea was not in evidence. It is strange but even on very black nights there is normally a faint line of surf or phosphorescent whiteness which you can discern separating land and sea.

On this night it was not there and thinking that the navigator might be a bit in error, we held on for a further five minutes or so, still with no joy. I then decided to complete the triangle on dead reckoning and get a QDM (magnetic wireless bearing) as I thought we were approaching the airfield. This plan worked reasonably well, I should not think we were more than ten miles out on our return, but as we approached the airfield I could see that some of the flares were actually blacking out. Heavy mist was drifting in from the coast at nought feet and, having been airborne for more than three hours, I had rather less than an hour's fuel to dry tanks. The thought of stumbling around blacked out

England with decreasing fuel looking for a place to land was extremely off-putting. So much so, that I performed a very tight circuit indeed, lined up with the only two flares visible and commenced to land. At 300 feet or so we sank into mist and I had to gulp hard to hold the landing configuration — all my instincts said get up and get out of it. A hazy glimpse of a flare ahead encouraged persistence but there was that nasty feeling that perhaps there was a tall tree or so waiting for us. Tense as a tightly coiled spring, I caught another glimpse of a flare almost straight in front of me — and above? Fortunately not, just a scared optical illusion, it passed to the left of me. I pulled the throttles back and let the old Anson do a wheeler. We were down all right but in thick mist and I could not see far enough to taxi the aeroplane safely so, having turned left off the flare-path, I shut down engines and we alighted. It was very very quiet and extremely black and no one it seemed was going to collect us. We commenced walking in the dark mist in the general direction of the control tower and hangars and missed them by nearly half a mile. We did finally identify the perimeter track and walked on it until we arrived at the tower. Here I discovered that I was the only one who had got away with it — seven other aircraft were on their way to Wittering.

The winter of 1941 passed slowly without more than a short snap of excessively bad weather which occurred over the Christmas period and which provided an accidental, odd, and not altogether pleasant experience. I was duty pilot for 'B' Flight and the weather had stopped all flying for a few days. Ice and snow abounded, temperatures were very low and our unfortunate fitters and riggers were working outside on the aircraft, striving vainly to keep barely warm enough to perform their duties. My sole job was to move aircraft from shelters to dispersals and back again after their maintenance schedules had been completed. The senior NCO in charge of the ground crews was a very pleasant chap, one 'Tich' Tee, a balding, rotund little man quite a few years older than myself.

By 8 p.m. the ground crews were working in extreme difficulties, having to break off frequently for a warm up over the fat iron stove which Tich and I had got glowing red hot in the hut. I suggested that maybe conditions were bad enough to justify a rum issue but Tich was of the opinion that Chiefy Lonsdale in the stores would not want to know. I persuaded him to let me go and try my luck and off I went. Somewhat to my astonishment I was given a one gallon big brown jar of service issue rum — on signature of course. Walking carefully back to the flight hut, some half a mile away, I exhibited the prize and we commenced an issue there and then, one for all the ground crew due for a break and one for Tich and myself. The spread of warm inner glow was wonderful and the chaps returned to work if not with alacrity at least more enthusiastically than earlier in the evening. The next lot queued up for their issue and Tich and I joined them. By 11 p.m. all the lads on the flight had enjoyed a rum issue and Tich and I had joined them each time to be sociable.

At this juncture I had no idea that service rum was very different from that sold in any pub but I was soon to find out. Just before midnight, servicing was completed and I left the hut to step outside into a clear very cold night. Within a few steps the weaving started and it became impossible to hold a straight course for the Sergeants' Mess. I have no recollection of reaching it but I must have done because I came to the next morning lying on my bed, fully clothed even to my boots.

Upon staggering down to the Mess dining-room for black coffee with an appalling hangover, I heard numerous stories of how they had found the little man lying in the snow outside the Mess. He was now apparently being thawed out not much the worse for his experience. It was a damn long time before either of us had another rum issue.

By 27th February 1942, I had acquired a total of over 630 flying hours and was firmly in a non-operational rut. The arrival of a new Wing Commander Flying was the catalyst needed to spark off a new change of direction.

Ken Gardiner was a man of positive ideas and great energy of action and his arrival seemed to generate a great blast of activity throughout the flights. Rightly so, I was one of the first to be rousted out of my niche and on 1st March commenced my return to the sausage machine grinding out pilots for the bomber squadrons. After a couple of days' refresher in an Oxford, George Petty took me up in a Hampden and the whole miserable cycle recommenced. I was given 70 minutes of instruction and then let loose by myself for 45 minutes. I can still recall today the cold sweat and tremendous concentration engendered by those half a dozen circuits and landings. The big nagging thought was that I could not have any more trouble because of the three other lives I was driving with me around the sky. Hour after hour and day after day I practised high level bombing over the range at Grimsthorpe interspersing local flying exercises with circuits and bumps. Still I was frightened of the aeroplane and any subnormal attitude it adopted.

Courage is an odd quality; an RAF doctor (and deep thinking man) of my acquaintance expounded on it once to me in the spring of 1943. His opinion was that each man had a finite stock of courage and could keep drawing on it only up to a certain point. Past that point occurred a complete breakdown, a refusal to perform the actions requiring courage and an inability to come to terms with anything. God knows I had seen it happen to two men already and when it does happen medical theory comes slap up against service discipline and loses out every time. I recall one case of a Flight Sergeant gunner who had flown 33 missions, been awarded the DFM and yet could not face No. 34. His 'reward' was reduction to the ranks, loss of pay and flying pay and a skivvie's job at RAF Uxbridge, a 'hard' camp. Well, I had been to the bank of courage a devil of a lot in the last two years and had received endless encouragement from my fiancée, bless her, but here I was facing up to flying the Hampden again at night. Finally on 2nd April off I went and on my fifth circuit in the by now, black of night it all went wrong again!!

Turning on to my short cross-wind leg, eyes off the instruments, searching for the dimly lit flare-path, I must have inadvertently pulled on rudder and very gently pulled back the stick. The result was a classic stabilized yaw from which I only subsequently recovered a bare 200 feet above the camp. I landed coldly sweating yet strangely feverish, hands shaking, eyes blurred and all nerve ends jangling. Having taxied to the control tower, I climbed out, drew a deep breath and drew on my small stock once again by informing the Wing Commander that I could not safely fly the Hampden.

The ensuing blow-up was quite a classic because when the accusation of cowardice was finally made, a dreadful anger caused me to forget discipline and launch into my tirade. The substance was that as I had not yet experienced operational flying, how could I be afraid of it? What I was scared of was the bloody aeroplane, not the Germans. Somewhat taken aback Ken Gardiner said, "Can you navigate?" and with all the assurance of a six weeks' course behind me I said, "Certainly I can." "Good," said Ken, "you can start practising tomorrow, we will post you to a squadron as soon as the Wing Navigation Officer thinks you are fit." Thus I changed trades there and then and although there were a lot of sticky periods not far ahead, career wise I had begun to improve at last. The truth came home to me many months later, I was really a born navigator with an innate sense of direction, a love of ratios and a warm feeling of achievement when I directed an aeroplane to a chosen spot at a given time. On the other hand, I was unquestionably a lousy pilot. Funnily enough the biggest sense of relief stemmed from the fact that I had not now got several other lives in my incapable hands. The larger truth was yet to strike me, that every member of a bomber crew had every other member's life in his hands all the time.

All through May I flew as a navigator in a succession of Hampdens and after having notched up 667 hours as a pilot, I had acquired 14 hours as a navigator by 30 May when I found myself scheduled to navigate a Hampden on the first 1,000 bomber raid to Cologne. After a nail biting afternoon, we knew we were going somewhere because they had spent all day putting real live bombs on our aeroplanes, we were called to briefing. I had dutifully drawn up my charts, collected the beacon call-signs printed on rice paper and some emergency rations and emerged from the briefing room into a prematurely dark world — a thunderstorm was all but over the field. Worse was to follow. The Hampden was entered from the top hatch behind the pilot, you then slid down a panel at an angle of 40 degrees or so to enter the nose compartment where the navigator sat on his little round 'music stool'. I slid to the bottom of the panel, there was a click and a hissing noise. I was stuck fast at the entrance to the nose, on my back, with a Mae West rapidly inflating to make the unsticking impossible. I had snagged my inflation lever against a projecting piece of aircraft, resulting in the undignified position of a stag beetle on its back, arms and legs waving to no effect.

Looking back, I suppose it was funny but at the time it was the very reverse. To begin with I was dressed to withstand cold air at 15,000 feet over Germany whilst the close air of the thunderstorm outside had raised the temperature in the Hampden quite considerably. Secondly, there was the approach of our take-off time and with 1,000 aircraft to rise into the air from the east of England, everyone had their own allotted slot. I boiled, sweated, fidgeted and was eventually released by one intelligent soul breaking open the emergency exit from below. Had it not been for him I suppose I could have starved to death there, for I certainly could not move. By this time, of course, take-off time had passed and we were relegated to the back of the queue, which at least gave us time to reseal the emergency exit.

A half-hour went by as Hampden after Hampden roared across the airfield and disappeared to the south-east. Finally we got our own 'green' and by this time the thunderstorm was very violent and right overhead. Mac (my pilot) P/O McLaughlin drove us across the bumpy grass, bouncing, with everybody clinging to bits of aeroplane like grim death and thinking of the 500 and 1,000 pound bombs in the bomb bay and under the wings, until suddenly we were airborne. One minute later there was the most blinding flash I had seen to date — we had been struck by lightning. All communications had, at least temporarily, packed up. My eyes could not see the plot they were so dazzled, and Mac was having a job to see enough of anything to keep the aircraft upright. At this point we disappeared into pitch black cumulo-nimbus cloud losing and gaining nearly 1,000 feet in switch-back bouts of turbulence.

I was in a terrible state, my chart and instruments were scattered around the floor of the nose, the airspeed varied from just over a 100 to 190 m.p.h. which would not have assisted my dead reckoning plot much even if I had been maintaining one. Mac was steering by gyro-compass which, it should be known, had sufficient precession under ordinary smooth flying conditions to require resetting in agreement with the magnetic compass every 15 minutes. Consequently, 20 minutes passed whilst Mac battled out of the cloud, passing over the coast still in it and thereby preventing me from obtaining any fixed reference point of departure, and whilst I collected myself, chart and instruments (not necessarily in that order). It was only when Mac had come out on top in the clear and I had finally settled down that we noticed that the needle of the magnetic compass was describing lazy circles instead of firmly indicating the direction in which we were flying. This was the straw that finally broke the camel's back.

For over an hour we sought to orientate ourselves but with big black clouds hiding the stars, with turbulence and sudden squalls of wind and rain, we could neither fix position nor determine our heading and such rootlessness was becoming frightening. We obtained a QDM but with a crazy compass how do you fly down a bearing? Faintly on the horizon I spotted an intermittent red glow. We flew towards it, hoping it was our coast, and joy of joys it was a beacon near Orfordness. Having established this I calculated course, distance, and time to base. We set off and nearly half an hour later were back in the neighbourhood of the same beacon. The only solution was to look for other beacons inland, so by gradual beacon hopping and certainly not by the shortest route, we got back.

Two days later, in the same aircraft, we attempted to bomb Essen in the Ruhr and after a very sticky two hours we were back again at the airfield without having seen a thing and had experienced 'chasing the compass needle' again. There was definitely something wrong with that aeroplane, probably the magnetic deviations of the airframe had altered after the lightning strike. Be that as it may, two 'boomerangs' strengthened Ken Gardiner's suspicions and four weeks later after lots of bombing practices but with very little navigation training, I was posted off to a squadron. I was very unhappy that it was not a 5 Group squadron where all my friends and acquaintances were; I was sent to a squadron and to a place in 3 Group and I had never heard of either of them.

The next three months proved to be something of a nightmare. I arrived at Methwold in Norfolk to join 57 Squadron. The airfield was set in deepest, rural Norfolk — a pleasant wooded meadow showing at its green and peaceful best in the summer month of July. True, it had high trees bordering both sides so that there was only one way in and out of it. Administration resided at RAF Feltwell, a pre-war base some five miles away. The squadron had Wellington III aircraft which were much larger than the Hampden and although a bit slower had a very roomy crew quarters inside. But the squadron!! It was a demoralized unit which had taken a terrible pasting in recent weeks culminating in the loss of the Squadron Commander, Flight Commander and the specialist leader officers on the squadron. One squadron leader Flight Commander remained, as acting Squadron Commander, and daylight operations were being flown with the aid of cloud cover and with predictably heavy losses.

I reported to Peter Maggs, the acting navigation officer, and was quizzed about my arrival with no flying brevet on my uniform. This had arisen because on changing trades I had taken off my pilot's wings and substituted an Observer's 'O' wing. The Navigators' union informed me in no uncertain terms that an 'O' wing was the product of twelve months training which I certainly had not had. So I removed that too, and as at that time there was no other suitable flying badge, I flew badgeless for a spell. Peter was more concerned with giving me at least enough basic experience in navigation, to perhaps stand in for a wounded navigator. Consequently I practised plotting and using a sextant and got on to every training flight that was going. From the end of July until the end of August I worked and studied and managed to navigate two cross-country trips. I also saw more parties, piss-ups and fights than I had seen in my whole life up to then. Probably the rowdiest night was the evening when Lieutenant Richard Greene (later to act the part of Robin Hood) turned up with a numer of tank and armoured car crews at what the squadron regarded as its very own pub in the village. Many bodies were hurled into the duck pond that night.

With administration and discipline five miles away, with a heavy sprinkling of carefree Canadian crews on the squadron and with casualties still mounting, the unit was mostly a drunken rabble. At the end of August I believe that fact had impinged on the consciousness of 3 Group HQ and when a squadron was required to go to 5 Group and convert to Lancasters, 57 squadron was elected, and that turned out to be one of the luckier breaks in the war for me. Better yet we were posted into Scampton, my favourite station in 5 Group, and certainly the most famous airfield in Lincolnshire if not in the whole service. The elderly squadron Commanding Officer who had been appointed to effect the move now left us and an unknown quantity arrived to command us.

Wing Commander F. C. Hopcraft DFC, was a tall, rugged ex-public school boy who was given the task of making a rabble into a disciplined squadron. He was a man who led from the front, could take it, certainly dished it out, and was as straight as a die. My own first acquaintance with him stemmed from the fact that I had a date to marry my darling girl on the 12th September, and this had been fixed weeks before. Hoppy's first move was to cancel all leave on the squadron until he reckoned we had completed our conversion through Manchesters on to Lancasters and were operationally fit again. On receipt of this news, I was off hotfoot to the CO's office to apprise him of my marriage arrangements. The argument, respectful but firm on my side, unyielding on his, terminated when I stated that if I could not get the leave promised when I joined the squadron, by official means, I would certainly go AWOL (Absent Without Leave) at least until after the ceremony. The Old Man glared at me and then said something like, "Very well then, and only as a special case, I don't want to start life on the squadron with a court martial." Thus it was I made it to the church on time on the glorious 12th September. One week later, after a very short honeymoon on the coast at Parkstone dodging air raids by marauding FW 190s, I was back at Scampton to complete our conversion programme. This I did on 22nd September, only to find myself among the two crews of 'odds and sods' posted off as surplus to requirements or at least to establishment.

This was a crushing blow, I had got to know the blokes on the squadron well and although they were a wild bunch of Canadians, Australians, New Zealanders and from all corners of the British Isles, under Hoppy they were settling down into a damned good bomber squadron. Besides I loved Scampton, its history, its atmosphere and its institutions. Nevertheless off I went once again on what turned out to be a one month circular tour of Lincolnshire. On 28th September I travelled to and reported in at No. 106 conversion flight at Coningsby only to find the unit packing up for a transfer to Skellingthorpe next day. On the 29th I joined a scratch crew and helped to ferry a Lancaster to our new station just about five miles south-west of my starting point at Scampton. I actually spent as many as three days here flying mainly with Flight Sergeant Lou Burpee, a large Canadian pilot who later figured in some of the Dam Busters' exploits. By 2nd October I had joined a crew whose navigator had gone sick and under our pilot, Bill Piercy, yet another Canadian, we were all posted off to No. 106 Squadron at Syerston, down towards Nottingham, which was commanded by the legendary Guy Gibson. Here we were allotted an aircraft, tested it, and then flew it in a night cross-country around the north of England and two days later we did another one to the south of England. We were now figuratively champing at the operational bit and as yet had not figured on the Battle Order.

For some reason I cannot now recall, our crew was flown over to Coningsby to pick up a Manchester which we brought back to the squadron, and on the next day Bill Piercy found himself on the Battle Order. Not us — just him — it seemed that he was to fly as second pilot to gain enough experience on the trip to try and keep us out of trouble on our first trip. Poor Bill, his first trip was also his last, he never returned; along with the entire crew and aeroplane he was posted missing. This left us as a pilotless crew and as such our days on the squadron were obviously numbered. During this period between 11th and 18th October, a daylight raid was laid on and a volunteer navigator was required to stand in for a sick officer. I was still debating whether to risk a snub by volunteering, after all I was very green operationally, in fact one might say still a virgin, when the place was filled. That is why I was not among those present on the famous daylight raid to the French armament works at Le Creusot where the only aircraft lost blew itself up flying determinedly into the target below the safety height for dropping a 'Cookie' (4,000 or 8,000 lb bomb).

On 18th October we were on our travels again, this time back to the environs of Lincoln to 1064 Heavy Conversion Unit at Wigsley. Here, as a pilotless crew, we were to pick up a pilot and go with him through his conversion to heavy bombers, which meant flying the dreaded Manchester again as well as the Lancaster. It is strange that an aeroplane like the Manchester, twin-engined and therefore under-powered, a great central fin at the tail, plus two rudders and a heavy machine on the stick, could and did turn into the four engined thoroughbred Lanc. There were many incidents when the Vulture engines of the heavily ladened Manchesters caught fire in the air and if for no other reason they were not popular machines to fly.

Within a day of our arrival at Wigsley, I found my former 'B' flight Commander from Cottesmore, George Avis, crewless. He was now a Squadron Leader so I thought he must be up for a Flight Commander's job in a squadron and we ought to get to a squadron more quickly with him than grinding through the whole syllabus with a more junior pilot. Consequently I volunteered us and George very bravely took us on and on 1st November after 20 hours conversion flying, mostly at night, to my delight George was posted to 57 Squadron at Scampton to command 'B' Flight; talk about wheels turning full circle — and in only 33 days at that! We had enjoyed one rather weird night, flying a 'circuits and bumps' detail in a Manchester. We took off from Wigsley on the first circuit and as it was George's first solo in the Manchester he was working hard at it. I think he was working so hard at it that he flew too far away from the flare-path. We noticed nothing until after this first landing when it became clear that wherever we were, it certainly was not Wigsley. A quick check at the control tower and we established that we were at Skellingthorpe and by now somewhat disorientated, we took off again and landed at another flare-path only to find it an even stranger airfield. This time it proved to be Swinderby which, luckily for us, had a take-off direction which pointed straight at Wigsley and at the third attempt we made our first landing at Wigsley. This does illustrate how crowded nights could be in Lincolnshire during the height of the war!

Next day, we packed up yet again and moved all of ten miles back to the place I had started from 33 days before, good old 57 Squadron at Scampton.

The author and his bride — 'the greatest day of my life' — 12 September, 1942

CHAPTER THREE
Operations I — Still Learning

So our crew arrived at Scampton on 1st November 1942 and apart from George our pilot and captain and 'Susie' Sothern our Canadian commissioned rear gunner who went into the Officers' Mess, the rest of us Sergeants — Edwards, Flight Engineer; Gibson, bomb aimer; Phillips, wireless operator; King, mid-upper gunner; and me, the navigator — were billeted in an empty house of the peacetime Airmen's Married Quarters. It was a little weird to live in a house where there were beds in the kitchen, dining-room and sitting-room as well as the bedrooms, but we were content enough. The squadron had by now become fully operational on Lancasters and had already flown two or three operational sorties. We were by now awaiting our blooding, eagerly is not quite the right word, but we were certainly keen to break the operational ice and as George had by now taken over as 'B' Flight Commander, we had not very long to wait.

On the afternoon of 7th November our names appeared on the Battle Order for the very first time and in the late afternoon we attended briefing at that famous room which at Scampton was above the Airmen's Mess. The importance of the occasion was underlined by the presence of two Redcaps (RAF policemen) outside the doors; they admitted no one who was not named on the list and checked those that were by demanding production of our Forms 1250 (Service identity cards). So for the first time we entered the historic briefing room with its rows of chairs and navigators' tables, and with a large map of Europe covering one entire wall. There were maps showing where flak guns, heavy, medium and light were sited. Other maps indicated areas of probable fighter defences — the so-called boxes — and the covered map indicated tonight's target. When all the crews were seated, the squadron Commanders and the Station Commander, the excellent and much respected 'Charles' (J. N. H.) Whitworth DSO DFC, arrived. Finally the covers were removed from the route map and my heart sank into my boots — the string went south a very very long way across Europe and fetched up at Genoa in Northern Italy.

My depression was not from any sense of danger but from the length of that string and my doubts about my ability to navigate across 1,300 miles of Europe. I was acutely conscious of the fact that I had acquired a total of only 89 hours as a navigator and only just over 40 hours of that was time spent actually navigating and that none of it accrued from any kind of formal source and

43

because of that I still flew without a brevet on my chest — which probably summed me up at the time. Anyhow, to Genoa we were to go with two 1,000 lb bombs and eight small bomb containers each loaded with large numbers of 4 lb incendiary bombs. The target was the docks which at this time were one of the chief sources of supply for Rommel's Afrika Corps and it was our job to blow the stores accumulated there into tiny smithereens. I was still contemplating the prospect of flying over the (to me) uncharted Alps when two pieces of very cheering information were announced. First we were to skirt Geneva but would be close enough to see it and of course as the Swiss were not at war, it would be brilliantly lit and what a marvellous pin-point this was going to make for that hazardous journey over the Alps. The second piece of good cheer came from the weather man, he announced that a large col covered the whole of western Europe. A col is an area between two pressure systems where the air is completely slack. Consequently, if we accurately steered our tracks at given speeds, dead reckoning navigation would do the trick. My spirits rose tremendously and I began to look forward to take-off time.

With the fading daylight, bombing-up had been completed, all the tests had been made and here we were in the squadron locker room climbing into flying kit. There was a navigation bag full of instruments, a sextant, emergency ration kit, escape kits, signal data sheets and a chest type parachute to worry about and load on to the squadron 2-tonner which would take us out to our flight's hardstandings which were on the north side of the airfield, looking down on to Scampton village. On dismounting from the transport at the rear of our aircraft, Lancaster 'O' for Olive Oil, it was quite dark and there was a definite nip in the air on this late autumn Saturday night, two days after Guy Fawkes day. Being in the middle of a considerable war there had of course been no fireworks celebration — I rather thought that we were going to have our own display tonight. This waiting time before getting in and starting up was, I thought, the worst part of any sortie. The actual length of the wait was determined by so many imponderables that it was futile to plan to get out to dispersal with only the minimum ten minutes to sit around.

However, time passed, one last pee and then into the aeroplanes as the engines on the CO's Lancaster burst into life. Within minutes the airfield which had been so silent and desolate was full of the noise of revving Rolls Royce Merlin engines and the taxiways were teeming with red and green fireflies (we always put our lights on for taxiing, but made sure they were off when leaving the ground) crawling towards the up-wind end of the flare-path and take-off. We were tenth in line and by the time we had lined up for take-off all our ground checks had been completed, radios checked and compasses set. I experienced a mixture of feelings — some apprehension, some excitement and some worry about my part in the proceedings to come. In no time we were hurtling across the grass field until after a succession of jolts all became smooth as all three wheels left the ground and Scampton receded behind us with the faint shadow of a thought lurking — would we make it back?

Work now became the absorbing thing as we passed over the airfield on course for the south coast and over nine hours flying ahead in a very black, starless, but mercifully windless night. We climbed steadily whilst the temperature dropped lower and lower, approaching 20,000 feet it was a long way below zero and with no internal heating in the aircraft the long night's shudder commenced. Through a good clearance we spotted our out-bound coastal crossing point and I was much cheered to find that we were on track and on time. Riding in a bomber over a blacked out country on a dark winter's night is an eerie sensation because one feels absolutely alone. We all knew that there were dozens of aircraft all round us but themselves blacked out as we were, with exhaust stubs shielding the escaping flames from the engine exhausts, none were visible. Pilot and engineer sitting side by side gazing through the wide expanse of perspex in the cockpit and Johnny down in his enormous bomb aimer's office were our eyes to keep us out of collision trouble. Aft of the pilot, a great black-out curtain cordoned off the rest of the Lancaster and behind that curtain my feeble anglepoise light gave sufficient illumination on the chart to see where (we hoped) we were going. Next to me Phil's set glowed gently in the wireless apartment and then still further to the rear and out of our sight, 'Colonel' sat in his mid-upper gun turret with two Browning .303 machine-guns and right aft suspended out in space 'Susie' handled his four machine-guns. Out over the Channel George gave the order to test guns and all six made their clattering racket as they fired, unfreezing the sluggish oil.

Next came 'enemy coast ahead' from Johnny in the nose. I was to hear that call another forty-five times and I cannot pretend that it ever left me unaffected. Always there seemed to be a slight tightening of the muscles, a slight increase of pulse rate and a sudden breathlessness as if the oxygen had been turned off for a short spell. This first time one expected almost instant reprisal for daring to infringe enemy occupied Europe and it was curious to sit up here at 20,000 feet whilst down below was a hitherto friendly country crawling with hostile Germans. As always the adrenalin adjusted and heart and mind were back on the job, in this case to get the most accurate identification of the piece of French coastline we were now passing over. This was highly important, it might turn out to be the last positive identification position until we hit the Mediterranean coast — if we ever did, for as we flew in, searchlights began to wave around, and light flak stained the sky to our left. Somebody down in that hostile murk was alive to our presence but fortunately not exactly sure as to which piece of sky we occupied.

We flew on relatively undisturbed but by now tightly to attention as we penetrated the Luftwaffe's fighter box defences. Five pairs of eyes were quartering the sky for any sign of fighters whilst Phil concentrated on his wireless frequencies and I confirmed that we were on time and on track. So we ought to be; the coastal crossing confirmed that we were not being drifted by any wind at all. The col was right where they had said it would be and I just had to keep an accurate plot of heading and air speed and furthermore the weather was now clear. Popping out from the black-out curtain from time to time it was heartening to see no sign of weather in any direction. In the course of time the Alps loomed up ahead, a great black line breaking the skyline and visible from the pilot's cockpit. As we got nearer a wonderful sight came into view, the fairy-like necklaces of light that represented Geneva off to port and incidentally, another relief, right where they ought to be.

After leaving Geneva on the port beam the mountains rose higher and seemed to curve up towards us like an angry but petrified black sea. Turbulence started, the aircraft buffeting up and down in the currents of air until Mont Blanc disappeared nearly 5,000 feet below us and the high mountains began to descend to the plain. In twenty minutes the lad from London who had travelled very little up to now caught his first glance of the Mediterranean. I cannot honestly say that it struck me as the 'wine dark sea' of Byron's Greek adventure. Dark it certainly was and with no wind about, it was as smooth as a mill pond and correspondingly black, with not a single white cap showing.

We reached the coast at Savona Head, dead on time and track, which at least proved George steered good courses and that I was maintaining an accurate plot. We then turned eastwards parallel with the coast of the Italian riviera and within minutes could see the explosions of heavy flak ahead and the sudden flare-up in the darkness as bombs reached the ground. I had not yet acquired the dangerously won experience of later raids and consequently I thought that there was quite a bit of flak around, but it was not heavy enough nor indeed accurate enough to deflect us from the bombing run. At the aiming point was a large warehouse with the bonus of a ship of some 10-15,000 tons tied up alongside. Both appeared on our subsequent photograph taken by the light of a 20,000,000 candlepower photoflash. When these flashes exploded the ground was for an instant brilliantly lit and I never got used to these enormous flashes of lights exploding below us. Duty done, George pulled round on to the course for home and once again we began climbing to gain height safely over the Alps.

Nothing of any great moment occurred on the way home. We went through the muscle tightening process of entering the fighter boxes from the south, but saw no one. Eventually Scampton beacon hove into view (thank God for a windless night) and after a circuit we were down to a very nice landing nine hours and twenty minutes after leaving and sortie No. 1 was safely over.

Two nights later we set off for Hamburg for a trip which was to turn out vastly different from the first one. This time we left the ground to climb into thick wet cloud and climbed for what seemed like hours in a pitch-black turbulent world, finally emerging above clouds sitting over the top of it all at 16,000 feet. Confidence in my navigational ability still enthused the crew from the first trip and things proceeded smoothly up to the time of our last Gee (radar) fix before enemy jamming made further use impossible. Shortly after this the cloud shapes changed and the temperature took a dive. Furthermore the cloud rose towards our level and frequently enveloped us. From hindsight I now know that we had crossed a cold front and had I not been so ignorant I would have known that we had gone from warm sector stratus or layer cloud to cold front type cumulus or heaped cloud, that a drop in temperature and increase in cloud level indicated the crossing of a cold front. In my greenhorn ignorance, such matters were a closed book.

The problem was to secure a further confirmation of position by some means. A Gee fix was impossible, the radar screen was swamped with the grass of enemy jamming. Sitting over and sometims in 16,000 ft of solid cloud did not yield an enemy coast crossing pin-point. Quite rough turbulence also put out of the question any attempt to try my shaky astro-navigation from the stars.

Thus we fell back on navigating by dead reckoning, and there lay the catch. I was using winds which I had found before Gee went out and applying forecast changes of direction and speed. There were two things wrong with this method — first I had crossed a cold front and the wind had changed from westerly to northerly and secondly, the Met. Office had no knowledge of the cold front sweeping down the North Sea that night and consequently their forecast changes of wind direction and speed were completely wrong.

We wallowed on, in and out of heavy cloud, thrown about by turbulence and anxiously watching for ice on wings and engines. A few minutes before our ETA over Hamburg, we ran into clear air still with heavy cloud below, but ahead of us were the vivid explosions of very heavy flak. Somehow, I thought, we had made the target area and in support of this supposition elongated blobs of light weaved along the clouds as searchlights vainly tried to pierce them, and flashes of light in the cloud indicated bombs and photoflashes exploding beneath. There was no chance of seeing an aiming point through so much cloud so we flew into the middle of the thickest concentration of flak and searchlights and dropped our load (one cookie, a 4,000 lb bomb and 10 cans of 4 lb incendiary bombs, about 900 in all).

From the dropping point we set course for the short dog-leg to avoid Heligoland and ten minutes or so later altered heading for the long near-westerly drag across the North Sea to Lincolnshire. Ten minutes later, some twenty minutes from the target, we were still being enveloped in heavy flak bursts. How could this be I wondered when we should be over the sea? I went forward to check that George was steering 'blue on blue' on the magnetic compass — I had suspected that he might have got disorientated and was steering 'red on blue' in other words a reciprocal course taking us further east. But, as usual imperturbable George was on course for home, or at least was on the course I had given him. Sitting in heavy cloud with mushrooming explosions lighting up the clouds on each side, I was beset by a kind of desperation, we were steering westerly, there were no stars visible to check by, there was no possibility of seeing below through this thick murk. Turbulence added to our problems and indeed we were not sure that some of the turbulence may not have been attributed to near misses by the heavy flak we were flying through. It still had not penetrated my bemused brain that we were south of our intended track and were flying over North Germany. After a very frightening half an hour or so the cloud began to thin and soon I was hailed from the rear turret.

"There is a huge, squarish town on the south-west edge of a small lake," said Susie Sothern. 'Ha' thinks I 'a pin-point at last.' I must have checked every map I had from North Cape in Norway to damn near Gibraltar but no such configuration showed. As we flew west, Susie could see more of the land behind and he now informed me that the lake was more huge than the town, and at that the penny dropped, we had obviously passed over the Zuider Zee and Amsterdam.

A snap alteration of course to starboard put us across the Dutch coast and heading out to sea and at Noordwijk we left the last of the flak behind. A safe return to Scampton followed — there is some truth in the old adage that God looks after fools and drunkards! How much truth was not really apparent until we realized that there were only two surviving crews from the six sent out on the operation. The truth was further compounded on the next day when, with the assistance of our weather man, we reconstructed what had really happened. Illustrations 'A' & 'B' make it graphically clear.

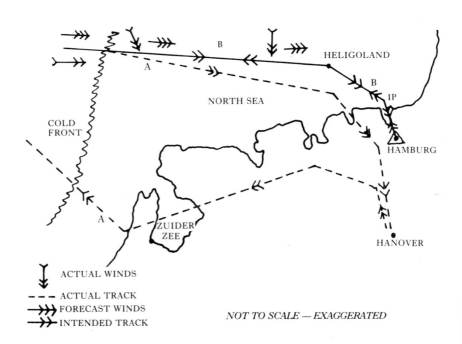

The passage through a cold front, unremarked by me, caused a nearly 90 degrees swing in the direction of the wind, resulting in excessive southerly drift and an increase in ground speed into the target. Thus at ETA target, we had overshot by many miles and had been lured to the flak defending Hanover whilst thinking we had made Hamburg. We had obviously turned well short of Heligoland and pursued a south-westerly track across — wait for it — Bremen, Bremerhaven, Brunsbuttel, Emden, Wilhelmshaven and all points in Germany up to Amsterdam. The marvel is that of all the shells fired at us from all those places, none actually hit. This lesson of not appreciating the weather lore and the dangers it could pose stayed with me all of my flying life and in the course of the next 23 years I became quite expert at aviation meteorology.

We landed back at Scampton after being in the air for just under six hours but it had felt like a lifetime and it was a crew with very mixed feelings. On the one hand was that indescribable feeling of relief — so huge a sensation as to compare with the size of the risk, our lives on the line as it were. On the other hand there was a mood of depression at the loss of four aircraft — 28 of our squadron mates, and you do notice the absence of that number of men from beds, dining tables and the locker room. However, with the resilience of youth, a few hours' sleep and some hot food restored the usual interests of life, like who was going into Lincoln tonight and who was playing football against 83 Squadron, etc.

Five nights later our names were on the Battle Order again and once more we went through the feverish preparations of a flying test, a check of all our equipment and, on my part, more mugging up of flak maps and the situation of German flying fields acting as bases for their fighters. We arrived in the Briefing Room and in due course the curtain was pulled aside and there again was that enormous piece of string stretching right down to the Mediterranean. The target was Genoa again and the reason for the raid was the same, for by this time Montgomery's 8th Army and Rommel's Afrika Corps were locked in furious battle.

In the dark of a dry but cloudy November night the noise of taxiing Lancasters rang out over the airfield and soon the winking green at the end of the flare-path was for us. Dragging our large bomber, seven of us, a bomb load of a cookie and incendiaries, thousands of rounds of ammunition, our four Merlins bellowed at full throttle as we gathered speed across the grass and, after the usual rumblings and bumpings, heaved us into the air. Once airborne, things became smooth as we climbed steadily to the height needed to traverse France and the Alps. Half-way across France the cloud broke and we flew on into a fine night with lots of visibility. Once again, passing Geneva to port, we headed for Mont Blanc and over the top we went. A nice steady run ensued at 4,000 feet above the Italian Riviera coast and there ahead was the target criss-crossed with heavy and light flak and searchlights. On the run up to the docks and warehouses which were our target it was noticeable that about 80% of the flak dried up, and I guess the gunners were seeking shelter. This time —

and very rarely it happened — we, or some of us saw the bombs strike. The cookie straight into the roof of a large warehouse and the incendiaries scattering across it and the surrounding docks. We got a beautiful picture with our camera with the aid of a 20 million candlepower flash and along with all the other crews we really did paste the Genoese docks. The return trip was uneventful and after 9¼ hours we were down again, safe again, and had completed the third sortie of the tour.

The weather had been kind, vital pin-points had been visible and given these assets, my navigation had been good. Both the crew and I were gaining in confidence but there was still a long way to go and still a lot to learn.

Towards the beginning of the second week of December we were sent to Turin to try and slow down the tank and aero engine production in their big factories. This was a testing trip because the weather was terrible, typical European winter weather of icing cloud, seemingly extending hundreds of miles and thousands of feet high. We saw nothing on the ground, staggered over the Alps anxiously watching ice forming on the wings and even on the Mediterranean side of the Alps failed to break through cloud into the clear. There were certainly some breaks over the target area but not enough to ensure a concentrated attack. After another long miserable haul back we made it in nine hours and despite everything I had found us the way there and back — chalk up four!

Five days before Christmas we were to fly another raid and this time it was to be our christening in Happy Valley, as the Ruhr was known in Bomber Command. This time we climbed into the cold, black air with a load of fourteen cans, each containing ninety-six 4lb incendiary bombs, there was obviously going to be a hot time in town tonight for them as well as us. We climbed to 16,000 feet, levelled off over the North Sea and as before got our last Gee fix just over half-way across to Holland. The difference this time though was that the night was fairly clear and I identified Noordwijk as we crossed the coast, on time and on track.

Now you could almost feel the tension in the aircraft as five pairs of eyes scanned the night sky for fighters. As we flew at what seemed a snail's pace across Holland, there were reports from the tail and mid-upper gunners of other Lancs close in all around us. This produced mixed feelings; it was good to know that I must be navigating accurately to be among so many, and it did mean that we would get a split second warning of an attack as the bombers to port and starboard opened fire. On the other hand we were flying at about 180 m.p.h. and undulating slightly in a little turbulence which did offer a considerable collision risk. In fact, looking back from hindsight, I am awfully glad that some of the later raids we did with eight hundred plus bombers were done at night — I am sure it would have frightened us to death if we had seen them all round us.

At last the flashes ahead of bomb explosions and the very bright camera flashes told us that we were approaching the target and that the first wave was at work. Within seconds the sky was afire with flak flashes, I stood between the pilot and engineer (navigation unnecessary for the next five to ten minutes) and wondered how on earth we could penetrate this dense heavy anti-aircraft fire and remain unscathed. Then whilst viewing this morale buster a shout came from 'the Colonel', "ME 110 closing from port side." George swept us into a diving turn to the left but the attack it seemed was not aimed at us and coming back on to an even keel, we continued the run in.

By now the aircraft was bucking in the aftermath of near misses from the flak and just as we had the bomb doors open and Johnnie's eye glued to the bomb sight, Susie called from the rear turret, "ME 110 closing from starboard." This time we could do nothing about it, we were on the bomb run which had of necessity to be as straight and level as George could manage and we had our bomb doors open which was creating a fair bit of drag. Everything then happened at a greater accelerated velocity. The ME 110 struck at an aircraft further away and our guns opened up. Johnny called, "Steady, steady, bombs away," and with a snap bomb doors closed and the Lanc was whipped away from the threatened attack. As a result we got no photo that night but we did have an incident (funny in retrospect) involving our bomb aimer. There had been some swift and fairly confused talk on the intercom when a JU 88 was identified behind us as we left the target. Finally Reg said something like, "He's sailed over," and Johnny thought that he had said something about "Bale out". In the dark he had made a frantic grab at his parachute, missed the cloth carrying handle and snatched the release handle instead. It took him ten minutes to come up from the nose which was enveloped in silk. I had no idea that there was so much silk in just one parachute. Finally a somewhat embarrassed Johnny appeared below Reg's feet and staggered up on to the flight deck. We never got another pin-point from the nose all night, I had to press my nose to the perspex blister behind the pilot to spot our coast crossing positions.

We landed safely back at Scampton four hours and forty minutes after take-off and spent some considerable time trying to collapse and collect that wretched parachute in the nose. The parachute section were not best pleased to see our heroic bomb-aimer stagger into them with masses of crumpled silk in his arms. However, we were safely back from No. 5, had sighted three enemy aircraft, which proved that our gunners were on top of their job, and we had survived the most thunderous flak barrage. We were all learning and learning fast. I had already discovered that if I compared the winds I found over the North Sea with those forecast for that area and then applied the difference between these two sets of winds to the ones forecast for the German side of the North Sea, I was getting relatively good track and time-keeping. After this trip we also had a discussion about intercom chatter and made a vow to tighten up our procedure in future — we really did not enjoy silk swathed fuselages.

Christmas was the excuse for a long and rather drunken celebration which turned into a debauch. Christmas Day was sacrosanct to Bomber Harris and he never mounted an operation on that day. Therefore when operations were fogged off on Christmas Eve, everyone knew that they were safe for at least 36 hours. In consequence a very wild party started on Christmas Eve which ran into Christmas Day and after our midday Christmas dinner, got wilder and wilder until as far as I was concerned it finally vanished into an alcoholic haze at about 4 p.m. that day. The last thing I remember was dodging a pint mug hurled at me — in friendship I may add — by our excitable extrovert and quite mad Canadian 'Doc' Lalonde. The next time I can remember anything at all clearly, it was the morning of the 27th. Apparently Scampton had been covered in fog throughout the Christmas and Boxing Day period and the party had continued right on. On the 27th I felt that I would never be well again — how could anyone survive such a splitting head and such a nauseous stomach! When I faced myself in the shaving mirror two eyes stared back like — as our lads graphically said — two piss-holes in the snow, the deathly white face being pointed up by the black stubble of a 72-hour beard. That day there really was a hush over the airfield. It was still too foggy to fly so that every crew room was occupied by slumbering forms and even our youthful resilience was severely tested — it took a full 24 hours to recover.

The following day we were ordered to Swinderby, south-west of Lincoln to prepare for an operation but again the fog won, and the raid was concelled. I have a log-book entry of a flight to Swinderby but not of one back. I can only suppose that another party developed and that we came back by road in a stupor.

The weather finally cleared on 3rd January, on which day we spent over an hour in the air leading a formation of Lancasters around Lincolnshire, and finishing up with some practice bombing at Waynfleet on the coast. Then the next day we prepared for another penetration to Happy Valley, this time to Duisburg, the home of many heavy industries and of the People's Car works. Our bomb load was again a cookie (4,000lbs) and 12 cans of incendiaries containing a total of 1,080 four-pound fire bombs. We soared into the black and still misty air and proceeded across the North Sea, climbing into and out of thick icing cloud. Then came Johnny's call of, "Enemy coast ahead!" and we were crossing into Holland and approaching the Dante's Inferno that was Duisburg under attack. Once again we flew — although it felt like crawling — into very heavy flak indeed. Almost immediately there was a jolting thump, a loud bang and the sharp acrid smell of cordite wafting through old Olive Oil. We had indeed caught a packet from a 4.5-inch shell — fortunately as we later ascertained the explosion took place beneath us, it must have had a proximity fuse. Thus instead of being hit with a large solid chunk of metal, we were lanced through by nearly a hundred metal shards. It certainly was not pleasant, I had a hot flush years before the male menopause, the throat constricted and every muscle seemed to clench. Upon the cry from the nose, "Bombs away," I found that I had been holding my breath for some time past. With the exhalation of air and the swinging round of the Lanc on a course for home, I became released from some sort of paralysis and started work on the navigational chart again.

Once again there was that ominous patter as of hailstones hitting the fuselage, but it was fine weather over the target. Take another gulp of air and ignore it, we are still flying and no one has complained so we must be all right.

And so back across the cold dark North Sea where only twenty miles off the coast from Cromer I received my third heart-stopping shock of the night. I was looking forward from the astrodome when a shower of red sparks went by outside like red dotted lines. What was it? German fighter? No — merely my skipper tapping out the ash from an illegal fag, and I suppose if the swear words were deleted, I said very little to George about it. This flight lasted five minutes under five hours and definitely blooded the virgins — there were dozens of tiny rents in the fuselage and wings which gave our ground crew a headache for a couple of days.

Which neatly brings me to the other half of our team, the fitters, riggers, electricians, armourers, etc., very ably led by Danny our ground crew corporal. Those lads worked some awe-inspiring numbers of hours in the crappiest winter weather we had had for years. Our old Olive Oil never left the ground in less than a perfect state and despite the trouble the aircrew got the old girl into, she never quit on us without there being some reason attributable to German nastiness. I have not got a clear recollection of the circumstances but as I remember it, we had been on a two-day party at the end of December and approached the New Year very hung over, only to find ourselves on the Battle Order and scheduled to go and lay mines in Danzig harbour. This was a terrible long way for a pissed young navigator to find and in our total state of health I do not think that we would have survived this trip. As it happened there was one engine being run up on Olive Oil as we approached from the squadron, it being quickly shut down as we appeared in view in our old two-tonner. We entered the aircraft, sat down, semi-collapsed and George started up and began testing magnetos. There was the most God-awful drop on the starboard outer engine and as there was no spare aircraft available that night, we had no option but to scrub the trip. We had had no trouble with Olive Oil before then and we had precious little afterwards, so I often wondered about that one engine running up as we arrived. If they did — then God Bless you chaps for our lives, I am certain we would not have survived a low level trip in our state. A great and truly important lesson was learned here — alcohol and flying do not mix and we never attempted to do so ever again. We had truly terrific ground crews on 57 Squadron and ours was one of the best.

I diverge from the tale of our return from Duisburg on the night of 3rd January. We were quite close to the east coast when we received a message which diverted us to Thorney Island down near Portsmouth on the south coast, apparently most of England except the south was fog-bound. We hurriedly back-tracked south of the Thames estuary and headed west down-Channel through a dark and misty night. There was no problem getting there, my Gee set was working perfectly until we arrived at the point where the German jamming stations interfered with it, and then it got troublesome. We were flying in thick mist, very little of the ground could be seen and I did not know exactly where we were. Arriving over Thorney Island on estimation, we called them up and were told to hold, there were so many aircraft trying to get in. I set off on a hold pattern not too sure of my whereabouts when suddenly there was a very loud rasping noise and unbelievably a barrage balloon passed down the starboard side! There was it seems a large area of Portsmouth and Southampton covered with balloons to keep low flying German aircraft up and away from the ships. Of course I knew they were there but I did not know that I was also. Some minutes later we were approaching Thorney Island on a QDM and finally in ever-thickening mist, now officially fog since the visibility had decreased below 1,100 yards, the flare-path loomed ahead, and gratefully we touched down upon it.

It was by now very foggy and taxiing on a strange airfield at night was always difficult anyhow. We followed as best we could the Controller's van which led us to the two torches of a marshaller and then the fun began. To have described the circle he was calling for we would have needed to be a London cab, the very large Lancaster just could not do it, so we stopped and George leaned out of the window and shouted. The two torch lights approached, swinging about, trying to discover where the aircraft was and why it had stopped. Finally the young naval airman picked up the slab-sided fuselage towering over him like some giant cliff and uttering a whistle of disbelief, he used his torches to explore the outline of Olive Oil. George leaned out of the window some twenty feet or so above him and shouted again and then he appreciated the size of the problem. On cutting engines after finally getting berthed he expressed surprise at the size of the Lancaster and explained that the naval squadrons at Thorney were equipped with the old Stringbags (otherwise and officially known as Swordfish).

The following day it was still misty but we found our way back to Scampton and thus a week later were in position for yet another sortie. This time the string, although very long, did not go to the Mediterranean but to the Big City (as Berlin was known in Bomber Command). As I looked at the map of Europe splashed with red coloured flak zones and green coloured fighter areas, that string seemed to go through an awful lot of both. The route plan was to fly low over the North Sea and Denmark, and then climb fairly rapidly on a south-easterly heading, clipping the corner of Sweden and crossing the German coast at Dassar Ort *en route* to Berlin. The load was similar to those we had carried to the Ruhr but as Berlin was so much further and we therefore had to carry a lot more fuel, it was reduced in weight by reducing the number of incendiaries carried. So we took a cookie of 4,000lbs and eight cans of incendiaries totalling 2,800 of the 4lb hexagonal type. This was to be our seventh sortie and we sure hoped that seven was our lucky number, because the Big City had an even worse reputation among our crews than did the Ruhr.

We took off and headed directly eastwards across the flat fields of Lincolnshire flying very low. We maintained the easterly heading and an altitude of less than 100 feet across the North Sea with the intention of staying under the German radar cover until we were in the Baltic. This had some considerable disadvantages from the navigation point of view, since Gee fixing would cease earlier than usual as we departed over the radar horizon quite quickly. I was able to pick up an occasional drift whenever white caps appeared on the sea but in the main the technique was to apply wind changes from those found to those forecast.

The following table makes this technique a little clearer.

Route Sector	Forecast Wind	Wind Found	Wind Used
Scampton 5°E	260/18	270/22	270/22
5°E Danish Coast	280/20	-	290/24
Danish Coast/Gothenburg	270/15	280/17	280/17
Gothenburg/Dassar Ort	240/12	-	250/14
Dassar Ort/Berlin	230/10	-	240/12

It was certainly not the perfect way to get there but it was a little better than sticking blindly to forecast winds. In the event, we obtained a pin-point over the west Danish coast, another on the east side and a third over south-east Sweden just as we started to climb. Minutes afterwards we discovered that we had got too close to Gothenburg and all hell was let loose as heavy and accurate anti-aircraft fire erupted. We altered heading slightly to starboard to steer a more westerly heading and get away from the flak a little quicker, but there was no doubt that the Swedes were firing to hurt, they certainly intended to demonstrate their neutrality to watching German eyes.

We levelled off at 16,000 feet and crossed Dassar Ort, a very distinctive cape on the Prussian coast, and the flak started again. For the next hundred miles or so intermittent flak blossomed around us but we just pressed on to that dark horizon ahead in which somewhere lay a huge sprawling mass of darkened buildings and more flak guns than one could imagine.

As always when approaching a target which was not yet under attack, time seemed to slow down so it was with some relief that the first flashes of bomb bursts showed pretty well ahead of us. With those bomb bursts came an unbelievable barrage. The whole sky seemed filled with mushrooming explosions and it seemed impossible that anyone could survive through this lot and live to bomb the target. However with gritted teeth, flexed muscles, and indrawn breath (no doubt a curious sight to a disinterested third party had there been one) we reached the target and commenced a commendably steady run which, as it turned out afterwards, gave us splendid aiming point photographs. (It always amazed me how time speeded up whenever one actually came under attack and everything seemed to happen at once.) With the cry, "Bombs away," George clanged the bomb doors shut and hauled old Olive Oil round in a G-filled turn to slap us on to a course out of there and in the general direction of home. The turn revealed the smoke covered red glow of the burning target area. I was to see such a sight many times in the future but that night in Berlin impressed itself on my optic nerves for ever.

A bombed city seen from the air is a fearsome sight, compounded of many colours and constituents. First and foremost are the fires from destroyed buildings which, contrary to what one might expect, do not burn with a steady glow but rather flicker, glowing brighter one moment and then fading, presumably because of the wind. Over all hangs smoke! Smoke from fires, from flak explosions, from smashed masonry, from those great camera flash bombs and later in the year poisonous smoke from phosphorous markers was added to the witch's brew. Shot through the smoky glare are the flashes of exploding bombs and every now and again the brilliant flash of 20 million candle power photo flares. As the fires take hold the grim Dantesque scene expands in area and in intensity and often from the astrodome I could see the red glow of a burning target on the horizon fifty to one hundred miles behind us as we headed home. Strangely enough the fact that thousands, sometimes tens of thousands, of Europeans were dying under our efforts, never broke through to our awareness and never really penetrated our consciousness. In retrospect I can only put this down to the major struggle we had ourselves to stay alive (the good old No. 1 syndrome at work again) against their defences, plus the fact that we were from three to five miles up in the air and had a sort of psychological detachment from it all. This would account for debriefings when replies to Intelligence Officers' questions were usually very laconic, such as 'good prang' 'good photo', etc. — 'wizard prang' maybe if it went very well indeed. Even then there was no sense of horror at it all, maybe we were all too young and immature in human experience, maybe too we had grown up with fathers who had suffered once already at German hands and certainly my youthhood was played out under the rising shadow of that evil man, Adolph Hitler. So when Britain was savagely attacked in 1940, there was a certain element of 'just you wait' stored away.

Be that as it may, we arrived back at Scampton scarred and nearly undaunted after the longest eight and three-quarter hours in the air I had yet experienced. It had been lucky seven — we now had the scalp of the Big City under our belts, or so we thought. Of course in a city of that size the amount of damage two to three hundred aircraft could inflict was limited, but at least we had seen the heart of Nazi power under fire.

Four nights later we were off to Happy Valley again, this time to try for the umpteenth occasion to destroy Herr Krupp's industrial sprawl in Essen. We did not then appreciate that we were in on the start of a long and bloody battle. It later became known as the Battle of the Ruhr in the history books and it lasted well into the late spring of 1943. It lost us hundreds of men and aircraft, the best there was of both, and it saw the stuttering efforts of the American 8th Air Force spring into powerful life so that the Reich experienced for the first time a little of the round the clock bombing which was to come. It also brought a change in our tactics to some extent, much of which was welcome to us. For one thing, we began to use the cruise climb technique, where you put the aeroplane in a climb using the minimum revs, pitch and mixture to keep it climbing steadily. No longer did we level off at 14,000 or 16,000 feet but went on climbing up to 21,000, 22,000 feet or even occasionally a little higher, and thereby in our unheated aircraft experienced temperatures below zero which heretofore I did not believe existed. The other major change was the arrival of Pathfinder squadrons, those bunch of heroes who turned from a sour joke in 1942 to a match winner in 1943. With their help in positioning flares for aiming at we could now bomb through thick cloud obscuring the ground, with a fair degree of success.

But I digress, back to the night of 21st January and our very hairy five hours or so to Essen and, most importantly, back.

The night was again very black with heavy cloud which had a fairly low base and somehow the blackness of the night always seemed to add to that silence which ensued when we had debussed at the dispersal points, packed our kit in the aircraft, and waited for zero hour. When the boss's engines started, the whole squadron started up and then the long line of Lancasters snaked its way round the perimeter tracks to the Chance Light at the downwind end of the flare-path. We always had a long way to taxi because our squadron was located at the north end of the airfield, atop the hill which looked down on Scampton village. Finally we were thudding across the grass seeking to lift us and our bomb load (the standard Happy Valley load of one 4,000lb cookie and twelve cans of 4lb incendiary bombs, totalling 1,080 in all) into the air. Over a period of time as we repeated heavily loaded take-offs, George acquired the knack of wrenching the Lancaster into the air with bare flying speed and then depressing the nose into the valley, picking up speed nicely before turning on to a heading for the long climb.

Steadily we climbed upwards and outwards towards the North Sea through thick winter clouds and at about eighteen thousand feet broke into a clear starlit night. There was a little light I suppose from so many stars but there was never enough for me to spot the aircraft all round us when I stood in the astrodome. Fortunately the gunners sitting out in uninterrupted darkness developed very good night sight and often picked up aircraft three or four hundred feet away. There was quite an armada of four engine bombers on the way to Essen this night, Lancasters of 1 and 5 Groups, Halifaxes from 4 and 6 Groups and Stirlings from 3 Group. After passing over the enemy coast at what I hoped was the right crossing point, the fighter attacks started and again quite incredibly no one actually attacked us. The gunners were reporting strings of flares dropping either side of the long lines of bombers, they reported exchanges of cannon and machine-gun fire from both of our flanks but did not have to open up themselves. Once more with muscles tensed, etc., we ran in towards Happy Valley and a veritable fusillade of flak poured into the night sky. It was a very rough ride in that night, one burst of flak was close enough to sprout holes in the wing, another penetrated the glycol tank of No. 4 engine and within a very short time the engine burst into flames. Thank God for Graviner and his switches, the engine extinguishers put the fire out but now George had to trim out to compensate for a dead engine as we made our bomb run. Somehow we survived the terrifying flak barrage, "Thick enough to walk on," said Reg surveying hundreds of puffs of smoke hanging in the sky. Smartly we turned away and started the long haul home.

In due time we crossed the Dutch coast and started to lose height to increase speed and to come down to a warmer altitude. A warmer altitude indeed! Warmer is a word of comparison but the comparison was between deathly cold at 20,000-odd feet, bloody cold at 15,000 feet and just plain cold below 10,000 feet. For this reason I suppose we must have looked somewhat odd when dressed for battle. We all had thick flannel shirts (no ties on, they shrink in water) even thicker white woollen aircrew sweaters, uniform coats covered by quite thick flying suits and topped off by flying helmets, oxygen masks, and in the case of pilot and engineer, flying goggles. Even with that lot on it was still unbearably cold and of course it made movement quite an effort so it was a good job that we were all young and fairly fit. Below ten thousand feet we were allowed to fly without oxygen on and so we could have a mug of hot coffee from the thermos and just begin to feel human again. I had obtained my first Gee fix clear of the German jamming and was moderately surprised to find I was on track pretty much where I had hoped to be. The wind I measured checked out nicely so that I could now relax with only a hundred miles to go to base. With the stopped propeller in view from the astrodome and the knowledge of the reduced ground speed thereby occasioned, thoughts turned to ditching. This was something I really dreaded, I was nothing of a swimmer and the thought of hitting that icy winter sea did nothing for my morale. My old friend Brian Woolston had once spent two days in a dinghy in the North Sea in the spring of 1941. He had drifted to within thirty miles of the Dutch coast, had witnessed a Luftwaffe/RAF fighter scrap overhead resulting in losses on both sides, and had finally been picked up by a RAF Air Sea Rescue Launch at some incredible distance off the Suffolk coast. I had heard from him at first hand and it had put me off ditching for life.

I was jolted from these gloomy thoughts by a cry of, "English coast dead ahead," and hurrying forward, I checked our crossing in over Cromer and the final course for Scampton. In talking about relaxing on the way home, it was a natural reaction from a lot of fright I suppose, but it had its own dangers too. The Luftwaffe had an unpleasant habit of inserting the odd JU 88 into the returning bomber stream and nothing is more disconcerting than being shot up again when you are back over Merry England. We landed at last and I suppose because we had had a fairly action-packed night, I had the greatest difficulty in staying awake through the debriefing, and the large mug of hot coffee laced with rum did not help a lot either.

A combination of some bad weather and the need for the Flight

Commander to space out his operational trips prevented us from going on any further operations until the day before my birthday. This resulted in my spending the early part of the day returning from one trip and sleeping most of it away so that I could be flying out on another trip the same evening. On the evening of the 13th February we were on our way out to the Atlantic coast of France to a very different target from the usual run of things lately. This time we were to attempt to assist in the Battle of the Atlantic by bombing submarines, German U-boats, in their concrete pens at Lorient and bombing the surrounding services — areas of wharfs, hangars, repair shops, etc. The trip went fairly well, some aircraft carrying armour piercing bombs and others cookies and incendiaries. Despite some fairly heavy flak over the target, the aiming points were bombed and many fires started in the service areas. In the early hours of the morning we landed back at base, debriefed, and were in bed by about 2.30 a.m. Seven hours later we were up, breakfasting and then down to the squadron for pre-flight checks. After lunch we attended that famous briefing room again. This time we were to go to the factories of Milan and at the end of the short winter's day we were assembled to fly again.

After a long climb through thick weather, we broke clear at just over 20,000 feet and having soldiered on through sporadic gun fire in Northern France, were now peeled for action from German fighters. Not one did we see and eventually we spotted cloud which contained Mont Blanc. As the mountains rose in height so did the cloud and at 21,000 feet we were flying in and out of icy wisps and casting anxious glances at wings and engines. The temperature was very low, minus 20°C, but the air was moist, damp enough to produce cloud and such conditions also produced ice on aeroplanes. If enough of it stuck to the aeroplane, it spoiled its aerodynamic qualities, weighed it down, and finally caused it to crash. The methods of combating it were fairly basic at this stage, mainly anti-ice paste spread over wings and fuselage. There had been quite a few nights when loud bangs had heralded not anti-aircraft shells, but large chunks of ice breaking away from wings and engines and cannoning off the fuselage. However on this particular night we brought our ice-encrusted Lancaster over the last big ridge and saw that the cloud ahead was thinning, and now we could descend to a warmer temperature.

The final run-in to Milan was made in much better weather with broken cloud at about 4,000 feet and once again that strange phenomenon was observed, that the sky was full of gun fire until the explosion of the first bomb. Magically, the volume of gun fire dropped by about 60%. Bombs gone we turned our backs on the Med and started a fairly steep climb to gain as much height as possible before arriving at those gigantic Alpine mountains again. Another cloudy, icy flight of three hours and we were among the fighter boxes in Northern France, but being in thick cloud, we escaped without a fight. Nine hours and thirty-five minutes after leaving we were back on the ground and having completed fifteen and a half hours flying in the last thirty hours just elapsed, perhaps we were entitled to feel tired.

What a way to spend one's 23rd birthday!

Sortie No. 10 had been successfully completed, the crew was now a strongly welded fighting unit and my own confidence was sky high. We had four times made return flights to Italy, we had been to the Big City and back, three times to the Ruhr, and once each to Hamburg and Lorient. This represented a total navigational effort of over 13,000 miles and I was beginning to master my trade. All in all, we felt that we had survived the bumps and maybe we could survive a full tour after all. It would take some doing because at this stage on the squadron, no one starting out from our reorganization in late August had yet completed one.

Lancaster bomber, preserved at RAF Scampton

CHAPTER FOUR
Operations II — Nearly Professional

At the turn of the year I had been promoted to Flight Sergeant and after three and a half years as an acting and then full Sergeant, the crown above the stripes felt good, besides I got a rise in pay of a shilling per day to 13/6d. At £4.16.6d. per week plus marriage allowance I was now on a reasonable rate of pay, particularly as Sergeants' Mess fees were low and the uniform was free. However, in the middle of February 1943, I had been recommended for a commission in the field and the next step was an interview with our CO 'Hoppy'. As luck would have it, Johnny Day, his, and the squadron's navigation officer, fell sick and Hoppy wanted to fly another operation. So as part of the assessment he nominated me to take Johnny's place and after a couple of hours' cross-country flying with the crew on the morning of the 25th, I found myself with them on the Battle Order.

The sortie was to be to Nuremberg — or Nurnberg as the Nazis called their holy grail — and it was typical of the Old Man that he would volunteer for what was likely to be one of the tougher trips. The target city lay well down into south-east Germany which meant traversing many lengthy flak zones and exposure to fighters for the better part of six and a half hours. As some sort of compensation we were going to visit the Nazi heartland, the stage setting for those obscene pre-war Nazi rallies when it looked as if a whole nation had gone off its collective head chanting "Sieg Heil" to the diminutive and slightly comic figure of Adolf Hitler. (Had we but known then!!) The bomb load was one cookie (4,000lbs) and ten cans of incendiaries (900 x 4lbs) which I suppose were chosen as Nuremberg was an old town, largely built of timber.

We were off and now, flying with the CO, I knew what it felt like to be first off — no slip-stream to avoid in front, the air ahead quiet and undisturbed. Soon we were settled in to the long cruise climb that took us up to 20,000 feet. Shortly we had crossed the enemy coast and were keenly aware of the German fighters harrying the flanks of the bomber stream, but as I seemed to have positioned us in the middle of the stream, no personal battles ensued. Across the German border, the Rhine and into Franconia and now the flak was increasingly heavy. At last ahead of us we discerned the target marker flares and commenced our bombing run across the town. My word, the flak was thick, it was apparent that the Germans had mounted heavy defences to protect their unholy city.

The boss held the Lancaster steady in his large capable hands and drove her across the city with bomb doors open and accompanied by flashes and explosions all round us. We made it and with the shout, "Bombs away," he had whisked us away on the return heading and in ten minutes all was dark and quiet again, but behind us was a red inferno. We were now flying above a thick belt of cloud which completely covered the ground and in a 1,000 feet high channel under heavy cloud above which totally obscured the sky. With no pin-point from the ground, no star shots from the sky and far too far east for Gee to work, we were once again on Dead Reckoning navigation using forecast interpolated winds.

Nearly three hours had elapsed with never a sight of ground or sky and Hoppy was beginning to become a little irritable with the continued uncertainty of our position and with the continual lowering of the fuel tank contents, revealed each time he pressed the fuel gauge buttons. We had several terse and rather snappy arguments in which he demanded our exact position and I replied with a Dead Reckoning one. On the last occasion we were both rude to each other and to avoid any further deterioration, I unjacked my intercom plug and naviated in silence until I had plotted our estimated position for the crossing of the south coast of England. I then rejoined the crew on intercom to hear the following cross talk between Hoppy and Pat Patterson, our Canadian bomb aimer in the nose.

Hoppy: "Oh for Christ's sake Pat, pull your finger out and tell me where that is."

Pat: (somewhat hesitantly) "I, er, think we are coming up on Manston."

Ah, thought I, if they can see the ground I should be able to recognize it and peering out of the starboard blister window, I did.

Navigator to Captain: "We are approaching Gravesend."

Captain: "What the blistering hell do you know about it?"

Me: "I was born and bred in London and have travelled all round it."

Hoppy: "What do you think Pat?"

Pat: "I think we are a bit further east."

Me: "No, we are about to cross the Thames at Gravesend."

Hoppy: "Ah shit, two of you are supposed to be able to read a map and you can't agree. For your information we have less than thirty minutes fuel left, where do we go?"

Me: "Steer 30° to Bradwell Bay, Beacon Code - -, distance twenty-eight miles, time twelve minutes. If you don't choose to do that, invent your own bloody course."

End of conversation, me incommunicado again.

Ten minutes later, once more plugged in, I could hear that the Old Man was calmer and could obviously see the Bradwell Bay beacon. Shortly after that we had circled and landed with rather less than 15 minutes petrol left in the tanks. The reason had been the consistently heavy head winds which we had met on the return leg which had knocked 30 knots or so off our intended ground speed.

The refuellers met us after we had shut down and we left the aircraft for the first time in seven and three-quarter hours heading for the control tower in thunderous silence. It suddenly occurred to me that it was now the 26th of the month and this was the day that I was due to be interviewed by my squadron commander whom I had recently been very rude to. I thought perhaps that I had better mend a few fences, so I fell in beside Hoppy and said, "I am sorry that you were worried on the leg back, sir, although I was fairly happy with the navigation and was fairly close to our intended track all the way back. We were never lost, just temporarily uncertain of our exact whereabout."

He replied, "Yes, well, maybe, but if you are flying a large bomber which glides like a brick-built shithouse, you do not want to run out of fuel, and we were bloody near it tonight so I reckon that that gives me the right to get a bit upset." I forbore to argue further with a pilot who was a great 'seat of the pants' man so that after refuelling had been completed we got clearance from the tower and departed for Scampton, arriving back at 5.50 a.m.

Eight hours later I tapped at Hoppy's door and was bidden to enter. He was still tired and leaning back in his chair with his feet on the table.

"What do you want?" was his opening shot, in response to my smart salute.

"Er, I've come, I, er, mean I was told to report to you regarding the possibility of a recommendation for a commission!" — it was out at last. The heels came off the table and down on to the floor with a bang.

"You have come to do what?" says he. I knew perfectly well that he had heard me the first time so I held my peace and we stood eyeing each other for long minutes. Finally he said, "All right Lovejoy I am going to recommend you, anyone who can choke off his CO like you did this morning has got plenty of gall, and we all saw how you can navigate."

"But, Sir," I said, "I was aware of and happy with our Dead Reckoning position all the time and at the end when we did see the ground, I was not very far off."

"No," he agreed, "you weren't, but I do like to know where I am rather than to rely on someone else's guesses." I did not take too kindly to this, but I had the sense to say no more. I realized I was dealing with a pre-war pilot who belonged to the 'seat of the pants' school and you can't really argue convincingly with them. Anyway, I'd got my recommendation and I liked Hoppy a lot so peace again reigned.

The final interview was with Sir Ralph Cochrane, AOC No. 5 Group, at Grantham Group HQ. True, I was in best blue but, as mentioned earlier, was not wearing a brevet. This caused some sharp comment from Sir Ralph and a telephone call to Charles Whitworth at Scampton to instruct him to post an order in DROs (Daily Routine Orders) to the effect that I had been given my Navigator's brevet — so from then on I wore an 'N' Wing.

The problem arose a week later when I found I had been awarded a commission, the man from Burberry's had been up and measured me for my uniform, but I could not get time off to get to London to pick it up.

Consequently I stayed in the Sergeants' Mess for the time being, until ordered out of it!

On 1st March we paid our second visit to the Big City, carrying yet another cookie and incendiaries. I was back with George again and the rest of my regulars, which was really as well as it was a thoroughly uncomfortable trip from end to end — all eight hours of it. Shot up over Denmark and Sweden, threatened right across northern Germany, fighting bad weather all the way, the only bright spot was that we ran right up to the marker flares, laid by Pathfinder Force (PFF). They had made a very good job of it this time, the IP and the target were well marked. However it did have the drawback of drawing searchlights to the area of the flares and as we arrived over the Initial Point (IP) to commence our bombing run we were coned by dozens of searchlights. I found out that it was a true description heard from the old hands earlier in our tour, you did feel like an insect on the end of a pointer. We fought those searchlights for five or ten minutes but could not escape until after the bombs were gone. On this occasion the bombs went wild because the longer we were held in the lights, the hotter and more accurate was the anti-aircraft fire exploding around us. Thus we did not obtain a decent target photograph on this wild night, but we did once again savour the scent of exploding cordite and liddite. Somebody could write a book about smells and the memories they trigger. I absolutely adored the smell of rubber, petrol and dope so prevalent in the hangars, I quite enjoyed the aromas from the Mess kitchens at mealtimes, but I loathed the smell of explosions — sharp, acrid and lingering.

Eventually as all things must, even the bad ones, it was ended. We landed at Scampton absolutely done to a frazzle, too tired to appreciate the necessity for another half an hour reporting what we had seen and done and almost too tired to appreciate the mug of coffee laced with GS rum.

I was duly gazetted as a Pilot Officer on 3rd March but was still unable to get away and obtain my new uniform. I stayed in the Flight Sergeant's battledress and remained in the Sergeants' Mess pro tem until Hoppy stopped me outside Squadron HQ one morning a few days later. The conversation was brief, terminating in the order, "Go to the clothing stores now, draw a new battledress on credit, sew on a thin blue stripe, and move to the Officers' Mess this evening." All this was duly accomplished and thus I stole modestly into the west wing of the Mess that evening at 6 p.m. only to find of course that I had been allocated half a room in the east wing. I thus had to pass through the centre of the Mess and whilst passing the 'Exchange' — the hatch from which the Mess Stewards fetched our drinks — a hand came out and placed itself on my shoulder, thus arresting further progress. At the end of the hand was the Station Commander, Group Captain Charles Whitworth.

He said, "You are Lovejoy aren't you, in Avis's crew?" I admitted that indeed I was and was prepared to explain why I was still in battledress in the Mess at 6 p.m. on a stand down night from operations. I never got that far. "Mr Ruth," said Charles to our Senior Steward, "this is Pilot Officer Lovejoy, open a bar book for him and put two pints in it," and thus I opened my commissioned career by standing the Station Commander a drink.

There was not a lot of time to dwell on my changed circumstances although I did come up against my Squadron CO Hoppy in the Mess over a game of shove-halfpenny. This was a game my father was very fond of and I had played with him on our board at home since I was about ten and consequently rather fancied myself at it. When Hoppy asked if I played the game, I replied brightly, "Yes, I've had a lot of practice at it."

"Have you indeed!" says he. "Right, we will have five games and loser buys pints." He must have seen me coming! He was an absolute ace at the game and won all five and so, somewhat crestfallen, I bought my Squadron CO a drink. As a consolation he did remark that I wasn't bad at it!

On 11th March we reported to Briefing to start another run of forty-eight hours on ops. The first trip was to Stuttgart, which was going to be a tricky one as it lay partially hidden among the hills in Franconia, well down into Germany. However we took the usual load and happily had a clear night for the bombing run, and with the assistance of PFF's markers we made quite a good run. Once again we met an absolute hail of metal and there was a severe jolt as we left the target. However old Olive Oil continued to pound away towards home so it obviously wasn't a serious hit. In the event, on our return we found two holes in the fuselage just — thank goodness — aft of the main body of the crew. A shell must have exploded right beneath us, the blast throwing us upwards, but the metal flying high wide and handsome and mostly just missing us.

This trip took 7¾ hours and after a fairly short lay in, we were up and about quite reasonably early on 12th March in order to prepare for a sortie into Happy Valley to have another go at the Krupps empire in Essen. This was to be our fourteenth operation and we all felt good at getting through that number thirteen, so we took off feeling fairly confident and able. And — doesn't the old adage say 'Pride goeth before a fall' — we were to find out this night that it was better to be born lucky than rich.

We reached the enemy coast at IJmuiden on time and on track and the night was black but clear and star filled. We got our usual doses of flak on the way in, but on arrival on the northern outskirts of the Ruhr, the shells were exploding so numerously and close together, that it did look as if you could walk on it. We stuck to the north/south run into Essen laid down in the Bomb Raid Plan and got the hottest reception we'd experienced so far. Poor old Olive Oil was rocking in continuous blasts of explosions above, below and all round us, even the normally imperturbable George was visually shaken and the raid plan called for us to emerge on the south side of Essen over the Ruhr Valley and return on a parallel track side stepped five miles to the west. Frankly I quailed at the idea and I wasn't the only one. Thus it was at my suggestion we turned east instead of west and flew along the relatively peaceful valley of the river Ruhr until we could turn north to the east of Dortmund, and then I set about closing the original track once we had safely left the heavy Ruhr defences astern.

It worked like a charm, our heavily riddled aircraft was not seriously fired upon again and so we came up to the Zuider Zee, Johnny was busy trying to dislodge an obstinately sticking can of incendiaries. They must have been well frozen on and even the axe hacking away at the ice on the cradles failed to release the box of nasties. Perhaps we were over concentrated on this problem for certainly nobody saw the twin engine fighter which discharged four streams of lethal cannon-fire which just cleared the nose of our Lanc. "Jesus Christ," exclaimed George pulling the nose up sharply, and almost simultaneously Sgt. Gilliver, riding as our reserve in the rear turret, called 'Twin engined fighter astern and closing." Saying which he opened fire with his four Brownings closely backed up by the Colonel in the mid-upper turret with his two. So hunter and hunted climbed towards the sky as if tied together with a piece of string.

The noise of 4,800 rounds per minute from six guns was tremendous over the intercom, but much more scarifying was the persistent thumps and clangs from the underside of the fuselage and wings as his shells struck home. He must have been a green pilot — he just closed in on us with no attempts at jinking and consequently he finally flew into the conjunction of those 4,800 r.p.m. and pieces of his aeroplane began to fly off. Three pairs of eyes had now identified him as an ME 210 just before he rolled over on to his back and commenced spinning down. I was too late into the astrodome to catch sight of the Messerschmitt but I certainly saw the sudden rosy blossoming through the thick cloud at 4,000 feet as he undoubtedly thudded into the ground.

The whole episode cannot have lasted more than seconds but it seemed a hell of a lot longer and now we could all draw breath and ascertain what our damage was. One thing was sure, we were still flying, albeit with a devil of a lot of vibration all over old Olive Oil. To begin with we discovered that the hydraulic lines had been cut somewhere and we had lost all our hydraulic oil and with it the power to the undercarriage and bomb doors. This left us in the awkward position of having the normally required services reversed. We had the bomb doors open instead of shut because they had been open when the fighter struck, to allow Johnny to clear the incendiaries stuck up inside. We had the wheels up as in normal flight but could not now get them down for landing. The wiring to the Gee set was sliced through, apparently by the heavy German flak, and we had overall vibration. However the engines were functioning well so despite the heavy drag from the open bomb doors we set course for Scampton from a pin-point I obtained on the west coast of the Zuider Zee.

As we wallowed across the North Sea, Johnny continued to attempt to free the sticky incendiaries, but with no success. We finally arrived over Scampton and called up the tower for a landing and were given the No. 4 slot. George replied, "I'd like to land quickly because we have no hydraulics, open bomb doors, locked up wheels, incendiaries lodged in the bomb bay, and a lot of vibration."

Back came 'Happy Day', the senior controller, "Olive Oil, you can bugger off to an emergency strip, we have twenty-six more aeroplanes to land and you are not going to foul up our flare-path."

"OK," said the imperturbable George, "where do we go?"

"Anywhere you like," says Happy Day, "as long as it is not here. There's Wittering, probably the nearest."

"Thank you and out," replied our Skipper and I gave him the course to Wittering.

It was now in the early hours, approaching 2 a.m., that time at which doctors always say that life is at its lowest ebb. There was nothing wrong with our survival instincts though. In the fifteen minutes or so it took to fly to Wittering, we had debated how to get the wheels down whilst Johnny still made frantic efforts to rid us of the can of incendiaries into the fields of Lincolnshire, all to no avail. We had meanwhile decided that the five remaining pints of coffee and about two pints of urine, collected from various strategically placed tins in the aircraft, should be poured into the forward end of the hydraulic system, hopefully ahead of the break in the line, and manual pumping we hoped would do the rest. It didn't of course, at least not quite, the wheels fell down with quite a thud but unfortunately would not lock. This put us in a position only marginally better than before. If they didn't lock on landing, the undercarriage would collapse and we would go sliding along a concrete runway on opened bomb doors, striking sparks into a can of incendiaries.

It was not a pleasant outlook but our marvellously practical skipper said, "The only thing left to do is to approach the runway very low and keep ramming the wheels on to it and take quick bursts of engine up and down again till they lock. If they don't lock, keep your hands on your seat belts and as soon as we have slowed down sufficiently, hop it fast." It was some comfort to know that the runway started on Kingscliff airfield and pursued its length through many fields to Wittering where it ended three miles later.

All was done as George said, as soon as he throttled back on came that rasping, penetrating noise from the undercarriage horn and on came red lights. He bounced and took off again, bounced and took off again and still the red light and the horn stayed on. Two miles up the runway on the ninth bounce, there was a click and out went the red lights in favour of green ones and all was silence.

We rolled on to Wittering airfield, were marshalled into a parking bay, shut down engines and just sat there in a kind of stunned silence. Minutes went by until there was a hullabloo at the rear door. We filed out, down the ladder and on to blessed terra firma where as the poet said there was more firmer and less terror. We looked over old Olive Oil in the light of many torches. She was a sad sight and we thought she would never fly again. The whole fuselage and wings were pockmarked with flak holes, the underside of the wings showed the results of cannon fire, and the fuel pipes were actually hanging down below the wings. How near we had come to total loss of fuel and a very possible fire!

After such an adventure, anticlimax followed in a big way. We were taken by truck to Intelligence Headquarters for debriefing before a squadron leader who was patently very annoyed at being woken and hauled out of bed. His first words were, "Let's hurry up and get this over and we can all get to bed, now what training mission have you been on?" Seven voices replied at once giving:

    a) A lurid bad language description of the mission,

    b) Advice on where he could now go,

    c) A request for an immediate return to Scampton.

The debriefing went well from then on. After a few hours' sleep, an aircraft came down from Scampton to collect us and we left Lancaster 'O' for 'Olive Oil' sadly behind, never to see her again.

Some days later I was called into Hoppy's office to face a fair dressing down. The gist of it was that our navigation plot had been analysed at Bomber Command Headquarters and they had disapproved of my novel idea to avoid a double dose of the Ruhr's flak defences. Through channels, I gathered that Hoppy had received a fairly terse message from Bomber Harris which stated that his staff were expert at tactics and he would be obliged if I did as I was bloody well told in future. I appreciated the reprimand for although avoiding flak I had certainly exposed us to radar clear of the protecting mass of our colleagues who were miles ahead of us, and that of course gave fighters a plum target. We could thank our lucky stars that a combination of good gunners and a greenhorn pilot had saved our necks for another night.

The following diagram makes the position clear.

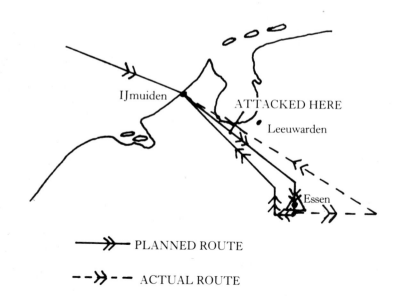

IJmuiden

ATTACKED HERE

Leeuwarden

Essen

⟩⟩ PLANNED ROUTE

- -⟩⟩- - ACTUAL ROUTE

Unbelievably we were scheduled for operations again for the third night in a row, but the weather intervened and the trip was cancelled, whereupon we were given fourteen days' leave. At this juncture after fourteen operations I, at least, needed it. It had been a long cold hard winter but spring was just around the corner and temperatures up in that high atmosphere over the German plain could now only rise and I was, and am, one human being who functions more efficiently when warmer.

On our return to Scampton it was April and a strange new unit was forming on the station, with the outlandish squadron numeral of 617. It did seem a unit with more than its fair share of highly experienced crews although our squadron provided several crews from 'C' Flight to make up their established numbers. We were to see a lot of them over the next few weeks and when Guy Gibson appeared to take command of this new unit, we all guessed that something special might be in the wind.

However, we had our own problems on 57 Squadron which had suffered steady losses throughout the winter attacks, mainly on Ruhr targets. This bitter war was sill being fought but strangely our first mission after leave was to La Spezia, a large naval base on the west coast of Italy. We were certainly getting to be long distance and even Italian specialists.

We took off on the late evening of lucky 13th April and headed south to the Mediterranean in the sure knowledge that this ought to be an easy one. The target was reputed to be not too well defended and we routed clear of most anti-aircraft guns so that the biggest menace appeared to be a fighter interception over northern France.

We crossed the enemy coast to the usual welcome of scattered flak and passed on into France. No fighters appeared and for once the weather was fine. We spotted the peacetime glow of Geneva's lights miles ahead, skirted the town and rode serenely over the serried ridges of the Alps in the clear air and finally slipped downhill to Savona Head on the Italian coast. We flew out over a calm Mediterranean Sea in comparatively balmy air and never before felt so warm, comfortable and at ease on an operational sortie. We were carrying four 1,000lb semi-armour-piercing bombs to ensure the penetration of stout dock side wharfs and buildings, plus the usual load of incendiaries.

Turning east, we headed for the Italian coast and La Spezia at a comfortable height of 4,000 feet. We must have been a couple of miles out to sea, west of the port, when there was a rumble like a London tube train and something very large flashed past and exploded behind and above us. This seemed to be the signal for every gun in La Spezia to open fire, and light and heavy flak, naval shells like the one just seen, Oerlikon cannon and even light machine-guns opened up. As we flashed in over the dockyard on our bombing run, the reason for all this unexpected commotion was seen, about half the Italian high seas fleet was in residence.

From being a doddle with no losses, it degenerated into a fire fight in which the force lost four aircraft. We were very low though and it certainly looked as if the port took rather a battering judging by the good photograph we brought back. Somewhere in that frenzied outburst of gun fire a small piece of metal lodged in a glycol tank and one engine packed up as we made the return climb over the Alps. The climb was no problem in a now much lighter aircraft but three engines had to be run at several notches above cruise power and by the time we were crossing the English Channel towards the Kent coast, fuel was running decidedly short.

There followed a dazzling display of emergency assistance for as soon as George had called, "Mayday, mayday," on approaching the coast, three separate sets of searchlights sprang up in cones above the airfields at Biggin Hill, Manston and West Malling, and the channels were cleared for us to communicate. West Malling was the nearest so in we went on our last few drops of fuel with barely enough to taxi and park. We had borrowed 'Q' for Queenie on this trip and we kept it away from the squadron for nearly thirty-six hours before we had debriefed, slept, lunched and taken off again. Ten hours and thirty-five minutes had been spent in the air to complete this trip which brought us half-way through the tour with over one hundred and eleven operational flying hours, and still luck was with us.

Two days later we had a new 'Olive Oil' and as we were also on the Battle Order for that night, we took her up for a thorough check out. Unfortunately after half an hour, the port inner engine failed so we returned to Scampton and had to take a reserve aircraft 'Z' Zebra on operations. In the briefing room the piece of string stretched right across Europe, all over land and crossing the pre-war borders of four countries, Belgium, France, Germany and Czechoslovakia. The target was to be the 'Skoda' arms complex at Pilsen and this time our load was a mixture of high explosives and medium capacity bombs — one cookie (4,000lbs) and two MC (1,000lbs).

We took off an hour or so after darkness had set in, and took with us Malcolm Crocker, an American, who had joined the RAF before the States had got into the war. He was coming for the experience and as he was a likeable extrovert, he was welcome aboard. We made our way across the coast of France and then south-east into the Belgium Ardennes with flak bursts lining the track of the bombers all the way. Across the Rhine, where I got a visual pin-point fix, navigation became all important because the route wound between some very heavily defended areas like Mainz, Ludwigshafen, Stuttgart, Frankfurt, Ulm, Nuremburg, and so on. Throughout this four and a half hours flight there were not too many minutes when somebody was not shooting at us. I recall standing in the astrodome to try and assess our position relative to Ulm and Augsburg from the surrounding concentrations of flak. We were in a quiet area where all was dark when suddenly to starboard, maybe a mile away, seven searchlights exposed, obviously guided by a 'Blue Master' and coned on a Lancaster. Very heavy flak commenced immediately and although the pilot tried evasive action, the blue searchlight remained on him, no doubt radar locked, and the bombardment continued. In not more than thirty seconds firing, probably less, the Lancaster was a mass of flames. The lights went out, the flak stopped and all became dark and quiet as before. Slowly descending through the skies were two burning arcs of fire as the aircraft broke apart. We did not, unfortunately, see a single parachute descend.

This episode kept us well on our toes even after being under fire for nearly three and a half hours and I, at least, was gratified to observe that fighter flares were being dropped and fighter attacks taking place on our flank. In other words, we were in the very middle of the stream and thereby escaping the worst. Now over southern Germany the cloud was thickening and as we approached the Danube at Regensburg it obscured the ground. Running up to Pilsen there were a few breaks but the target was very difficult to espy and the marking was not good. The outcome was a rather sporadic attack spread out over a considerable area, the hoped for concentrated drop on the Skoda works had not happened after all.

This of course did nothing to raise our spirits as we set off on the long long flight back through all those flak areas. There was a definite feeling of being buggered up and far from home. However slug it out we did against a strengthening north-westerly wind which cut down our ground speed and made the passage home even longer. At last in the wee small hours of the morning we were outbound from the enemy coast and over the sea. Then when nearly back to Scampton, came the warning, "Enemy fighters are infiltrating the bomber stream." Tired eyes and bodies came to a fresh alert but we finally did land without trouble with very nearly nine and a half hours flying.

Just over twenty-eight hours later, we had our new Olive Oil back and set out to give her a thorough air test, which this time she passed with flying colours. We now had sixteen bombs painted on her (one for every trip we had so far done) and a Swastika over trip No. 14 (for the 210 we had got) and she was ready for operations that night. At times like these a good night's sleep is at a premium, and it says a lot for resilience of youth that twenty-eight hours after taking a nine hour pounding, we were all on top form again teeing up for another trip. And where was it? Why Italy of course, and another nine hours plus.

This one started all wrong. Everything seemed to have to be done a little quicker than usual. We leapt into the air and climbed away to the French coast where we were immediately heavily engaged by flak and unknown to us, one small piece found its way into the deadly area of the glycol tank of one of our engines. It took some considerable time for all the coolant to leak or pulse out but when it did, half-way to the Alps, up went the engine temperature and down went the oil pressure. There was no alternative but to switch off and feather the blades. Now George had to open the throttles on the other engines a bit further to keep Olive Oil, us and our bomb load flying at 18,000 feet at 180 m.p.h. More RPM (revs per minute) means more fuel used so we throttled back again and slowly lost a couple of thousand feet in order to maintain our speed. Came the Alps, and we were down to 16,000 feet with the mountains rapidly climbing up towards us. This required more throttle and more fuel to climb a little to maintain our separation from the rugged mountains and stay clear of the heavy down-draughts above them.

Finally nearing Mont Blanc, we knew that the fuel would not take us to La Spezia and back that night, so reluctantly we turned around and headed back to lower altitudes in France. There were now two problems to solve, first where to jettison the bombs for it was becoming critical to lighten the load. We solved this one by heading for the middle and deepest heart of Lac du Bourget and dropping everything, one cookie (4,000lbs) and two semi-armour-piercing bombs (1,000lbs) into the lake. I apologize now for that midnight bang that must have woken up quite a few people in the little town and villages round the lake.

The second problem was not so easily solved. It was a navigational one, essentially its elements were: How long for the force to get to La Spezia, bomb it and get back to the southern edge of the fighter defence boxes in northern France? How long would it take us to get there on three engines? What time should we leave here to arrive at the fighter boxes with the bomber stream spread all round us? We circled a small town, I believe it was Chambery, on the edge of the lake for a further hour or so and then set course for home. We arrived at the fighter boxes in good order and with Lancasters and Halifaxes all round us. I felt quite bucked, if I could solve such a navigational problem so successfully, my ability must be improving! We finally arrived back at base absolutely drained after nearly nine and a half hours flying — nearly eight of them on three engines.

A week later it was our turn to return to the Battle of the Ruhr which was still being bitterly fought out. A strange episode occurred during this intervening week when we returned to the Mess after the cancellation of an operational trip laid on for one evening in mid-week. During this period, the newly formed 617 Squadron sharing Scampton with us were doing strange day and night training trips with peculiar loads. These trips had been going on for some time so that when we returned from our cancelled operation, 617 were sitting and lounging all over the best chairs in the ante-room. As we entered, one of our Singer twins from New Zealand — I could not tell if it was Pete or Tony — said, "Here they all are, 617 lay-about Squadron, busy again resting." With one accord 617 rose to its collective feet and set about the entering 57 Squadron crews and a right royal dust up ensued. The peculiar thing about this battle was that it was joined by junior officers and despite the considerable noise no senior officer appeared on the scene. I was amazed when, many years later, I saw that the incident had been included in the film 'The Dam Busters' — it was news to me that outside of we junior officers anyone was aware of it. At any rate, after the dust up there ensued one of the best impromptu parties we had ever had in the Scampton Mess — and we did have quite a few.

I see that I have not yet mentioned Scampton's big bang — probably the biggest in RAF airfield history. It came about like this. Thirty-two Lancasters of 57 Squadron, all bombed up, fuelled and ready to go, began filing along the perimeter track to the end of the flare-path. Progress was slow because thick mist was becoming thicker by the minute and we were being guided along by a 'Follow Me' truck and waving torches. Hoppy in the leading Lancaster reached the end of the flare-path and lined up for take-off. He did not get the expected green light to go — instead it was red for 'do not go'. The thirty-two Lancasters spread out in an arc behind the Boss were all standing using fuel and filling the evening air with the noise of 128 slow running Merlin engines. Apparently Hoppy got the signal to 'cut' and so closed down, and so, one after another, did we all. The planned assault on the Ruhr was cancelled for that night much to our relief, because by now one could not see the proverbial hand in front of one's face.

Thus Hoppy decided that to attempt to taxi right around the perimeter track back to our hard-standings was too risky in the all-enveloping fog which now shrouded the airfield and I must say that we all agreed with him. It did however leave the Lancasters in a nose to tail position, curved around the best part of a mile of the airfield and this was definitely against Command Standing Orders which stipulated a minimum of one hundred yards separation between aircraft in order to minimize the effect of any sudden air raid. Not that there seemed much chance of that on a night like this — if we could not see on the ground, no Nazi pilot was going to see much from the air! Besides to try and move them was impracticable anyway and we therefore rode off to the Mess to start a party celebrating our escape from operations for another night.

Next morning after breakfast, I was groping my way through thick fog down to the squadron when there came the most earth-shattering explosion which was sufficiently powerful to cause a tremor in the wall of the building I was clinging to. Anxious to find out what was what, I hurried forward to the squadron and was greeted by more immense explosions out in the fog. Pale, scared faces began to arrive at the squadron from the direction of the explosions and we learned that our aircraft were blowing up and catching fire. The first thought of course, was that some kind of enemy raid was in progress but as that was palpably impossible, the true story began to emerge.

The cold, damp fog had caused a short-circuit in the firing mechanism of a 20 million candlepower photo-flash on the Boss's Lanc. The photo-flash had fallen from the bomb bay, ignited, and burned unseen in the thick fog. This blaze set light to the aircraft, the heat caused the 4,000 lb cookie to explode (first bang) and shattered the Lanc causing burning fragments of it to be scattered far and wide. The burning pieces set light to three more aeroplanes which eventually blew up and scattered yet more burning debris down the line. By dint of hurried (and I thought very brave) action by our pilots, the burning aircraft and those as yet safely behind them were taxied apart and the flames quelled with fire extinguishers. When the fires were finally out, the squadron had lost four Lancasters totally destroyed, four aircraft burned to write-off stage and many more damaged. Our total serviceable strength was in the end, eight Lancasters. Of course, all-out efforts were made to make the remainder serviceable but even when a few days later, the ground crews had worked miracles, we were still eight under strength. It took some little time to obtain replacements; you see there was a strike at the aircraft factories at the time and so our covering strength was somewhat thin for a week or two.

The remainder of April passed with two more operations to Happy Valley, the targets being Duisburg and Essen. The Battle of the Ruhr rolled on with its usual accompaniment of heavy flak, hundreds of searchlights and snarling fighters diving on to us out of the darkness. Our Guardian Angels worked overtime again and twice more we returned unscathed, which was now beginning to be truly remarkable, since well over half of the chaps we had started with five months before were gone, whilst we were nearly two thirds through our tour. It was odd that even now we had the feeling that the 'chop' was for other people, not us. I can only put it down to inexperienced youth which had not appreciated that there is an immutable kind of deadly certainty attached to statistics — that, in simpler terms, the crock will, sooner or later visit the well once too often.

Be that as it may, the nights were getting shorter, the evenings longer and the weather becoming summery. I well remember a two hour 'shop' session on the steps of the Officers' Mess one beautiful May evening. The 'hangar doors' were wide open because among us were men of the calibre of Micky Martin, Dave Shannon and Bull McCarthy who had an awesome total of operational hours behind them and were well worth listening to. The merits of low flying into Germany to the targets were propounded by Micky, argued against by Bull and then re-argued by Dave. We had our own theorist on the squadron, 'Holy' Hudson, a great and good man and a practising Christian. He held that jinking over the target wasted time and fuel, that one might just as easy fly into a flak burst as away from it and so he made a straight run up to the target. He truly believed that if his time had to come, he would go, jinking or not. We firmly adhered to the view that God helps those who help themselves and we kept our arse-end moving from side to side and up and down all the time except for the final run-up to the target. Johnny got very cross if we did not get that last bit straight and level as we approached the target. I do not know if our theory did us any good but it certainly felt as if you were doing something to protect yourself by movement. I hate to say it but poor old 'Holy's' theory exploded on their sixteenth trip, I think it was, when they did not return from a trip to Happy Valley.

Lovely May days and shortening May nights meant a further series of shorter trips to Happy Valley — we were still very coy of showing ourselves in daylight over Hunland so could not raid the more distant targets during the span of a short summer night. So on the night of 4th May, we set off to Dortmund and stretched our luck to the uttermost during the course of this operation. Things went very smoothly up to the crossing of the enemy coast at IJmuiden and shortly afterwards we were crossing over Utrecht which flung up its usual barrage of heavy ack-ack fire — but this time we did not slip through it frightened but undamaged. This time we were frightened — and hit! The shell exploded close to the starboard wing-tip and produced the usual spread of deadly steel shards, several of which entered the starboard outer engine. With so many hits, it did not take long for the glycol to drain away and a very rough running engine finally failed. On four engines, we had been combating a very strong head wind reasonably successfully but on three were definitely limping along some 70 m.p.h. slower than before. On the approach to Dortmund, the port inner began to run very roughly indeed and within minutes the temperature was off the clock and oil pressure going down fast. There was nothing for it but to feather the propeller and close down the engine, which had probably picked up some stray pieces of shrapnel.

We were now in a fairly parlous state, ten miles or so short of the target, facing a stiff 50 m.p.h. head wind and with two engines out, reduced to a ground speed of just over 110 m.p.h. — more important, losing height too. Johnny spied a night-fighter base despatching its aircraft off from a dimly lit flare-path a mile or so to port of us and we decided to lighten our load by making them a present of our 4,000lb cookie. A quick run up to the airfield and two tons of amatol and baratol left the Lancaster to liven them up. It was a beautifully clear night, the wind was too strong for clouds to linger, and we all saw the brilliant flash of an explosion in the middle of the airfield. On reflection, it probably did little more than blow up acres of grass but it did put their lights out so at least they had had a scare and a few less fighters got off to get amongst us.

Like a wounded rhinoceros we turned and charged at the target, now all alight from the attention of the earlier arrivals, and of course from the later ones all rapidly overhauling us. We lumbered through the exploding shells, smoke and searchlights and miraculously delivered our remaining load of 1,080 four-pound incendiaries into the target area without meeting a fighter or sustaining further damage. As soon as we had turned on to the homeward leg, the gale force wind got behind us and the ground speed encouragingly increased. It was a long haul home on two engines but we finally made it back to Scampton nearly six hours after starting, and after our usual rumble and bump landing, we made it just to the turn off at the end of the flare-path before the remaining two engines cut from lack of fuel.

A week later we visited Happy Valley again and this time it went like clock-work, even down to delivering our cookie and incendiaries on to Duisburg, bang on target and bang on time. But such is the strange variety of experiences on each raid what was easy for us must have been very hard for others, for the force lost a relatively large number of planes and crews that night.

At this time strange goings on were observed at our companion squadron on the base. Large spherical objects covered in tarpaulin were being received by 617 Squadron giving rise of course to many ribald jests at their expense. We did wonder why they were doing so many night cross-countries, we did not know that these flights were always to narrow, twisting lakes and reservoirs. But signs of feverish preparations were obvious in the couple of days after we returned from our last Ruhr operation. Finally on 15th May 617 Squadron were called for a briefing in the utmost secrecy whilst we spent part of the day doing some high level practice bombing with 11-pounders at the range at Oglethorpe. By the time we landed the airfield was closed, no one in and no one out. As we heard the roar of eighteen Lancasters starting up we all poured down to the flare-path to cheer them off and saw by the light of the Chance Light the ugly great ball of a bomb supported in special crutches and unprotected by any bomb doors. We cheered them all off and left the scene for the Mess wondering what the hell they were going to do with just one bomb each and at that the most peculiar bomb we had ever seen. The rest is history, described by far better word-smiths than I.

However there is an interesting footnote to history which I witnessed, at the time ignorant of the background events. We were called early from our beds in the Officers' Mess to find the remnants of 617 Squadron scattered about the Mess, pissed and exhausted. Dizzy Davis, our Station Commander, for the first and only time, had allowed the bar to open after 617's debriefing and emotionally and physically flogged as they were, it took but a pint or two and the proverbial sniff of the barmaid's apron to put them out. 57 Squadron assisted them to bed, I personally put two very eminent members of the squadron into their cots and then repaired to the dining-room for breakfast. In the ante-room we beheld the quite astonishing sight of Guy Gibson sitting in a straight-backed chair with a cup of tea in his hand, steady, cool, and not a hair out of place. Since we had quickly learned that eight out of the sixteen aircraft to reach the targets were missing, we knew that they had had an appalling night, 50% losses. There was a very quiet Mess that day and I believe 617 were very lucky to have 'Chiefy' Powell as their Flight Sergeant Admin — I knew his worth well — after all they had pinched him from our squadron! At Methwold, he had shown his mettle and was a tower of strength during our move to Scampton.

A few days later I had lunch with King George VI.

I like that line and it is intrinsically true, if not materially so. The King was with the Command and Group Chiefs and Gibbo on the top table and I was, as a pilot officer, on the very junior table forty feet away. But at least dining in the same room and at approximately the same time.

The next week or so passed in anticlimax. We on 57 Squadron did some rather desultory training until the morning of the 23rd when we were all on the Battle Order. The target was once again Dortmund which, as it turned out, was some kind of Jonah to us. We started out with our standard Happy Valley load of one cookie and 1,080 4lb incendiaries. All went well as far as the enemy coast where I had managed to guide us on track and on time, but it was a very heavy raid and there were hundreds of bombers in a relatively small area of sky, so Jerry decided on 'hose-pipe' tactics with his flak. It came up at us almost literally in a curtain of steel and of course it got heavier and heavier the closer we got to the target. In the end the inevitable happened and we caught a real packet. After the tremendous bang, several shaky voices piped up on the intercom to establish who was or was not in one piece. We were very fortunate, George collected one piece of shit which went through a wrist and this we put a field dressing on. No one else was wounded but there had been some very near ones. Some perspex had gone so there were draughts of wind sweeping through the aircraft and I was the proud possessor of a piece of 105mm shell base which had scored the instep of my flying boot, leaving an interesting scar across the leather. We delivered our load and turned for home and incredibly in flak barrages thick enough to walk on, we were not hit again and our incredibly tough old Lancaster took us safely back to Scampton.

We were now approaching the summer solstice when the nights are remarkably short and quite often very clear. The Battle of the Ruhr still waged and although we were suffering losses, sometimes very high losses, we felt that we must be winning — I still don't see how those German workers stood up to the terrible pounding we were dishing out. As a crew we were now within seven or eight more trips to the end of our first tour of operations — thirty operations being the magic number — and some sort of hope of survival was springing up. It was a sensation to be wary of, several crews had reached this stage only to 'buy it' in the next one or two. Nobody from the start of our tour with the squadron, some six months or so back, had yet completed a tour, so the omens were not good as yet, but we definitely felt hopeful at this stage, springing from a belief that we were now a fairly professional outfit, and to prove it we flew two good trips to Happy Valley.

On the next trip to Cologne, our Base Commander, Air Commodore J. N. H. Whitworth DSO, DFC decided to ride with us. For his benefit we exerted every effort to ensure a successful trip. My navigation was absolutely spot on; as we arrived at the Initial Point (known as the IP or lead in point to the target run) PFF flares descended in front of us a mile ahead and dead on time. The flak was very severe but George, mindful of who was sitting beside him, held Olive Oil steady for far too long, we thought, on a bombing run and lo and behold, we not only delivered dead centre on target, but had a camera picture which later proved it. Charles Whitworth seemed to enjoy the operation which was conducted in the thin air above 20,000 feet which was, as he said, a change from wallowing through at 12,000 feet in a Whitley. We all breathed a sigh of relief when after nearly six hours flying we delivered him safely back to Scampton.

For the next three days I flew a variety of odd trips. First with the Boss, Hoppy, to Prestwick and after a landing back again. Good navigational map reading practice this and the Boss seemed very happy this time. Next our crew climbed into a spare Lancaster — 'O' Olive Oil was still having flak holes repaired — which was then climbed to 20,000 feet, from which height we attempted to drop a stick of four 11lb practice bombs on a very small white triangle. We pulled Johnny's leg unmercifully that trip because, unhampered by either flak or fighters, he only achieved a 300 yards undershoot. Next

George and I took an Oxford out on a flight to Newton where we landed and then on to Cottesmore for another landing, then all errands completed, back to Scampton.

The following day we were on the Battle Order again, and it was for a return trip to Cologne which we had bombed four days previously. At this juncture this was to be my 26th operation and, although I did not know it then, my last of the tour. We took off on a fine summer's evening on 8th July and flew eastward into the spreading dusk. Visibility was good and we were bang on track crossing the coast of Holland and although others around us were having brushes with enemy fighters, we flew on unmolested and once again delivered on target. On the return home, just after leaving a blazing Cologne behind us, I suffered acute stomach pains and I do mean acute. It was quite a job to remain compos mentis, which I managed to do with difficulty and with disastrous effects on the navigation. We made it into the south coast, miles off track, where I promptly collapsed. George got us safely back to Scampton where I was carried off the aircraft on a stretcher, not wounded, which might at least have been fairly heroic, but bloody ill!

An ambulance hurried me off to Nocton Hall RAF hospital where an X-ray showed an abscess on the appendix, so in hospital I had to stay while it was reduced, mostly it seemed to me by starving it! I got back to the squadron two weeks later to find that Command had called it a day for us. I was four short of thirty, George one short, Reg three short and so on, due to flying with other crews now and then. So rather than break up a crew, Hoppy had arranged for us all to finish.

There was a fairly healthy party as a result, particularly as Ron Croston's crew had finished at the same time and we reckoned an escape from the Grim Reaper was worth a celebration, although in my weakened state my drinking prowess was somewhat curtailed.

Posted as we were to Station Headquarters strength to await disposal time did hang a bit heavy. I therefore volunteered for a couple of trips as navigator in a gash Halifax Scampton had obtained. The first flight was to Westcott where we delivered Hoppy to become Wing Co Flying of a Heavy Bomber OTU (Operational Training Unit). The second trip I shared with another navigator — I took the Halifax down to Northolt where I left it for a weekend's leave — and he took it back. That was the last time I saw Scampton for the weekend was in between postings.

It is difficult to describe the change from living with the dark angel looking over one's shoulder to a stint as an instructor at an OTU where the arrival of tomorrow is a confident bet. That of course was the big gain in finishing a tour of bomber operations, but there were losses also. A Lancaster crew in wartime was the closest most self-sufficient group one could meet and beyond it was its family, the squadron. No training unit could ever achieve that cohesion by the very nature of the transitory courses through it. But as was always the Service way, you thanked God for the big gain and accepted change of place, face and job with good grace and got on with it.

CHAPTER FIVE
Betwixt and Between
(August 1943 — August 1944)

I reported into 83 OTU at Child's Ercall deep in Shropshire on the 29th anniversary of the start of the Great War. The station was so deep in rural Shropshire that it was quite difficult to find, but what beautiful countryside surrounded it. The flat lands of the east had been replaced by the rolling hills to the Welsh Marches. This made bad weather flying a bit exciting in this neighbourhood, especially with the 1,200 feet high razor-back of the Wrekyn, a few miles to the south of us. However I was to find my flying opportunities very limited in the next few months for I was a ground instructor, a lecturer, and setter and marker of examination papers. I suppose like all who had gone before, I was determined to make the young blighters on the course appreciate what a tough life they faced and therefore to compel them to make the most of good advice and instruction.

I plugged away through three courses or so as winter came in, getting no more than a very occasional hour in the air in one of our Wellington 111s or Xs, the old Wimpy. There was a slight interruption for an appendectomy in Putney hospital, the old trouble flared up in mid-September, at the beginning of fourteen days' leave which was spent in the hospital. I got the fourteen days after though which evened things up. I ploughed through an advanced Navigation Course at the Group School of Navigation at Tilstock and by the end of the year had done a hell of a lot of talking, but only spent less than four hours in the air since leaving Scampton. Finally in January 1944, I got into the air to screen a trainee navigator around a five and a quarter hours trip all over the southern half of England.

On 6th January I suffered a crushing blow, a telegram to say that my mother was gravely ill in the South London Women's Hospital at Clapham. I hastily secured some compassionate leave and by dint of a motor cycle, motor car and train from Derby, arrived home six hours later to find that I was two hours too late to see her. A most unhappy week followed, it was extra hard because my firstborn, her first grandchild was due in two months or so. I got back from the funeral to find that I was now to go to another Wellington OTU much nearer home at Westcott, near Aylesbury, Bucks.

Here I found myself a Flying Officer and appointed Ground Instruction Organizer which meant that instead of talking to students myself, I organized other talkers. Fortunately I had a very helpful and able No. 2, Flight Sergeant

Strickland who took over the rather monotonous day to day running of the programmes so that I could go flying. In this way I chalked up another ten hours flying by D-Day, most of it visiting other stations to meet old friends.

At this period I became interested in politics and religion and this was due to Flight Lieutenant Desmond Donnelly, and the padre, the Reverend Maughen. Many, many discussions with the first nearly persuaded me to stand for the Commonwealth Party of Sir Richard Acland and as many discussions with the second led to the padre's appearance at our local parish church to christen my son. The padre was a lovely man, a scholar in Greek and Latin, dragged from a Norfolk flock to minister to the RAF roughnecks. Unfortunately he really could not relate to what was happening on the Bomber Squadrons and his sermons did therefore lack bite, but I remember him with a great deal of affection.

On 24th June I departed to a Heavy Bomber Conversion Flight at Shepherd's Grove in Suffolk, crewed up once again and preparing for a second passage of arms. The conversion flight was for our new skipper's benefit. Flight Lieutenant Roy C. Earl from New Zealand had completed his first tour on Wellingtons in the Middle East and had never flown four-engined aircraft. Mysteriously I thought, we had been assigned to rural Suffolk in order that he could learn about fours on the old Short Stirling, although it was a racing certainty that now being members of 3 Group, we would finish on Lancs, and that of course is literally what happened. We spent from 4th June to 25th July flying Stirlings and nipping over to Stradishall to learn all about the mysterious and, I thought, somewhat overrated H2S equipment. We pounded the circuit with Roy for ten hours by day and six and a half hours by night, and at the end of it he was handling the huge Stirling with reasonable precision. Then we pursued hours of flying, practising our H2S map reading, although at this time the definition on the radar screen was not a lot to write home about. After just over thirty-seven hours flying we were sent up to a Lancaster Finishing School at Woolfox and here we once again pounded the circuit with Roy flying a mix of Lancaster Is and IIIs (Rolls-Royce or Packard engine). Then we did a cross-country, starting in daylight and finishing in the deepest darkness of blacked out England and authority decided we were fit for the fray again. On 12th August as grouse shooting would have started but for the war, we started off for our shooting match and arrived at 75 (New Zealand) Squadron based at Mepal, half-way between Ely and Chatteris, to the side of the big Peterborough Drain stretching up to the Wash, and the wettest place I had ever been in.

CHAPTER SIX
Operations III — The Professionals

There were seven of us, all about to start a second tour of operations, carrying very varied experiences from the first; starting from the sharp end there was Dicky Rich, F/O Bomb Aimer, Flight Lt. Roy Earl, Pilot and Skipper, Flt. Sgt. Taffy Howells, our very knowledgeable engineer, myself, F/O Finnegan, our Wireless Operator, up in the top turret was Wally Brown DFM and right out in the dustbin F/O Bill Goodridge DFM and, although I say it myself, there was a fair sprinkling of experience residing in we seven bods — enough we hoped to keep Roy out of deep trouble.

Wing Commander R. A. J. Leslie was our New Zealand CO, and indeed about 70% of the squadron was composed of New Zealanders, which was fair enough I suppose as its full title was 75 (NZ) Squadron. We were the only second tour crew on the squadron at this period in August 1944 but I've never been really sure what that signified, there were of course other individuals on a second tour. Be that as it may, we were on the squadron a full four days before going on to the Battle Order, and in that time had watched with some amazement squadron crews clocking up three short daylight operations totalling rather less than one trip to Berlin in flying hours. This was the post D-Day period when sorties were required in support of the armies in France and we were looking forward to operating in daylight at long last. But it was not to be just yet — our Boss man figured that if our crew was experienced then they were better used on the difficult long distance night operations. Thus we went to Stettin on the night of the 16th which was once again a severe test of my navigation, made no easier by constant bilious sickness as a result of a night flying supper of corned beef fritters — chunks of corned beef fried in fat and assisted down by chips! One thing I did learn over the years was that the type of food consumed before and during long and difficult flights has a definite effect on performance. However we delivered our 2,000lbs M.C. bomb and 360 large 8lb incendiaries on target. It was cheering to see the guiding flares of Path Finder Force dead ahead of one and on time. It meant that they were doing well and so was I. We arrived back at Mepal in the early hours of the 17th and promptly found ourselves scheduled to go the following evening.

This time the target was Bremen and once again we had a good trip enlivened only by very heavy flak over the target, but we still managed to get our target photograph. A few days later we were off to Russelsheim in

Franconia just east of the upper Rhine and in a collection of very well defended towns like Mannheim, Frankfurt, Stuttgart, Darmstadt, etc. The trouble started with a mistake in the identification of Saarlouis for Saarbrucken on the H2S screen. Working from this mistaken information, I calculated a drastically incorrect wind which meant that our actual ground speed was somewhat different from what we thought it was and with so many blobs of towns on the screen, Dicky Rich found it difficult to identify the target. After stumbling around the districts to the east of the Ruhr for some time, we gave up H2S navigation and got down to some 'seat of the pants' map reading and eventually located our target burning merrily from the assault of several hundred Lancasters — twenty minutes earlier. It was no wonder we had the undivided attention of the searchlights and flak. Somehow we survived to deliver the cookie and incendiaries and obtain a photograph. Then with a correct pin-point to work on we turned north-west and skedaddled for home.

Three days later we were operational again and we were beginning to feel rather put upon. It was Stettin again and here we were on the fourth trip of the tour and had not as much smelt a daylight operation. Whilst many crews on the squadron were amassing sorties but not a great deal of operational hours flying doing the 'milk runs' across the Channel. We all told Roy in no uncertain terms that after this trip we wanted a change!

The sortie itself was a highly successful one. Stettin received a very heavy and quite concentrated raid and this time the flak was much lighter. This I think was connected with the massive fighter attacks made on us all the way from the east coast of Denmark, across the Baltic Sea and right into the target. We were surrounded by long lines of bright slow moving flares which silhouetted the bomber stream for the fighters. Although we had no personal engagements our guns were in action raking across the fighters as they swept in at right angles, wave after wave of them. Once again we delivered and obtained a good target photograph and crawled into de-briefing after a very hectic nine and a quarter hours in the air.

In the afternoon of the following day the whole crew's discontent surfaced. We had completed four very tough night operations, spending a total of thirty-one and a half hours in the air to do it. Some crews on the squadron in the same time had seen little or no night action but had garnered eight and nine sorties towards their tour end. Roy agreed to talk to the Boss and an hour later came back to say that we were going to do our first daylight operation on the next day, 31st August. It did seem as if the old man was rubbing it in a bit but it was what we wanted, a change of scenery and tactics, so no one complained.

As it turned out, I would not have missed the chance to clobber this target for the world! It was a large flying bomb base at Pont Remy and with a wife and child evacuated and badly treated to boot, because these horrible things were exploding all over London, I had a very personal interest.

It was odd flying out over the Channel in the full light of a summer's day, but it made navigation so easy that I had time to climb into the astrodome and look around. It was thus I saw the enemy coast approaching in full daylight for the first time in the war and of course the green fields and hedgerows were little different from southern England, but for the first time in my life I was actually seeing a 'foreign' land. My musings were brought to an abrupt end as we swung in over the coast of the Pas de Calais to be greeted with the great puffs of smoke denoting heavy flak. The target, a ramp, V1 storage dump and back-up services was not very far inland — in fact a matter of a few miles. On this bright clear day, map reading was easy and in a few minutes we were on the bombing run.

As there were only a handful of bombers on this job each had the bomb run to itself and riding through the flak bursts, we delivered our 11 x 1,000lb and 4 x 500lb M.C. bombs spot on target with very satisfactory explosions and flying debris resulting. In no time we had landed back at Mepal and the whole thing had taken only just over three hours. I thought this was a great way to get through a second tour, but daylight sorties were few and far between for us.

We did another one five days later, but this time it was to deliver a hammer blow to 5,000 German troops surrounded by the Second Army who had hemmed them into the dock area of Le Havre. We carried the same load, 15 M.C. bombs, and about one hundred Lancasters attacked almost simultaneously. From my view in the astrodome, I saw the whole area disappear under smoke and dust with, here and there, erupting flames as yet another bomb hit the deck. The attack lasted minutes only but the demoralized troops were then captured by General Dempsey's men within the next few hours.

Then for the seventh trip of our second tour it was back to night operations, with the difference that this was a tactical target and not a strategic one. It seemed that the German army was using Moersdyck Bridge over the River Maas to bring up tanks and troops each night to reinforce their brethren on the west bank. We were to attack and destroy the bridge by the light of a fairly full moon, and by doing it at night we hoped not only to have some cover for ourselves but also to catch a tank squadron or a battalion of troops actually crossing the bridge. Whether we did so, I never knew, certainly the roads at each end of the bridge seemed quiet and empty as we approached at a fairly low level. We were to attack down the line of the bridge which it was hoped would give a line target rather than a small section of the bridge in sight for seconds only, had it been attacked broadside on. The idea was a good one in the planning room at Bomber Command Headquarters but in practice it took us over a nest of guns guarding the approaches at each end. For what must have been relatively few guns they certainly pumped up a lot of steel. There were only a few aircraft on the operation and each got individual attention from the German gunners and I must say that although it was brief, it was certainly hot! I have to admit that I saw no sensational outcome of our attempts, no bridge collapsed, no span fell into the water, but by golly we must have frightened that bridge. Our bombs struck the edge of it somewhere near the centre but I imagine that even if now rather shaky, it was probably usable with care. I do not count this as one of our successes.

On the very next night — 17th September, now a historical date — we flew on what I then regarded as the daftest operation of the entire war. First of all, they would not tell us what our bomb load was. Secondly, they said go and fly up and down on a line from Emmerich to Kleve across the Reischwald on the German/Dutch border. On each run they said, press the bomb tit once and thirdly, whilst you are doing it, make as much noise as you can, roaring up and desynchronizing engines, etc., and turn your exterior lights on and off. Up to now, our whole object on night raids had been to remain as individually anonymous as possible, and here we were being asked to draw attention to ourselves.

Well, we did it — flew up and down over the forest, released something on each run, flying low, making lots of noise and flashing lights on and off. Ground fire was very sparodic so it wasn't too dangerous but at the time it did not make much sense. That night of course some miles away, our big attack on Arnhem commenced. I did not discover our part in this business until after the war, and then by accident. I came home from India on a troop-ship in 1946 with, of all people, the No. 3 Group Weapons officer of September 1944. He it was who told me that on a clear night we had been dropping dummy parachutists into the Reichwald in order to create a diversion and draw the Germans away from the Arnhem and Nijmegen areas. It was by all accounts partially successful but I suppose was nullified by the accident of the German tank laager being in last minute residence around Arnhem.

A few days later it was back to horrible old Happy Valley and night operations. The target was Neuss marshalling yards close to Dusseldorf and it was attacked using our blind bombing technique, because the yards were covered in a heavy blanket of cloud. Under these circumstances one does not know for some time how successful efforts have been, reports have to filter through from agents on the scene and by the time the Command Bulletin is issued, it is ancient history to us.

Late in the month we made daylight attacks on successive days on some really heavy (105mm) guns sited around Calais. The first was reasonably successful whilst the second was a total failure. We were forced to abort this one since the area was covered in rain and cloud and we certainly did not want to drop bombs upon our French friends.

October opened with a precision raid on the sea wall of the Dutch island of Walcheren. The Germans were thick upon the ground on this low lying island and were putting up stiff resistance to all Second Army's attempts to land there. Some sixty Lancasters were therefore detailed to neutralize the German positions by breaching the sea dyke, thus allowing the water to flood in and wash them out. We were in the van of the attack and with only small arms fire to contend with, the bombs were laid extremely accurately. In no time we had dropped our load (one cookie 4,000lbs, six M.C. 1,000lb and one M.C. 500lbs) and in the short time that the raid lasted the sea could be observed to be seeping in through the breaches we had made. I have been to Walcheren in recent years and was very impressed with the ancient town of Middelburg, which fortunately escaped the water, as it is on a slight rise in the middle of the island. I was also pleased to see how attractively Flushing (Vlissingen) had been reconstructed. To the people of both towns who had to suffer from our actions, I offer my regrets, but the nature of the bloody war made it necessary.

Next came a night attack on the marshalling yards at Saarbrücken which, although we circled it for some little time in hopes that the cloud would break, was in the end abandoned.

On the 14th, I achieved a personal record. I had always thought that I would finish my bomber operations without ever seeing Happy Valley in daylight or at least without seeing it in anything but its night-time colours of roaring red fires, strings of flaming onions, and the twinkling bursts of flak overall. Very early in the morning of the 14th October, about 3 a.m. actually, we were roused and crept down to our Nissen hut briefing room in the very chilly morning air. When the curtain over the map of Europe was removed there, incredibly, was a red route marker straight to the heart of the Ruhr. I must admit to a bit of a sinking feeling, we had now grown accustomed to short penetration behind the lines of enemy positions on tactical raids by daylight. However, this was by any standards a fair penetration for night bombers to make to a well defended strategic target in daylight. As if to underline the prospect, half-way through the briefing came a loud explosion as yet another V1 plunged into East Anglia, not too far away.

By 7 a.m. we were climbing out of Mepal on an easterly heading on a reasonably fine morning although it was still chilly. By 9 a.m. we were over our target Duisburg, in company with several hundreds of four-engined bombers. The sight was an awe-inspiring one, Lancasters as far as one could see, with vapour trails behind them, over them and around them as the German fighters roared into the attack. Approaching the initial point to the run up, I was standing in the astrodome when I saw what I now know to have been an ME 262 jet aircraft. At the time it was utterly astonishing. The thing travelled like a bullet into one side of the bomber stream, firing cannons as it arrived, and out of the other side in a blur of movement, its speed was simply unbelievable. In the meantime, thousands of angry black puffs filled the sky and the going got a bit rough. By 9.15 a.m. Duisburg under a pall of smoke looked like a burning wreck from the air as we headed home.

It still felt rather unreal to be over Germany in broad daylight but it certainly made for more relaxed navigation. The Rhine was easily visible and pin-points could be obtained which made life easy. After four and a half hours in the air, we were down and taxiing to a stop in the dispersal bay, we got the surprising news that after a few hours' sleep briefing for the next operation would be at 3 p.m.

On attending the briefing at the ordered time, we were staggered to find that we were going back to the same target and that zero hour was to be exactly twelve hours after the first one that morning. The bomb load, which was the same as that morning's, was a very untypical load for the Ruhr. It consisted of eleven M.C. 1,000lb bombs and four 500lb bombs which indicated that we were now more concerned in smashing up buildings than setting fire to them. By 7 p.m. we were streaming east again but this time in darkness and so we were not really aware of the hundreds of Lancasters grouped around us. We crossed the coast of Holland, on time and on track, and there navigation virtually ceased for dead ahead of us, one hundred miles away was the most frightening red glare. Duisburg was still burning from the morning raid and although, as usual, the German gunners stuck to their task well, poor Duisburg received another huge battering lasting about thirty minutes or so. The immense smoking fires could again be seen all the way back to the Dutch coast. We all thought that perhaps it was a case of gilding the lily a bit but after all Happy Valley had harassed, killed and wounded us for years, so the feeling basically was that we had this day got some of our own back!

Four nights later we did a really punishing six hour flight to Stuttgart. Although we saw no fighters on this trip, we were under almost continuous heavy ack-ack fire through the whole flight over enemy territory. We arrived back safely with slight flak damage and very very tired.

The month finished in style with a daylight tactical raid on some 105mm guns sited on the sea side of Flushing. These guns were used as heavy artillery and had been firing across the Schelde pinning down the Canadians of the Second Army outside Breendonk. Unfortunately for us, they could also use these monsters cranked up to the vertical, as very heavy anti-aircraft guns.

We flew in from the North Sea in close packed formation vics of threes, which whilst making for concentrated bombing on small target areas, also left us very vulnerable at a mere 6,000 feet or so. The almost inevitable happened on the run in, the blighters got our range and the sky was suddenly filled with great steel splinters. We had just opened our bomb doors and were thereby exposing our 14 x 1,000lb bombs; open doors over intense flak fire is guaranteed to tighten up the sphincter muscles. I was standing in the astrodome on the look-out for fighters and saw all that happened next, although it was stupefying in the speed and utter completeness of the catastrophe. Johnny Johnson was flying a wing span away on our port side. A 105mm shell struck him square in the open bomb bay and there was the most tremendous explosion which lifted the remainder of the formation forcibly upwards and to the right.

I was jammed against the side of the dome with the force of the blast and to my utter horror was gazing at a few dark pieces of debris drifting down to earth where a split second before several tons of Lancaster and seven men had been. By flying mostly at night I suppose we had missed the spectacle of horrors like this, but seeing it happen close to was an experience to shake one clear down to the soles of one's shoes. We did for those guns, the push over the river started as soon as we had finished, but it was a rather silent and melancholy journey home. Suddenly just three trips from the end of my second tour, it had come back to me strongly that life in a Lancaster bomber was really pretty fraught.

The day before Fireworks Day we set off on another daylight raid to the Ruhr, to Solingen in fact, Happy Valley's Sheffield. I did not like the trip at all. It was flown in tight formation with leader navigation which meant that I was merely monitoring. It was also arranged to bomb *en masse* on the leader's GH fix, which meant that when he did, you did, right or wrong. I never used GH so I do not know how difficult it was to handle, but I do know that we did not bomb Solingen that day. By some freak of conditions over the Ruhr area I was getting fixes on my Gee set and on return at debriefing I was forced to report that in my opinion we had dropped our bombs under orders some seven miles from the target.

The other thing I hated about this trip was the report subsequently written by the Sunday paper correspondent who came with us on the sortie. To begin with the target area was blotted out by huge banks of cloud and although there may have been fighter activity, we saw none, only the angry red flashes of flak searching for us in the clouds. Our correspondent in the engineer's seat beside Roy Earl was jumping up and down with excitement so that when he saw a 'scarecrow' he nearly went incoherent. I should explain that a scarecrow was fired up from the ground by German gunners and as it had the appearance of Lancasters disintegrating all over the sky, it was supposed to shake our morale. By now though I knew the difference between one of them and the actual paralysing incident they attempted to portray. To stop our man going barmy up front, I carefully explained all this to him. Having got back to Holland, nothing would satisfy him but that we go down low under the cloud and have a look at Walcheren Island which we had 'sunk' the month before. Truly enough it presented a wretched spectacle, all under water except Middelburg, the only movement visible was from groups of people sculling boats about. So back to base.

The following day, being a Sunday, saw a front page headline report by our correspondent and our unmerciful ragging from the rest of the squadron started.

Even in thick cloud, the clown had seen fighters swooping to the attack, factories disintegrating under the weight of our bombs, debris flying high in the air, and so on. Worse yet, he reported getting the 'wind up' about the scarecrow only to be reassured by our young veteran navigator — followed by my full name. Finally he had, he said 'persuaded' us to fly low over Walcheren so that he could see the hole in the sea wall which we had made. Needless to say, the whole damned front page wound up in the squadron 'Line Book' and we had to fork up for many beers for the inexcusable crime of line shooting.

In the middle of November we went on another tactical daylight raid to a place called Heinsburg on the east bank of the Rhine. It seems that the Germans were entrenched in the town and their guns were sweeping the river, thus preventing the Americans from launching their rubber boats for a crossing. It was decided to turn the heavies loose on the town which ought to remove guns, tanks, infantry and anything else in the way.

We set off into a bright winter's day and found the little town without difficulty, because by now we could fly relatively very low over Germany since the Allies were in possession of all of it west of the Rhine. Approaching across the river at a modest height all hell let loose and on the run in we were hit very severely by several large chunks of iron. However, old 'C' for Charlie kept on going and in a matter of a few minutes the little town was a smoking ruin. The Yanks were massing for the crossing even before we left, which I thought was a touching demonstration of their faith in our ability to remove the obstruction. So once again, mortality had come near to being demonstrated, but, we only had one more sortie to do to complete that second tour.

We were not kept waiting too long, exactly a week later, on the 23rd November 1944 (a date written large in my memory) we were on the Battle Order for a daylight raid into the Ruhr. If you've got to go, you may as well go out in the grandest style I suppose, but Gelsenkirchen in the heart of the Ruhr was not our idea of a good target to finish a tour on. In daylight too! I have never known a crew so short on words and long on silence as we were that morning. It was to be another radar directed attempt and we were to dump one cookie of 4,000lbs and fifteen 500lb M.C. bombs on to a group of factories in the heavy industry belt.

Briefing over, we ambled out into the watery winter daylight and boarded the coach for our squadron hard standings, for the last time one way or another. Soon afterwards we were climbing away up into the crisp icy air and formating over Mepal until the squadrons were all formed up. Then joining the already very large 3 Group formation, we set off for Germany for the last, and in my case forty-sixth time. Our monosyllabic crew were still taut with unreleased tension as we made our way across the North Sea. As we crossed the enemy coast the perversities of operational life were demonstrated once more. No one fired at us, no fighters were to be seen and Germany lay beneath us in the winter sunlight. Yes, it was that easy — straight into the target through heavy gun-fire, but none of it seemed to be near us, and not a German fighter to be seen — it was hardly credible. Still there it was, we were on the way out and all talking happily again. After just four and a half hours in the air operation, No. 20 of our second tour was over and that was, we knew, our farewell to Bomber Command.

After a very satisfactory celebrational thrash in the Mess and in Cambridge, the crew began to break up as postings came in. I had secured Christmas leave for the second time in the war and thus it was early in 1945 when I reported to a peculiar outfit equipped with Dakotas, called 238 Squadron of Transport Command. They were based at a place called Merryfield in Somerset and no one knew what rod was in what pickle for us.

I was naturally a little sad, although relieved at still being alive, on parting from Bomber Command. A lot of my life and energy had gone into it so far and it had, after a chequered career, yielded me a commission and a Distinguished

Flying Cross, of which I was very proud. I cannot say I was sorry to leave Mepal though, I had been wet through for the past two months from the condensation and leaks in the Nissen hut. It had also been very cold and windswept. Nothing is more discouraging than waking up in damp blankets, stretching your feet out of bed into two or three inches of water (very cold, of course) and then, blue with cold, climbing into damp clothes. The only time I dried out was when flying, when all the moisture froze and movement brought cracking ice noises. No, Mepal was not my favourite spot, and I know now that the squadron doctor was right when he said, "Never mind lads, it won't hurt you until you are thirty or forty years older."

CHAPTER SEVEN
Overseas Posting

So Merryfield had to be an improvement — or was it? Once again dark and weathered Nissen huts were our quarters and when I actually had a rat run over the bed clothes one night, I thought officer accommodation had reached rock bottom. There were still some bloody spots to come in the future did I but know it, but the rat was the last straw. We at least got attention on that score.

I made the acquaintance of the Dakota with an Australian pilot, Flying Officer Johnny Bateman. I loved the aeroplane but discovered that all our training was shaped to one end, the perfection of astro-navigation and I was a real greenhorn at it. We had tried but seldom had a chance to fly straight and level for astro fixes on bomber operations. I had only four cross-countries out to sea, three by day and one by night, to master the art. Unfortunately I did not and consequently was posted off the squadron. The reason was given by the Squadron CO. It appeared that the squadron was Australia bound, but because of the Japanese war and the fact that they were picking up new aircraft at Dorval in Canada, they were going to do the trip westwards. This would necessitate a route from San Francisco to Hawaii and then on to a refuelling stop on a very small island named Canton. Reasonably accurate astro-navigation was therefore required to get within beacon range of Canton. Miss it and you ditched (and died) in the limitless tract of the Pacific Ocean. After a very good party I left for a few days' leave whilst they figured out my next move.

The telegram arrived whilst I was at home — 'Report to Victoria Air Terminal with a maximum of 40lbs of kit on the morning of the 5th April.' I bade my loved ones farewell and sallied forth. Upon arrival a very eager Squadron Leader greeted me with, "Thank goodness, you can be OC Troops for flight No. 450." I was then issued with an air ticket and introduced to my No. 2 for the trip, one 'Jenks' — short I think for Jenkins — a recent arrival from Bomber Command. He was a gunner in Pathfinder Force and had just completed his last operational tour and was now going to be a Passenger and Freight Officer in India with Transport Command. As was only to be expected I suppose, P & F Officers were known as 'Panic & Flap'. The mystery was where were we going to go — apart from the knowledge that it was India, we were very much in the dark. My ticket simply said 229 Group HQ and I had no idea where in South-East Asia that could be. However that was something to worry about when we arrived in four days' time, for now I had other things on my mind.

My 'troops' were twenty or so brand new Pilot Officers, aircrew fresh out of training school in Canada. We shepherded them on to a coach bound for Paddington which in true Service style delivered us there a full hour and a half before the train was due to leave. Train? To India? Ah well, the Service has its own way of doing things. Seizing the last opportunity for who knows how long to sample English beer, I sorted out the Pilot Officer with the smallest service number which in my book made him the senior man, and deputed him to secure two corner seats for myself and deputy OC Troops. We then departed up the ramp to The Load of Hay just outside the station and just over an hour and twenty-five minutes later, well loaded, caught the train by the skin of our teeth and subsided into our corner seats. We were woken up by the young sprog in temporary charge when the train drew into Swindon. The penny had by now dropped, we were to be flown out from Lyneham, the premier airfield of Transport Command.

Having arrived there, flying kit and main baggage were taken away for loading and we were left with sufficient for overnight stops. After a coach ride through the rural lanes of Wiltshire, we fetched up at the Marquess of Lansdowne's country house near Calne. Here we were supposed to remain until the following morning as we had already cleared Customs and Immigration and officially 'left' England. It was very dull in the Mess, absolutely no life there at all and seemed definitely no place to spend one's last night in Blighty until God knew when. Consequently, Jenks and I found our way over the wall surrounding the grounds and wended our way to the Lansdowne Arms in Calne where we spent a very beery and satisfactory evening playing skittles with the locals.

We found our way back and spotting that the bar was still open, decided on a nightcap. Looking neither to the right nor the left, we marched in and in loud alcoholic tones demanded pints of beer. The barman made no move to serve us but remained attentive to a knot of officers at the other end of the bar. This, of course, only resulted in louder still demands for beer. The altercation was stopped only after we had been ejected from the Mess and been told that our behaviour had severely displeased the new Transport Command Commander-in-Chief, Sir Ralph Cochrane, who had been in the centre of that knot of officers at the bar. No doubt, we were told, he will wish to see you in the morning. I felt that this was very unlikely as we were to rise very early in the morning and were scheduled to be off long before the time one would expect C-in-Cs to stir abroad.

So it proved. We were airborne just after 8 a.m. and he apparently left at 10 a.m. All the way through the 6,000 miles flight we were ahead and so no interview actually took place. On arrival at Karachi, Sir Ralph suffered a dose of the local tummy trouble and by the time he had recovered we were elsewhere.

The flight out was in a good old Dakota and having ushered my charges aboard, I relaxed and dozed for the next eight hours or so until landing at the recently captured Italian Air Force base of Elmas, near Cagliari in Sardinia. Here we were once more ejected from the Mess really before the evening had got well under way. The altercation this time was with some Italian Air Force officers who it turned out were flying a Caproni bomber on Air Sea Rescue missions. They had a special table reserved for them in the Mess as there was apparently no fraternization. Unfortunately no one had advised us of this fact and we both resented being told to buzz off and find another dinner table by our recently defeated ex-enemies.

Take-off was again early next morning and this time we dozed fitfully through a long and boring flight over the Mediterranean, starting the first hour in darkness and after a refuelling stop at El Adem, Libya, and landing at Cairo West nearly ten hours later. Being so near Cairo, I think it was about twenty miles, we had to visit the fleshpots but in the end tiredness beat us, so we settled for another booze in the transit bar only a couple of hundred yards from a bed.

The next morning we were off early again crossing the Pyramids as the early sunlight fell on them like a spotlight. Then we flogged for hour after hour across the deserts of Palestine and Iraq, faithfully following the oil pipe line until it branched off to Habbaniyah, where we landed in the early afternoon heat. I looked around with interest because there was still plenty of evidence of the station's encounter with the forces of the insurgent Raschid Ali, a couple of years or so earlier. Things like pock-marked armoury walls from field gun shell explosions, a written-off Oxford which had flown out to bomb the rebels and had been severely shot-up in the process. Jenks, strong, able-bodied Welshman that he was, elected to take the ninety mile taxi trip to Baghdad. I had a very entertaining evening in the camp cinema where a group of ENSA led by Paula Green gave us a two hour show. I marched my charges down to the aircraft and got them aboard at 1 a.m., when the air was relatively cool and flying was likely to be smooth. At 1.30 a.m. we were about to leave Jenks-less when around the corner came an ancient taxi bearing the lad himself in fine alcoholic fettle. We poured him aboard where he promptly fell asleep on the mail sacks at the rear of the aircraft. I volunteered my assistance to the captain and navigator, Flight Lieutenants Flint and Thomas. I was allowed to take star shots with their sextant and it was a great experience, for the air was very still, visibility down the Gulf was unlimited, and all the conditions were there for good astro-navigation. I enjoyed the shooting and the resulting calculations and we continued on our happy way until landing for breakfast at Bahrain.

It was a very different place in those far off days, lonely, muddy, and smelling very strongly of fish and shrimps. The principal town was then a very small place and the island's only importance was as a fuelling stop. After breakfast and a refuel, we were off again passing such exotic places as Bandar Abbas and Jiwani before entering the Indian Ocean which, in the morning sun, was very blue and very calm. Ten hours after leaving Iraq we were landing at Mauripur, just outside Karachi. The date was 9th April and a full month of unsettled living was about to commence — a period of acclimitization and of stumbling from one unwanted posting to another until I finally got what I wanted.

The trouble started when I reported in SHQ brandishing my posting notice, I asked for transport to 229 Group HQ, not knowing where this was. The reply was somewhat startling — "229 Group HQ is in New Delhi — 1,500 miles away — and everyone is posted there as a holding posting. Check here daily for further news." Now there was nothing salubrious in living in a tent on sand on the outskirts of Karachi. To begin with I was a full one and a half miles from SHQ or anywhere else for that matter as it turned out that Mauripur was an enormous size. Some chaps maintained that the building contractor had misread his building scale and made it three times larger than it was meant to be. Be that as it may, it was a long hot and dusty walk to and from SHQ. So much so that by the seventh day I was burnt to a painful brick red and began to have some kind of hallucination during this daily walking fry-up. I was certain that the ever-present noise of the cicadas emanated from insects on my uniform and as I could see none on the front of it, I stopped a passing airman and asked him if he would brush the insects off my back. With a stare that spoke volumes he said, "There are none there, Sir." I thanked him, walked on for some distance and looked back. He was standing in the middle of the road gazing after me and his expression plainly said, "That bloke's Dulally Tap" — the local expression for round the bend.

On the eighth evening came my first encounter with my life's aversion — snakes. I had an Indian bearer (batman) who was supposed to keep the tent clean and swept and light the lantern on the tent pole at sundown. He had not been very thorough in any of these duties over the preceding week, but this night took the biscuit. I arrived back from the Mess to find the tent in darkness which was a poor start since I had now to find the lamp in the dark and a box of matches and bring the two into close enough proximity for the lamp to be lit. I managed it eventually and brought the lamp over to the charpoy (bed) to find something squirming under the mosquito net. A second closer look verified what I had at first believed incredible — it *was* a cobra and it *was* coiled up on my pillow. I broke all records for that two hundred yards to the Mess and spent the night curled up in the chair in the ante-room.

Next morning I gave my bearer what for in no uncertain fashion and got a change of bedclothes, and I must admit I approached tent and charpoy very carefully that night and finding them clear, climbed in and slept very badly. The nightmare was over the next day. My original bunch of sprogs were also still with us here at No. 9 Transit Camp and when I went, they went, with me as OC Troops once again, only this time on a train!

I cannot pretend much sorrow in leaving Karachi, the town was like any large Indian town, crowded and incredibly noisy. The surroundings were sandy to say the least and the heat in April quite remarkable; even harder to bear for the rookie fresh out from England, was the harsh glare. I really do not know why, but of all the places I visited, India had the brightest daylight. The other thing I learned to avoid was walking under a camel's head, or even close to it. Karachi had hundreds of camels pulling all sorts of vehicles and many of them seemed to park during the afternoon hours leaving the camel sleepily contemplating the distant horizon. Pass close to one as he decided to yawn and you inhaled the fetid odours of what hell must be like — urgh!

Anyway, there we all were at Karachi Central Station with a large train awaiting to be drawn by a great snorting steam-engine of the Great Northern Railway (GNR). I shared a first class sleeper (two cots either side) with three other RAF officers and our first experience of the inside of the carriage led us to believe that it was probably hotter than the air outside. When a pedlar hawking ice blocks appeared we eagerly purchased two enormous ones and stood them on the floor in the centre of the compartment. At around 1 p.m. we pulled out of Karachi station and by 1.30 p.m. both blocks of ice were pools of water on the floor and by 2 p.m. even they had dried up.

For journey misery of a high order, I can recommend crossing the Sind desert in a railway train during the hot season. We stifled, we sweated, we changed position to stand, sit, or lie unrelaxed. The desert was flat, hot, sandy, uninviting, and monotonous. Cards soon palled in this heat and even conversation became difficult with the temperature in that carriage hovering around 110°F. The boredom was broken by the arrival of dinner-time, which entailed the train stopping, all first class passengers climbing out and walking along the line to the dining car and re-entering the train. An hour or so later, the procedure was reversed as we trudged back to our hot prison for the night. Two further unscheduled stops were made so that uninvited sacred cows could be pushed and pummelled out of the train's way. Finally, at around midnight we reached Multan and so stretched our legs for ten minutes or so, the temperature had by then dropped to a mere 100°F. Who said deserts cooled off at night?

Hour after weary hour we trundled on leaving the Sind behind and entering scrubland and finally some vegetation and scattered buildings. Our welcome to Lahore was a row of Indian backsides presented to us as their owners answered the call of nature just outside the station. Thirty-six hours after leaving Karachi we were puffing through Waziristan, home of the fierce fighting warriors — and those crowded on to the train certainly looked it. The train by now was not just full but definitely overloaded. There were Indians on the running-boards, sitting out on window-frames, and even on the roofs of the carriages — the combined load reduced the train's speed up gradients to little more than 10 or 15 m.p.h. Late in the second evening we arrived at our destination, Gujrat, well up towards the north-west frontier. Here we disembarked under the guns of armoured cars. It seems that the town football team had played against RAF Gujrat on the day before and lost heavily. The inevitable riot ensued and we were de-training in the atmosphere of the sullen aftermath.

Upon arrival at the camp I discovered that I was to join a course which would train me to navigate Dakotas for supply dropping duties in Burma. I was a little surprised at this since, when I left the United Kingdom, I had received the official pat on the head and had been told that I would not be required to fly operationally again. Whilst not being all that keen to fly in against Japanese anti-aircraft gun-fire, I figured that it could not possibly be as bad as Germany had been and so settled down to it. Lo and behold, on the third day I was rescued! Told to report to the Station Adjutant, I hurried there to find an irate cable from 229 Group Headquarters summoning me there forthwith and asking why I had not reported there four weeks ago.

The urgency and tone of the summons ensured my rapid departure from Gujrat by the evening Frontier Mail Express. I have two abiding memories of Gujrat. There was the afternoon in the lecture room when we were attacked by a swarm of hornets, which battle we won, swatting numbers of them and driving the rest off at the expense of several nasty arm and facial stings scattered through the course. The other was standing before the open window of my hut in the mornings and looking out across mountainous country to the distant snow-capped tops in the Hindu Kush range. The air was very clear and pure and, in the early morning, like wine.

Departing Gujrat at 5.30 p.m. I shared a first class sleeper with a Muslim gentleman who at last and first lights took off his footwear and facing west rocked back and forth in prayer for several minutes on each occasion. His navigation must have been good too for I reckon that he was facing Mecca both times. Hot, sticky and tired, I reached Delhi Central at just after 8 a.m. on a Sunday morning and sought a conveyance to 229 Group HQ situated somewhere out in New Delhi. Upon arrival at the huge block building shaped like an H, quite close to government buildings, I dismissed my gharry and started inside to report. There was no activity going on inside yet this was the end of April 1945 and furious battles were still being fought in the Arakan in Burma. I was to learn that Staff Headquarters made their own hours which certainly did not include early Sunday mornings. By this time I was more than a little annoyed, rudderless in a strange town with no Urdu at my command. Hearing voices coming from a room marked 'Orderly Room' I pushed in to find a corporal addressing remarks to another man sitting on a window ledge with the sun streaming in around him. The corporal, turning as I blustered in, said, "Can I help you, Sir?" I replied very angrily that yes he bloody well could. After arriving dirty and tired, not met at the station, and plainly nobody interested in my arrival at Group HQ, why the so and so had I been dragged hotfoot for sixteen hours by such an urgent cable?

The figure in the window heaved himself forward and revealed himself to be Air Commodore Jarman, the second in command of the Group, who said, "Whilst I appreciate your sentiments Flight Lieutenant, kindly cease to take your frustrations out on the corporal." He was rather more succinct, but that was the gravamen of his message. I thought 'Oh hell, what a good start!' and accepted his offer of a lift to the Mess.

The rest of Sunday passed quietly and on the next morning I reported in only to fetch up eventually across the desk of the Group Deputy Navigation

Officer, one 'Tiny' Lewis, an old acquaintance of mine in Bomber Command over the last five years. I do not like rowing with friends but when he announced that I was to be station briefing officer at RAF St. Thomas's Mount in Madras, a row erupted. I told him in no uncertain terms that I had not come over five thousand miles just to be grounded. Tiny, being the good-natured giant that he was, allowed that if I could find someone on either the Dakota or Liberator squadrons stationed at Palam, some three or four miles out of Delhi, who was willing to swap jobs, I could do it. I did not think there was much chance of such a fortunate circumstance occurring but I had only one day to do it so I got transport laid on and made Palam for lunch.

Nobody on the Liberator squadron was remotely interested in my deal but to my delight and surprise I found a navigator on the Dakota squadron, No. 353, who had had a bellyful of flying in the Far East over the last five years and we swopped on the spot. I rushed back to Tiny's office with my find, got the paperwork done, collected kit from 229 Group Mess and was back at Palam in time for dinner!

CHAPTER EIGHT
Squadron Life Again — Air Line Crew

353 Squadron's task was in effect to fly all the routes in India which, were it not for the war, would be flown by Indian National Airways (INA). The squadron had to cover five standard routes as follows plus a flight twice weekly to Jiwani to supply this airfield in remote Baluchistan.

Route 1.   *Westbound Circular.*   *Elapsed Time . . . One Week.*
Palam — Jodhpur — Karachi (Mauripur) — Bombay (Santa Cruz) (Day's slip) — Bangalore (Yelahanka) — Sulur — Cochin — Colombo (Ratmalana) (Day's slip) Colombo — Madras (St. Thomas's Mount) — Vishakhapatnam — Cuttack — Calcutta (Dum Dum) (Day's slip) — Allahabad (Bamrauli) — Palam.

Route 2.   *Eastbound Circular.*   *Elapsed Time . . . One Week.*
As for the westward but in reverse, omitting Cuttack and Madras and calling in at Bangalore.

Route 3.   *Via Central India.*   *Elapsed Time . . . Four Days.*
Palam — Allahabad — Nagpur — Hyderabad (Hakimpet) — Madras — Trichinopoly — Colombo.

Route 4.   *To North-West Frontier.*   *Elapsed Time . . . One Day.*
Palam — Lahore — Rawalpindi (Chaklala) — Risalpur and return.

Route 5.   *Non-Stop Night Flight.*   *Elapsed Time . . . Two Days.*
Palam to Calcutta (Day's slip) and return following night.

We also would occasionally fly specials which were laid on by 229 Group Headquarters in New Delhi. We carried freight of an urgent nature and invariably a full load of passengers, officers and men (and women) of the three services, government officials of all shapes, ranks and sizes and occasional Foreign Office bods. Our passenger lists were nearly always full, there were even names on a waiting list for the longer routes. It was on this squadron that I made the acquaintance of passenger and freight manifests and all-up weight sheets for the first time. It was important to see that the freight was stowed with due regard to the centre of gravity of the aircraft and that the maximum all-up weight of 29,000lbs (about 15 tons) was not exceeded.

I navigated my first flight out of Palam starting 5th May on a Westbound Circular. It was still dark when I made my way to the Mess for breakfast at 4.15 a.m. The air was pleasantly warm and the sky completely devoid of cloud as was usual at this time of the year. Our crew, Flying Officer Eric Thompson AFC, Warrant Officer Wood and myself, climbed up into our Dakota and carefully stored our baggage, divested ourselves of navigation kit, sextant, signals information, manifests and the like and started up in the Squadron Lines at first light. We rolled easily across the airfield to the terminal building, checked off the passengers as they boarded and minutes later lifted off into a gloriously bright morning with the sun rising fast. In the two hours it took to fly to Jodhpur the sun climbed higher and it became very hot even at 6,000 feet above the parched brown fields of the Indian summer.

Navigation in Northern India at this time of the seasons is no problem. Visibility is almost limitless and one could see the one and only railway line for miles converging towards our track when many miles away from it. I identified the tiny Merta Road station when it was still twenty miles away. We landed at Jodhpur to find the sun glinting off the pink walled palace of the Maharajah, always a splendid and fascinating sight. After a small exchange of freight, a few passengers off and some more on and off we went again bound for Mauripur in Karachi. This part of the route gives one a view of a most unusual geographic division — the wiggly line drawn across the face of the earth marking the stark change from the burnt brown of the cultivated area to the bright yellow of the Sind desert. It is most marked at the airfield of Chor where one end of the strip is surrounded by umber coloured fields and the other runs out into the brightly coloured sand of the Sind.

We were now over the Sind desert, an enormous expanse of sand with very sparse scrub, the home of the Hurs for whom, reputedly, we carried our 'Goolie Chits'. This was my first acquaintance with this piece of insurance, it stated that if we were to be found wandering in the desert or wherever, those who found us and returned us to the British Raj would be well rewarded. I am glad that I never had to put the efficacy of this scheme to the test. Nearly three hours after leaving Jodhpur we landed safely at Nauripur and left the aeroplane in the blazing sun to be refuelled whilst we went off for a surprisingly good three course lunch in the Passenger Terminal Restaurant. I always enjoyed lunch here for the fish course invariably served some delightful little flat fish caught off Karachi that same morning and grilled in breadcrumbs.

After lunch we returned to the aircraft only to find upon entering that we would have been cooler stepping into a baking oven. The aircraft temperature gauge showed 130°F and opening doors and windows had little effect, the metal walls of the aircraft simply threw back the heat. Our pristine white overalls of the morning were looking a little the worse for wear now. In such conditions of course, one has freight loaded well before time and we delayed emplaning our passengers until the very last minute. With twenty very hot passengers aboard and with every window in the cockpit wide open, we roared off into the brassy sky, heading south.

The west coast of India hereabouts is indented with hundreds of little creeks and inlets and as we proceeded further south over the Kutch, they ran into one another forming a vast flat stretch of salt marsh. From the air it looked extremely desolate, but here and there tiny settlements showed and one wondered how they supported a living.

Leaving the Kutch behind the passing over Surat with its myriad cotton mills, the earth was becoming more lush although we still bordered the Arabian Ocean. At last among the profuse palm trees and tropical vegetation we fetched up with the railway line running south to Bombay and soon were over the town itself surrounded by inlets and islands. Our objective was Santa Cruz airport which was notorious for the huge vultures or kite hawks which lazily flapped around the circuit. They were there because numerous Parsee towers of silence surrounded the airport and the Parsees allowed their dead to lie atop the towers to be picked clean by the birds of prey.

We landed at last and having put the aeroplane to bed, boarded a coach which was to take us out to an aircrew hostel at Juhu beach. After a half an hour's drive through Bombay's busy and down at heel suburbs, we arrived at our night stopping place where a cold shower, followed by a cold beer, was very welcome. The beach at Juhu was enormous but, although safe for swimming, it did seem to attract large numbers of jellyfish and the occasional Portuguese man-of-war, all of which could and did inflict stings of varying severity. The evening meal at the aircrew hostel was not one of its attractions and often enough we hired a cab to take us into central Bombay for a meal. In time our favourite restaurant became the one opposite Churchgate Station where their 'steaks' were bigger thicker and juicier than any I had yet seen. Since the cow was considered a sacred animal in India, I often wondered where the steak came from, yaks probably. Next morning, again before it was light we were up, breakfasted, and on our way to Santa Cruz. After collecting the weather forecast, which predicted a uniformly fine day over the whole of southern India with only broken cumulus cloud here and there, we sallied forth to the aircraft, loaded up and climbed away south-south-east over the Western Deccan until we were sitting comfortably in fairly smooth air 5,000 feet above the plateau.

This part of the country in May was beginning to look parched as it waited for the monsoon rains of late June, July and August. One began to realize the immensity of both the country and its population when looking around to all horizons. Even in areas relatively inaccessible to all but ox carts, there were settlements and people — always people. In due course Yelahanka loomed up, this was the airfield serving Bangalore, the town which housed the Headquarters of the Indian Army's Southern Command. This airfield was infamous to all RAF aircrews who used it. The runway was level for a couple of hundred yards or so and then shelved steeply downwards, bottoming out and slanting gently upwards at the far end. Some said it dropped twenty-nine feet in two hundred yards, certainly it took some landing on at night or in poor visibility if one was not to give one's passengers a hell of a jar on touchdown. It was a bright, brassy day this time and Eric duly lost flying speed before the hill so that we stayed on the runway after landing. Driving into Bangalore from the airfield was a pleasant if slightly unnerving experience. The road ran between an avenue of palm trees and was bordered by lush vegetation but also bordering the road were hordes of baboons of uncertain temper. Often you drove unmolested, but occasionally one or two would alight on the roof of the car or van and hammer it unmercifully. The town itself, like a number of the larger Indian towns, had a very pleasant centre giving way to overcrowded and noisome suburbs.

However, not having visited the town on this trip, we were quite quickly away after the exchange of some freight and passengers. We were now flying over southern India and in Equatorial latitudes, and the vegetation was most definitely greener, although obviously in need of water. The trip to Sulur was a relatively short one of an hour or so and after a brief stop there we were airborne once again, heading south-west to Cochin on the coast. This again was a relatively short trip but it entailed a climb up to 10,000 feet in order to pass safely over the mountains bordering the coast, just as on the approach to Sulur we had been compelled to fly at 10,000 feet to pass safely over Ootacamund. The magical country around Ooty, as it was known colloquially, although high in the mountains enjoyed a remarkably soft climate and it was said that anything would grow there. Certainly they produced marvellous strawberries and cherries which found their way to Sulur and Coimbatore bases via the ubiquitous ox cart down the winding road from the mountains. The tall ranges before the coast were known as the Ammamalal Hills — one wondered what height a mountain would be in this region.

Once over the hills, the descent to Cochin was of necessity steep and rather sudden as it had to be encompassed in about thirty miles. The approach to the airfield was over mangrove swamps and sullen looking brown streams. The runway itself appeared to float on water and when a large ship was in Cochin harbour, it was often moored close to the end of the runway, thus completing the illusion that one was landing on an aircraft carrier. The stop here on this occasion was a brief one but it was enough to have opened the rear door to deliver a small piece of freight and to experience the hot humidity which hit one in a wave and felt rather like being immersed in warm mud.

Having left Cochin behind we were now on the final leg to Colombo and I was curious to see something of Ceylon, often described as a jewel of an island. We passed out of India over Ramnad and beyond lay Adam's Bridge, a line of coral islets joining the island of Pamban in India to the Mannar peninsula which pointed westwards from Ceylon like an indicating finger. There was a ferry service operating across the gap known as the Palk Strait between the two countries and although from our height of 8,000 feet it looked as if a giant could use the 'bridge' as stepping stones, in reality they posed quite a navigational problem to shipping. Shortly after crossing the coast of Ceylon, the huge rock of Sigyria could be seen rising from the surrounding plain like a great petrified whale. Thereafter the ancient ruins of the old summer capital at Anuradhapura could be seen and finally the harbour of Colombo appeared, crowded with shipping as at that time it was one of the busiest ports in the Far East.

We landed at Ratmalana, some five miles or so south of Colombo and after putting the old Dakota to bed were free for 36 hours until early morning take-off on the day after tomorrow. I made for the guardroom and a taxi to Bambalapitya, two miles south of the capital, where my brother resided with a number of other Admiralty types who were serving the naval port of Colombo harbour. My brother's particular responsibility was the naval stores and armoury of which more anon.

I could think of worse places to be than that bungalow! It stood behind a fair sized garden fronting the main road from Colombo to Galle and its rear garden gave on to tumbled rocks fringing the Indian Ocean. All kinds of vegetable and animal life thrived in both gardens. To reach it from Ratmalana, one had to pass through Mount Lavinia which was an area of very lush coconut plantations ending in a sheer drop into the sea on which perched the Mount Lavinia Hotel, a favourite spot of the British from Colombo.

After a very pleasant day seeing the sights of Colombo, lounging on the immaculate lawn of the Galle Face Hotel and watching the sun set from the front garden of the bungalow, it was back to Ratmalana bright and early in the morning. After packing them all in, off we set for St. Thomas's Mount in Madras in the south-east corner of India. It was a smooth ride early on in a nice bright clear day. I looked with interest at Tommy's Mount for here but for the grace of God and 'Tiny' Lewis, I would have been station navigation officer. All I can say that although it seemed quite a reasonable station, I would not have swopped my present job for a station ten times better equipped.

After leaving Madras behind we were crossing the huge estuaries of the mighty Krishna and Godavari rivers. At this dry time of the year they were disappointingly small trickles in wide salt and mud flats. We circled around the very high hills surrounding our next port of call, Vishakhapatnam and as the sun was past the yard-arm, it was now very hot. Rising currents of warm air combined with breezes gusting between the hills made the approach and landing a very bumpy business. However Eric took it all in his stride and we spent the refuelling interval slaking considerable thirsts with 'nimbo pani' (lime juice and water) from the airport canteen. After take-off we paralleled the Orissa coast up to Cuttack where we landed and made an extremely short stop, before completing the leg to Calcutta. We arrived at Dum Dum Airport in the early evening, some ten and a half hours after leaving Colombo and having finished for the day, boarded our aircrew bus which was to take us down town to the flat leased by the squadron as a transit Mess in Middleton Street.

Middleton Street was a reasonably quiet residential road off the Chowringee, Calcutta's main thoroughfare. One aspect of this city impresses itself upon you at once — there are too many people in it! In fact enormous crowds everywhere jostle for every square foot of space and it was appalling to discover that huge numbers of people were homeless. Late in the evening, thousands prepared their bed for the night in shop doorways, entrance halls to flats and hotels and, when all else failed, in the streets. At this time it was estimated that Calcutta had a population of some seven million souls and fully two million of them slept out of doors. Well, granted it was warm but sometimes in the monsoon season it was very wet. Worst of all to my mind, was the constant disturbance to the slumbers of the would-be sleepers as returning hotel guests and flat residents returned to their rooms and stepped over the recumbent bodies.

Of course where you have such masses of people living in insanitary conditions, diseases are not far behind. Annually, Calcutta had its plagues of typhoid, cholera and various other fevers. In the passing crowds one could see evidence of beriberi, glaucoma and elephantiasis. In fact I believe that India had every disease known to mankind — except yellow fever and their efforts to keep this disease out of the country all but choked us to death at Karachi on many occasions, as they burst in to the aircraft discharging anti-fever aerosol bombs.

Anyway after a day of sightseeing around the town, Chowringee, Howrah Bridge, Dalhousie Square, Outer Circular Road and so on, we were out of bed well before dawn, breakfasted and motored out to DumDum for the last leg of this round-India trip. Having secured our passengers and freight we were off in the still early morning and climbing out north-west over the Bengal coalfields.

A lovely flight at 8,000 feet above the Ganges, with not a cloud in the sky and visibility almost limitless, saw us through to Allahabad. A few miles east of our destination we flew over the many temples of Benares and contemplated the sight below of hundreds of pilgrims bathing in the 'Father of Rivers', the Ganges. After an hour on the ground we were off again, leaving the Ganges to make its stately way westwards whilst we struck north-west over the River Jumna. By the time we were flying over the beautiful towers of the Taj Mahal the afternoon was very hot and with so much visibility that we could make out the hills to the north where the British, in the old days, were wont to repair during the hot season.

After landing at Palam, disgorging the passengers and freight and then putting the Dakota to bed, the lengthening shadows of late afternoon had arrived and there was time to reflect that in the past week we had circumnavigated the sub-continent over deserts, jungles, mountains, plains and famous rivers, seen places which had figured in my school history and geography books and had, in that one round trip, spent thirty-six hours in the air. The Londoner had indeed come a long way.

Four days later we set off to the south-east, bound for Allahabad and Calcutta. On this trip I had decided to measure the height of a whale-back hill, south-east of Gaya, marked as Parasnath, on the map which rose sharply out of the river plain to a height of 6,400 feet. It was marked on the maps of the time as some two thousand feet lower and although at this time of the year one could see it from a good fifty miles away, I felt that it might be rather a menace in thick monsoon cloud later in the year. If all it took to avoid hitting a stuffed cloud was an accurate measurement, then I was determined to make it. The Indian air maps were in places notoriously inaccurate, but as they were based upon a Royal Engineers' survey of the 1890s, it was not perhaps too surprising.

We duly flew level with the monster, Parasnath, and having recorded an exact a height as was possible with one altimeter set on QFE (height above ground) and the other on QFF (height above sea level), we flew on over the coalfields towards Calcutta. The Ganges became the Hooghly river and then that river became many as it divided into The Sundarbans at its delta. I heard that the largest Royal Bengal tigers were to be found there, but never ventured to find out if it was true.

CHAPTER NINE
On Indian Weather and Airfields and Further Travels

Early in June, on an Eastbound Circular, we had left Karachi and were approaching Jodhpur. Away to the east was a sinister looking black line which would have to be crossed if we were to complete the final leg and reach Palam. Climbing out of Jodhpur, the sky got darker and darker, and flying conditions were getting very rough indeed. We were in fact flying into one of those giant walls of sand which seem to gather together in the hot cloudless summer days and then travel across the Sind desert, getting hotter and lifting more and more sand as they progressed.

Visibility was nil, the aircraft was rocking from side to side and tossing up and down, sometimes simultaneously, and our poor sweating passengers had to remain tightly belted to seats to remain relatively safe. The wind strength was quite enormous but the huge dust storm travelled remarkably slowly. Navigation was very difficult because one could only see the ground directly beneath and very hazily at that. The medium frequency beacon receiver was having extreme difficulty in locking on to weak signals which were severely hampered by strong static. By dint of the radio receiver and some luck we made overhead Palam and there it became obvious that we simply could not land in that inky, squally mass of sand. A static-interrupted conversation advised us to divert to Agra, a hundred and fifty miles down the Jumna to the south-east. "And," the voice added, "hurry up, the storm is headed their way."

We turned south-east without seeing a thing, obtained a back bearing on Delhi beacon, and set off for Agra. Three-quarters of an hour later we broke free from the sand wall to see the river Jumna over on our left instead of dead ahead. Making for the now visible Taj Mahal, we located the American base at Agra and landed. The sandstorm was fully visible and heading our way. There was just time to lash the Dakota down, unload everyone into a large communal tent containing little else but loads of charpoys (the peculiarly unluxurious Indian bed) and get our heads down before the storm struck. The light disappeared and daylight became a sand-filled brown fog with the wind plucking at the tent with a terrible banshee wail. The tent stood for about ten minutes, then guy ropes parted with a high twanging noise and it took off in a south-easterly direction. We were all now face down on the beds, resisting the force of the wind, and doing our best to avoid grains of sand lodging in our eyes and mouths. It felt as if that storm lasted for hours, but it was probably no more than two hours or so before the wind started to abate.

When the stinging sand particles had moderated it was just possible to move off the charpoy and see one's shape outlined in dusty sand. There was a long queue for showers and baths but eventually all returned to the aircraft, cleaner and fed, and in the now rapidly clearing air, we took off and homed back to base. In the two full days before my next flight out I was constantly resurrecting sand from every body orifice and the gritty feeling between the teeth was still there days afterwards.

From 5th May, my first flight on the squadron, to date (6th June) I had flown right round India four times, spent over 126 hours in the air, travelled some 23,000 miles, and seen a great deal of India and Ceylon.

My most abiding memory of India was the harsh light — it really did seem to be blindingly bright, except perhaps at the height of a sandstorm or on a day of heavy monsoon cloud. We experienced another sandstorm during an afternoon when I was between flights at Palam. Our working day when back at Palam during most of the year, began with breakfast at 7 a.m., continued with the Station Parade and then commenced work on the squadron at 7.30 a.m. until 1 p.m. when the sun was high in the sky, heat was tremendous and every step of the mile to the Mess for lunch was an effort. From 2 p.m. onwards it was too hot to do anything but lie breathless on one's charpoy and watch the chameleons change colour against the curtained windows, which like the door were wide open to catch the non-existent breeze. This particular afternoon the sky began to grow quite dark at about 2.30 p.m. and standing in the doorway, my room mate, Johnny and I, watched the advance of a terrifyingly high wall of sand. It stretched across the limits of the horizon and came out of the north-west, having its birthplace in the Sind, no doubt. By 3.30 p.m. we were engulfed in the hot choking breath of the storm. It was incredibly hot with doors and windows battened down and yet, despite this, that sand got through. Even after several showers, one still found sand between toes, under armpits and in various other interesting places, and the damned storm went on for hours. Looking through the window one could see the sparse trees and bushes being tumbled this way and that in a roaring, furious gale. All in all, what with the darkness, noise and heat, it is probably the nearest environment to hell that can be found on earth.

On a cloudless hot season day, the sky was the deepest blue you ever saw and in our camp close to Delhi, we were too far from water sources or mountains for any cloud to appear during that period. In consequence, visibility in the northern plains was almost limitless. Comes the monsoon, and how things change. I have suffered under the monsoon in many various parts of India and its severity is tempered only by latitude and topography. At Palam we were in the north of India and consequently were in the last area which it reached and, because of the vast sandy areas around us, it often reached us spasmodically. On the other hand, down in Ceylon (modern Sri Lanka), it reached the low latitude of Colombo in the early part of June and was present for the best part of three months instead of the three weeks around Delhi. The most severe monsoon storms I ever saw were around the lake north of Colombo, over the Western Ghats south and east of Bombay, and off the Travancore coast.

The first occurred as I was travelling back from my brother's bungalow to the airfield at Negombo, north of Colombo, in a car. It had been heavily cloudy with half-crown sized drops of rain falling slowly when I had left Bambalapitya and once through Colombo and running alongside the lake north of the town, it suddenly became very black, followed by the heaviest downpour I have ever seen. The lake rose by about an inch within the hour and the road was inundated by a foot of *rain*-water. Such intensely low pressure area storms were fortunately of short duration but the amount of water deposited on the ground in a short time is nothing short of phenomenal.

To be airborne in one of them is quite frightening. On one morning in July, having flown for some time in thickening and lowering cloud, from Bangalore to Bombay, we found ourselves in a genuine monsoon storm where the cumulo-nimbus storm clouds towered to above 30,000 feet, whilst the cloud base dragged along close to the ground. The turbulence within this cloud was unbelievable. It threw our fifteen tons of machine around the sky like a feather, every instrument toppling and racing madly around its indicator. High, high up we went at 2,000 feet plus per minute, then down into the black gulfs as fast. Knowing that the mountains of the Western Ghats towered up to 4,000 feet or so in the stuffed clouds below, we headed due west to find the sea and then descended so that contact could be kept with the surface. Navigation by instruments in these storms was just not possible, turbulence and static made them just about unusable.

There is something particularly unnerving in descending through thick turbulent cloud to what you sincerely and piously hope and believe is the sea below, especially when the altimeter is unwinding height at a quite alarming rate but no surface can be seen. At 200 feet, shreds of clouds separated sufficiently for a confused mass of white, heaving foam to be seen — the Indian Ocean disturbed and angry and driven by a force eight gale. Chris pulled the Dakota out on to an even keel at about 150 feet and we proceeded up the coast, bumping and squirming with each gust and feeling that the swirling sea below was about to reach up and engulf us. Every now and again vicious squalls of rain would blot out all visibility and we would climb to 300 feet for greater safety and fly blind. After nearly an hour of this stressful flying, we arrived over the inlet and Elephanta and were within spitting distance of Santa Cruz. After several circuits, outside the Parsee towers of silence, the sky cleared sufficiently for a landing. There was no doubt about that good feeling of being on terra firma again, but somehow that never stopped us pushing off into the murk when it was time to go.

The third really hairy storm was off the coast of Travancore when, having encountered heavy cumulo-nimbus building up inside the coast, we had elected to fly out over the sea and descend. Once again it was a case of low level flying in very poor visibility but, as before, aiming at a landing on an airfield very near the coastline, in this case Cochin. The force of the rain drumming on the fuselage was sufficient to drown out the noise of the engines, in fact it had something of the general effect of shrapnel arriving, oh evil memories! Cochin was flat, running across mangrove swamp but there was some high ground only twenty to thirty miles inland, so it behoved one to stick to the sea and cross reference the coast on the starboard side until the island loomed out of the murk. This time we made a very low straight in approach and motored on to the runway without having to make a correcting turn. By this time I had assimilated one very important fact in the matter of survival and this was — and is — that a thorough knowledge of meteorology makes for much safer air navigation. I was also interested in the subject for its own sake for there were so many factors which could produce bad weather, and if one could isolate the factors or constituents of it, it seemed to me that you would know when they were present and therefore be warned to expect sudden deteriorations.

So, flying the routes busily, the end of June came and the weather was still holding up all over India, blue skies, light winds and very high temperatures. At the end of the month I embarked on a 'Special', a non-scheduled flight ordered to pick up a large cargo of equipment at Lahore, to the north, and ferry it down to Minnerlya in the centre of Ceylon. We duly flew off to Lahore where the Dakota was laden to the gills with equipment and stores of the widest variety. The hour and a half flight to Lahore was followed, after the two hours loading period, by a flight of all but eight hours to Hakimpet, the airfield for Hyderabad in Mysore. This was a long continuous flight by the standards of the scheduled routes, and what a variety of topography was flown over. The fertile land of the Punjab, the scrub and near desert around the northern Jumna, more fertile crop growing country in the old United Provinces, jungle in the centre and finally the open spaces of Mysore. After a working day of twelve hours, we judged it prudent to spend the night at Hakimpet. It must have been a very dull evening, because strange to say I cannot recall anything about it.

We were off early next morning flying south for the best part of five hours, passing over Ramnad and Adam's Bridge, before landing at Minnerlya. This strip, hidden deep in the jungle of the flatlands in Central Ceylon was the base for a very hush hush outfit which flew Liberators. With extra tanks these monsters had a phenomenal range and from Ceylon they were apparently doing very long range surveillances and dropping strange loads in places as distant as the Andaman Islands, Burma, Siam and even the approaches to Singapore. Thinking of the tens of thousands of miles that they flew over shark infested waters, I wished them well and was duly grateful for my station in the life of South-East Asia Command. After unloading, we headed for Colombo and a night's stop, which meant another visit to my brother's bungalow.

After a very pleasant evening, we reported into Ratmalana and found that we had become a scheduled flight back to Delhi. The difference was that we headed straight north up through the centre of jungly India and on arrival at the Ganges near Benares, turned left for Delhi. This trip with stops at Trichinopoly, Madras, Hakimpet, Nagpur and Allahabad involved thirteen hours flying and was a very interesting navigational one in which the drift sight played the most important part. There is nothing like the arrival over a really big river — which means it can be the only one you think it is — for reassurance after you have been flying for a couple of hundred miles over trees — trees — trees. One tree looks the same as any other and similarly so do clearings containing small villages, but if your drift angle remains correct, you must arrive at the Ganges, it is so wide even in the dry season that there is never any doubt about it. Strangely enough it is not always easy to pick up such land marks all that far ahead of arrival over them if you are in thickly vegetated country. The long green carpet of vegetation being quite a long way off the ground tends to hide clearings, rivers, etc. until you are almost up to them.

On the following day I flew up to the north-west of India for the first time. True it was only as far as Lahore, but this is warrior India over the Punjab to Waziristan. To a young man brought up on Kipling and tales of the Khyber Pass it was exciting enough to catch glimpses from the air, which you could never capture on the ground, of far off battlegrounds of the previous century.

On arrival at Lahore, we loaded the Dakota to the gills with every conceivable kind of stores and in company with a second work horse similarly loaded, set off to the very centre of India to unload and help set up two summer stations. One was at Bilaspur and the other at Raipur, and both were a hell of a long way from the stores base at Lahore, about seven hours flying time in the old Dakota. We did the whole round trip in one sizzling July day, interrupted only by a slightly shifting load *en route* which entailed landing at Palam so that the Panic and Flap experts could secure the multifarious stores properly. This was a day of intense heat, temperatures well over 100° with the sun virtually over one's head. Incidentally, being interested in this kind of calculation I often worked out at what latitude between 23½° and 5° north the sun would be overhead on a given day. Then if we were landing at any place on that latitude, I would observe that I cast no shadow as I walked. It was just one more little experience to add to the growing number of fascinating things happening in this hot, sprawling, teeming country.

On the 13th July we had flown up from Bombay to Karachi, and after lunch set off for Jodhpur and Delhi. We got no further than eighty miles west of Jodhpur before running into a 10,000 feet high wall of sand. This time there was no battling the elements as we received a message from base saying "Return to Karachi" — all of the base and its alternates were blotted out in the giant sandstorm.

I spotted a waterspout for the first time during this month. Back at Palam, as the long hot dry days passed, we were accustomed to seeing local — and they were very local, some being only a few feet wide — areas of low pressure develop into a 'dust devil'. This twirl of sand, perhaps six to ten feet high, would ripple across the landscape quite quickly. Waterspouts originate in much the same way from small centres of intense low pressure, but they do tend to be much bigger. The first one I saw was off the west coast of Ceylon which we were paralleling about three miles out, on the way to Colombo. It was towards the end of a long hot day on 30th July and we got close enough to the twister to observe that a very tall column of water appeared to be held in suspense whilst being transported across the surface of the sea at a speed of about ten knots. I thought it was an uncanny sight but it proved to be the precursor of a very nasty line squall which we met on the approach to Negombo airport and Reggie had a hell of a job to hold the Dakota straight against the buffeting assaults of the wind. As usual we made it safely!

Another experience I had during this month was my first visit to the Red Fort in Delhi. This had been the scene of fierce fighting during the Mogul Wars of the eighteenth century, indeed it had been the residence of the last Mogul before he came to terms with the besieging British. It is a resplendent building in heavily Oriental style and oddly enough saw some quite violent scenes to witness the end of the British Raj in India. Over 160 years had passed between the two incidents!

By now the monsoon was in full blast across the southern half of India and for those who have never experienced it, the word wet is really not quite enough. The rain comes in blocks of several days of heavy and persistent downpours so that you and your possessions don't get just wet, but saturated and saturated again on top of saturation. The temperatures modify somewhat it is true but they remain fearfully high and with the monsoon comes enormous humidity — 100% is quite often the case in some places. Wet clothes in these conditions had to be dried out before packing away, otherwise you pulled out a mildewed and rapidly disintegrating article of clothing next time out. The constant drumming of rain on the roof-tops induces a depression of the spirit so that one longs to be somewhere else. The humidity is also a dreadful nuisance. In Calcutta and Colombo, to name but two places, it can and often does reach totality — 100%. For example, you would arrive in Calcutta after a long hard day in the air, damp, crumpled and sweaty, until after a lengthy session in the shower, you would emerge feeling cleaner and somewhat fresher. You would then put on freshly starched and laundered bush jacket and drill trousers and within the confines of the lounge in our Middleton Street flat, the three fans going full belt would keep you reasonably dry and cool. But step outside for the ten minute walk to the Lighthouse Cinema and before you had covered one hundred yards, you would be walking in a pool, nay a halo, of sweat which would immediately saturate your nice new clean khaki drill. Upon entering the cinema, which in 1945 was about the only building in Calcutta with efficient air conditioning, your sweat would freeze on you in five minutes and although you remained deliciously cool through the performance, you often woke up to a bad cold the next day. India does nothing in half measures.

Whilst talking of the Lighthouse, I well remember the Monday evening when the week's new film came to an abrupt end half-way through. Calcutta was the leave city for the 'Forgotten Army', Slim's 14th. Hundreds of them were present in the Lighthouse when 'Objective Burma' starring Errol Flynn was shown. The film had not reached its half-way point when burly soldiers began to uproot their seats and with other missiles like beer cans and fruit, bombarded the screen. It is a shame that so much damage was done that night, but fancy showing Errol Flynn capturing Burma nearly single-handed in front of fever-racked underfed swaddies who had 'enjoyed' (if that is the word) over two years of jungle warfare against the Japanese.

As far as the flying goes during the monsoon, it was quite simply a nightmare. Nowadays with vastly superior navigation equipment and flying at the sort of heights which would get you above even monsoon cloud, I do not suppose that it offers more than an inconvenience at the start and finish of each flight. But in 1945, most navigation and nearly all piloting was 'seat of the pants' stuff. Our instrument panel was the basic surviving to this day — altimeter, airspeed indicator, turn and bank indicator and a radio compass receiver. All of it put together was barely sufficient to fly in a good old-fashioned 4M monsoon storm.

Consider the facts. Cumulo-nimbus cloud extended from a hundred or so feet off the ground solidly to between 30,000 and 40,000 feet and it had been known to top 40,000 feet. Inside this cloud are currents of air in murderous up and down motion, reaching one hundred miles per hour in each direction. Thus, when flying straight and level in profile, we would often ascend as if in a giant lift, many thousands of feet at something like 3,000 feet per minute and even at rates exceeding this on occasions. Your altimeter would show wild increases of height which would be followed equally suddenly by fast unwindings which, with the Western Ghats beneath, was often 'heart in the mouth' stuff.

In the blinding flashes of lightning all around, it was often impossible to see the instruments continually and the accompanying noise used to create an illusion that both engines had stopped. The only worry we did not have — and there were plenty of others — was that of icing because at the sort of altitudes we flew, 6,000, 8,000 or perhaps as high as 10,000 or 11,000 feet, the temperature remained well above zero.

Navigation was extremely difficult because in the world of electrical storms, radio compasses and medium frequencies fared very badly with electrical interference and static making nonsense of their readings and responses. So July and August in particular were months of real sweat and hard work on our routes. My system of navigation then was to obtain a pin-point through a hole in the clouds based on a dead reckoning position calculated for the top of the climb. Having eventually secured one, we would fly a course based on the Met Office forecast wind until another sight of the ground could be obtained amid the roiling cloud. Calculation of a track and ground speed wind was then made, cross-checked with an airplot wind found from the dead reckoning position estimated from the courses flown, a comparison obtained with the Met Office forecast wind and the differences applied to future forecast winds. OK so far, this got us to the vicinity of our desination, but how to get down?

If a vicious storm was in evidence over our desination, then we could circle for half an hour or so if the alternative airfield was not too far away but bearing in mind the size and vast distances in India, alternates for many of our desinations were too far away for delayed decisions to be practicable. We would therefore decide that one go was on or, more usually, return to our departure point or a suitable alternate if there was one and wait for the destination to clear, meanwhile topping up with more fuel so that there was plenty for emergencies.

Having made the decision to go, we would try to advise the Control Tower of our intention and to receive their consent through the heavy static always present on the R/T at these times. Then it was a case of a slow descent through thick turbulent cloud with eyes on stalks for a first sight of the ground. We would often come out of the bottom of the cloud at about 300 feet and make a very low level circuit in order to find the end of the runway. It was fortunate that the Dakota, although heavy when fully loaded (some 15 tons) was also very manoeuvrable and many was the landing in bad weather when the wings were straightened out just as the wheels were about to touch down. I agree that it was split-arse flying, but lacking modern or even comprehensive instruments to assist such landings, it was all that could be done. Perhaps it should be noted here that our squadron pilots were magnificent — no accident was ever recorded on 353 Squadron.

In conjunction with talk about landings, a few words on the variety of Indian airfields and their approaches might be in order. Firstly our own home base of Palam. This was a pretty level runway, as it ought to be, considering the many thousands of Indian feet I saw treading the core base into a flat tableland. Our base was expanding all the time and in time became the largest airfield in the Delhi area and eventually, of course, the Delhi International Airfield. The alternate we used whilst our runway was under construction was a strip called Gurgaon. This was some way out of Delhi near a village of the same name and take-off took place between fields of growing crops. The chief difficulty at this field was to retain possession of the 'glim' lamps put out at intervals along the runway for use of night flying aircraft. These lamps made for excellent lighting in Indian huts and being portable were easily removed. A permanent guard was established after one or two hairy incidents of landings in patchy darkness had occurred.

Jodhpur too had a level runway but the approach was over low hills which fell away to the runway so that whilst being very close to the ground at one minute, once over the threshold and you were suddenly 40 feet or so higher up. Landing there in the early morning when the sun was low was a lovely experience. The air was still and cool and the sun's rays lit up the pink and gold façade of the Maharajah's palace like coloured spotlights.

Mauripur near Karachi was flat, sandy and invariably hot. Approaches varied from over the Arabian Sea or from the Sind desert according to wind direction at the time. The airfield was a sprawling area of widely separated camps, Messes, operational buildings, hangars and so on. It was, however, easy to find and allowed ample space for the landing of crippled aircraft.

Bombay, Santa Cruz was fascinating and a little dangerous at times. The approaches were usually either from the flat sandy beaches of Juhu bordering the Indian Ocean or over the river estuary and strange protuberances like Elephanta. Around the airfield stood the Parsee Towers of Silence complete with circling vultures. This is what made it dangerous occasionally even in clear weather. We once collected a shite-hawk in the port engine during the down-wind leg and having made a rather lumpy, under-powered one engined landing, we discovered that the big bird had passed into the engine, severing fuel lines and smashing cylinders thus making that engine absolutely unusable again.

I have already described Yelahanka strip which was really quite unique. I 'arrived' on this strip with a variety of pilots who had different methods of dealing with this landing. Reg used a slow approach and a wheeler landing to ensure that his wheels were firmly on the ground with flying speed lost before the dip. It was a good technique even if it did require a 'firm' landing. Chris would make a normal approach and fly in over the first 200 yards and then make a three-point landing on the slope. This was all right too although more difficult to judge, as any error was punished by a 'float' followed by a shuddering thud on contact. Manch used to dive in like a hammer striking a nail, pull everything back and invariably missed touching down before the slope started. With him we did make some thunderously heavy arrivals. Of course all this theory went by the board on night landings where it was a case of getting down as easily as possible despite the flare-path lights disappearing down the dip.

Sulur was approached over mountains nearly ten thousand feet high so that the end of the approach included a fairly steep let-down. The runways were level but on dry days the texture of the surrounding flora would generate quite bumpy air around the circuit.

Cochin was down on the Travancore coast, hot, steamy and very humid. The approach was across a couple of miles of crocodile infested mangrove swamp. There were very few *under*-shoots at Cochin. Often enough at the far end of the runway a large unit of the Royal Navy or Royal Indian Navy would be moored so it really did not pay to over-shoot either.

On the east coast of India among our regular ports of call were St. Thomas's Mount at Madras, Vishakhapatnam, Cuttack and Dum Dum airfield just north of Calcutta. St. Thomas's Mount was a wide flat airfield with a few minor hills to one side. The runway was wide and level and even Manch landed us here with no more than a bounce or two. Vishakhapatnam was a very different proposition set as it was nearly at sea level with high hills all round it towering up to several hundred feet. There was only one approach, down a valley. You arrived over the top of the hills at about 1,000 feet and then looked around for the deep and narrow valley that cut into the hills and led eventually to the airfield. Often enough in bad monsoon weather there was no way in and it had to be given a miss. It was strange to land from the approach down the narrow valley as once you sunk below 300 feet, you were in deep shadow.

Cuttack in Orissa was a terribly isolated airfield across the river from the little town of the same name. It was surrounded by wild country sporting very tall elephant grass. During the time I called in there, the CO was a rather eccentric Wing Commander whose favourite ambition as I recall was to shoot the man-eating tiger who was menacing the town's watchmen (chowkidars). On one visit I made there, the Wing Co. spent the evening laying plans to catch the marauder but despite a pressing invitation to do so I decided that he could manage without my help.

Finally, Dum Dum — large, nearly international standard even in those days and superbly equipped for night flying. Armament factories surrounded the area and this is where of course the name came from for the outlawed nicked bullet. It had perhaps two drawbacks as far as I was concerned; it was too far out of town for comfort and one had to traverse Barrackpur in order to get into town. As Barrackpur was the main suburb for the criminal element of Calcutta's crowded population, it was rare to go straight through the town without some incident occurring. These could range from stone throwing to jeering and spitting into the transport if it got caught in a traffic jam. It was always a very uncomfortable feeling to be a sitting duck for insults, etc. It was easiest after dark when no doubt a large part of the population of Barrackpur was engaged in more nefarious enterprises.

August was the month in which the monsoon reached furthest north and this was signalled in places like Karachi and Delhi by the arrival of a large percentage of the annual rainfall. Our living quarters, a collection of huts, was at the bottom of a gentle slope from the Mess and about half a mile away from it. I well remember one thunderous afternoon when during a storm the skies opened and rain fell in a blinding deluge. We were dry inside our hut until ten minutes after the deluge started when the monsoon ditches could hold no more water and a flash flood enveloped us all. I had been very damp during my tours of duty in the last month or so but to get wet indoors back at base was a bit too much. We retreated to the Mess at the top of the hill and cheered ourselves up with a Nimbo Pani (Lime Juice) followed by a stiff J.C. (John Collins).

On 15th August I set off for the real north-west frontier, Kipling country, within nudging distance from the Khyber Pass. We called in at Lahore and Chaklala (Rawalpindi) on the way north and at the latter place they were giving the Gurkhas their early parachute dropping lessons. The classic story goes that the brave and usually imperturbable Gurkha Scouts were gathered outside a Dakota and showing little inclination to emplane. This lack of keenness puzzled their officer and he attempted to discover the reason for it. At the end of the subsequent conversation he assured his men that they would have parachutes to jump out of the aeroplane. This cheered up the troop no end and they then exhibited their usual cheeriness and determination to be first in. I could believe it, I had met them several times in various places and a tougher bunch would be hard to find. There is another story that a Gurkha lay in wait in the jungle for a Japanese sniper and having pin-pointed him, he crawled towards the sniper drawing the famous kukri. With one slash he attacked the Japanese — "Ha, missed me," said the Jap. "Not so," replied the Gurkha, "try nodding your bloody head."

Between Chaklala and Risalpur, the full grandeur of the mountains of the Hindu Kush could be seen. Snow lay on the high peaks even at this latitude in mid-August. We had aboard a retired Resident Officer for that area and he related the story of the tribe who live at the bottom of a narrow valley in the Hindu Kush with surrounding mountains so high that they shut out the sun from the valley. In fact, he said with perfect logic, "They never see the sun because at this latitude (28° north) the sun never arrives directly overhead." True or not — it makes a good story and when looking at the massive peaks to the north and north-east it looks perfectly believable.

On a wide sweep to Risalpur we took in the army towns of Campbelpore and Peshawar and even got a good view of the southern entrance to the Khyber Pass. My imagination ran riot. I could picture the regiments of Victorian soldiers entering the pass in good order to pass through and capture Kabul only to return within two years with uniforms in tatters and ranks sadly thinned, still pursued by a motley band of Afghan and Pathan sharp-shooters.

Risalpur itself was really only another section of the vast cantonment covering the approaches to the pass. It was a crowded little town with a mobile and very lively population. Guns were in evidence everywhere probably secured from that quaint arsenal at Kohat. I must say that the Pathans certainly looked the part, just as warrior-like as Kipling had described them. We were airborne for a total of seven hours for the return journey and with the two stops made in each direction, we put in a twelve hour working day. It was enjoyable though because it had taken me away from the very hot plains into the much cooler, crystal air of the high country of the mountains and I know what they mean now when they say 'the air was like wine'.

CHAPTER TEN
Leave — An Interlude on the Cocos Islands — Brushes with Thieves

A day or two later I set off on my first leave in India and worked my passage down to Colombo, determined to enjoy twelve days of sight-seeing in Ceylon. My brother could not get this particular period off but two of his colleagues, with whom I was now well acquainted, had the same period and wanted to do the same things as I did. These included a visit to the Peradinya Gardens, a night in Kandy to see the Peri Hara procession from the Temple of the Tooth, something which only happened every four years, and then a spell at Sonny Bevan's Guest House at Nuwara Eliya. Here we intended to cool off at a height of 7,000 feet above sea level, play golf, climb Mount Pedro and above all drink good, drinkable beer at last.

We proceeded to the Fort Station at Colombo and entrained for Kandy but had already decided to break the journey at Peradinya to see the world famous botanical gardens. Some of the agriculturists from our own Kew Gardens had been the originators of Peradinya in, I believe, the 1880s, and the first incentive had been to see if rubber trees would grow in Ceylon — they did and they do. Having passed through the flat coastal belt, the train commenced its climb towards the highlands and when about half-way up, we left it for the visit to the gardens. Many years have elapsed since that visit but I still recall that it was one of the most colourful sights that I have ever seen. Frangipani, bougainvillaea, mimosa — anything with colour was there. In addition I saw my first tropical rubber trees and tobacco plants looking very healthy and strong. After a fascinating hour or so, we boarded the next train to Kandy and spent a couple of hours enchanted with the breath-taking views of the deep valleys and tree-covered hills, passing the occasional tea plantation. We wound higher and higher and at about 4,500 feet above sea level, Kandy came into view. We alighted at the quaint terminal station and made our way to the Queen's Hotel.

After all these years I am not exactly sure on which day the Peri Hara procession took place, it was certainly a Saturday in August 1945, somewhere about the 18th. Since it was only to be seen at intervals of four years it was definitely not to be missed. We were extremely lucky as we had rooms facing on to the main street and every room had a veranda. We had comfortable chairs, a supply of beer and a perfect view and watched the sun sink behind the mountains in what looked to be a very fine night for it. Just after 9 p.m. the head of the great parade began to pass by.

First came men in fearsome looking costumes cracking enormous whips on the ground and this we were told was to ensure that the evil spirits would be driven off the street so that the procession could pass safely. They were followed by Kandyan dancers who tirelessly and gracefully performed their ritual dances which entailed placing their limbs in very strange postures. There were ninety-three elephants in the parade, all richly caparisoned, there were warriors, priests and hundreds of ordinary folk all streaming past our vantage point. After about three-quarters of the parade had passed, there appeared the largest elephant I have ever seen. Nearly all of the huge beast was covered in cloths of the very finest quality and in a small howdah on its back was the splendidly jewelled casket which held the tooth of Buddha. In between these four yearly parades, this priceless relic was kept in the Temple of the Tooth on a hill overlooking Kandy. Altogether it was an impressive and fascinating occasion which lasted two hours before the last person passed by — hurling fire-crackers about.

After a day exploring Kandy, a small town but an engaging mixture of architectural styles from the Summer Palace of the potentates of old to the small huts on the outskirts, we caught the night train which climbed even higher into the highlands. Arriving at Nuwara Eliya after midnight, we roused the sleeping form of the solitary taxi driver and gave the address of Sonny Bevan's Guest House, higher still in the hills. We had already enjoyed hours of beautiful scenery seen from the train in the light of a full moon. The ride up a series of twisting, looping narrow roads produced even more breath-taking views, marred only by the hair-brained driving of the weedy looking Tamil in front whose breath imparted either the fumes of drink or drug on the summer night air and whose driving was none the more assuring because of it. Arriving at the guest house we were shown our rooms, and for the first time in many months slept deeply with a blanket on the bed.

The next morning we rose quite early and after a fairly gargantuan English type breakfast, were out on the golf course at 9 a.m. The morning was misty, fairly cool and rather humid, the golf was pretty terrible, the players were definitely not up to the standard of the course! I played in shorts only and made the remarkable discovery inside of an hour that the prickly heat which had been annoying me for the past month in India, was all gone.

Sonny had a very civilized habit of having a broached barrel of beer on its trestles in the lounge. The pint glasses ranged around the barrel were for use not ornament and they were used to considerable effect. The beer they made down in the town of Nuwara Eliya was as good as English draught and after existing on Solon's beer for four or five months it made a very welcome change. Solon's was made in Calcutta, hauled for days across India to Delhi in hot trains and when opened, deposited half of its contents on the ceiling. The remainder tasted very vinegary and I always felt that it was the squadron's masochists who drank most of it.

On the day following, we climbed Mount Pedro, the highest peak on the island. I like the sound of that, it sounds so professional, easy and natural. It was far from that. The narrow dirt road led up through the foothills of the mountain and then petered out into a path between stands of thickly foliated trees. Indeed the light was considerably reduced in the trees on the lower slopes. Having at last struggled up to the tree line at just over 8,000 feet, the mountain top suddenly seemed very bald by comparison. Up here the trees had blackened and carbonized into bent and unfamiliar shapes. The view was tremendous from the top, Colombo was in view from the west and looking around to the east, Trincomalee could be seen and just to the north of us was Adam's Peak, a little below. Within ten minutes we were in the cumulo-nimbus cloud which formed over the mountain top just after noon each day. The effect was of being in fog and without a compass, direction finding was difficult, which really explains why our little party of four came down the mountain by four different routes — and only one of them was the right one!

Speaking for myself, I descended through the petrified trees in a mist so thick that each foothold had to be searched for. About 300 feet down the mist suddenly cleared, I had descended below the cloud base. I found myself in a dense stand of teak trees, so dense that the light was really gloomy, almost like that of early evening. Despite uttering loud "Hulloos" there were no answering cries and up here the silence was absolute. Making the big decision, I reckoned to go straight ahead as at least that way it descended and must, I hoped, come out into the foothills at some point. An hour later, after a considerable slog through the trees and increasingly thick undergrowth, I came up against an impenetrable wall of greenery which forced me to divert sideways. This in turn led to green-covered slopes of easier gradient where the trees were beginning to thin out. Fifteen minutes later I was out of the foliage and in clear view of the roofs of Nuwara Bliya — a mile or so away. We replotted our various paths down that evening on Sonny's large scale map. In the course of it he uttered the casual remark that Ernie and I had descended through areas in which the panthers resided!

The rest of that very pleasant break passed in a haze of alcohol (in my case beer), pipe smoke and a green baize card table. Two or three times standing up from the table during the interminable games of slippery Sam, solo or blackjack, and drawing back the curtains for a breath of air, it was slightly shocking to find that the dawn had arrived and it was broad daylight outside. A lie-in during the morning was generally followed by a long walk or a game of golf. Then as early evening set in, so Sonny's barrel of Nuwara Eliya beer started its nightly punishment.

I returned to my base in India on the 1st September 1945, refreshed if not rested. A day or so after arrival back our sister squadron 232 suffered many casualties as one of their Liberators was lost with all hands just after doing a night take-off from the Cocos Islands *en route* to Perth, Australia. Somewhat to my surprise I was detailed to go down to the Cocos and convene a Court of Enquiry. I left in one of 232's Liberators on 9th September, with a case full of the aircraft's documents, service sheets, engine and prop logs, specification sheet and the like. An unexpected stop ensued at Colombo for a couple of days due to aircraft unserviceability, and then on the 12th — my third wedding anniversary — I set out in a Skymaster DC4 on the longest sea crossing I had ever made up to that time.

Just under eight hours later we circled the small group of five islands thousands of miles out in the southern Indian Ocean that formed the Cocos and landed on the coral based runway on the West Island which could just comfortably take these big aircraft. A couple of hours later I watched her depart for Perth, wishing that I was aboard.

I duly assembled the Board of Enquiry and listened to the eye witness accounts which all seemed to agree on one thing, that the aircraft started to turn to port after having just risen into the air. The turn to port apparently began to become steeper and eventually the aircraft rolled over and dived into the very, very deep depths of the sea outside the coral reef running round the islands. Having heard all the evidence, I talked it over with my fellow board member and we spent a day combing through all the aircraft papers. We discovered that on three successive trips the artificial horizon had given trouble, had then been checked and found serviceable.

An unserviceable artificial horizon in the bright light of a day in the Far East is no problem, but surely it could be deadly on a take-off from a small island on a dark cloudy night when sky and sea join with no visible line. On such a night a pilot must have faith in his instruments and maybe that slow port turn was initially a correction made to try and straighten the wings on a false display. We both thought this to be the most reasonable explanation for the action of a very experienced pilot and reported to 229 Group Headquarters to that effect.

Thus the Board of Enquiry was completed but now came the problem of leaving the place. Masses of aircraft were being deployed in ferrying the Australians home from the Japanese POW camps, and after the suffering these men had endured, they deserved, and got, top priority. However it did mean that aircraft were being diverted off the routes to do the job and although plenty were going to Australia, none came back that way. I was stuck at the camp on West Islands visible but not visitorable!

In the Mess tent lounge there were about a dozen well thumbed paperback books, most of which I had read before but which provided a couple or so hours a day of diversion from the huge sky and seascape all around. Sunset seen from the beach was something to wonder at, even that colour-mad artist Gauguin could not match the colours in it. Flaming red was followed by pale orange and broken tints spread across the calm sea until the sun slipped below the horizon when the sea turned from silver to pewter to darkness. Another occupation was gathering coconuts. 'Gathering' is not quite the right word since it was first necessary to knock them off the tops of the extremely tall palm trees which grew in a line along the top of the narrow beach. It required a large stone of about half a pound in weight and a very accurate throw but the successful result brought a large sweet and milky nut.

Then there was the lagoon, only three feet deep or so and extending for a hundred yards out from the beach where it ended on a raised coral reef, outside of which heavy surf pounded and the bottom almost dropped out of the sea, or at least for some thousands of feet. Outside the warm shallow lagoon lived all the varieties of fish one had ever heard of, ranging from tiny pilot fish to extremely large porpoises and sharks. I well remember awakening from a doze on the sand by shouts and yells coming from two young airmen frantically swimming for the reef. They had apparently had the brilliant idea of cutting an old drop fuel tank in half and making it into a small catamaran. Shortly after launch over the reef and into the deeps they were attacked by a swordfish moving at full speed. The fish was quite large, his 'sword' even larger, and it penetrated the light metal of the drop-tank, throwing both of the lads into the sea. Thankfully they both made it to safety but any temptation to swim in deeper water than the lagoon left me at that moment.

Five days after the conclusion of the Court of Enquiry I had exhausted all the delights of West Island, read all the books in the Mess and collected innumerable coconuts and still no chance to go either to Australia or return to India. It was then that an Australian Padre arrived for a short visit to the heathen on West Island. He was a short, rubicund man of immense good humour and although I cannot now remember his name, I was and am grateful for his cheerful company which made the next few days bearable. We spent hours putting the world to rights and in deep divisive arguments about religion. Finally, on 22nd September, the day after my beloved's birthday, I got off the island, having scrounged aboard a Liberator as supernumary crew. The airplane was returning to its base in Ceylon at Kankesanturi, miles from any connection to India but I figured Ceylon was at least a bit nearer base and I'd worry about the next leg when I got there. Ten and a quarter hours later we had arrived and after a good night's sleep in this camp in the jungle, I managed to talk the Flight Commander into extending the air test he was going to make to take in a landing at Colombo so that I could find a connection home.

Once in Colombo, I reported sick with a very painful toe-nail which had turned a strange colour. It was septic after a kick received in a football match and necessitated the removal of the toe-nail. This was such a minor thing but it had results out of all proportion to the ailment and as a result I was put off sick in Colombo for a week. It left me with a bandaged foot encased in a carpet slipper and it was in this state that I paid a visit to the French cruiser *Trouville*. The ship had called in on its way to French Indo-China to assist in what was to be the French exit from this corner of the world. My brother had responsibility in Colombo for armament supply to our Indian Ocean naval units and it seems that he had stored away large amounts of French shells and other ammunition which had been seized during the capture of Dakar. Now came the opportunity to sell the stuff back to the French navy since the *Trouville* could use it all. My brother, Ernie, had no French, the *Trouville*'s Gunnery Officer had no English but as I had schoolboy French, I was elected as interpreter at the meeting at the shore supply base. Thereafter we were invited aboard the *Trouville* for a rewarding drink and so embarked on a tender from the ship which crossed the harbour and arrived at the foot of a massive companion-way containing God knows how many steps. Up the flight I hobbled, slippered foot, walking stick and all, only to have to shift the stick smartly to the left hand in order to salute the quarter-deck amidst the din of bosuns' welcoming whistles. We duly had our drinks hosted by the Gunnery Officer, a genial giant of a man and an hour or so later made the return journey feeling no pain.

On 29th September I returned to India aboard one of our own squadron aircraft and after a night in Bombay on the way, arrived in Delhi on the 30th. It was now October and weather was definitely improving all over the sub-continent so that I spent more complete days in the air than on the ground during the month, and achieving a total of over 90 flying hours. The following month provided a bag of mixed experiences. It opened for instance with a trip to Bikaner with an unforeseen bonus to it. It seems that there was a Japanese prisoner of war camp somewhere out in the desert from Bikaner and the strip called Nal was the nearest point of transport to it. Thus on 3rd November we welcomed the Delhi Area Commander and his staff aboard our Dakota and flew them up to Nal, which took an hour and forty minutes. A reception party awaited our distinguished passengers and whisked them off into the desert whilst we three, Chris the pilot, George the wireless operator, and me, were driven into that part of the Maharajah's palace which served as a transit hotel for visitors. Our escort was a very pleasant young captain of the Bikaner army who was also an ADC to the Maharajah.

Upon arrival we were served a sumptuous British type breakfast and an hour later the ADC appeared to ask whether we would like to visit the Maharajah's palace. Such invitations do not come one's way very often so that we all jumped at the chance. There followed three of the most enthralling hours one could spend. We started with the State Apartments, enormously proportioned reception halls with marble floors, and then passed on to a throne room at which the mind boggled. The entrance door, some seven feet high and six inches thick was made of beaten silver. The two thrones for the Maharajah and the Ranee were of gold and inlaid with a multitude of precious stones. The dressing-table in the State bedroom was also inlaid with gems. It is rather overpowering to see so many diamonds, rubies and emeralds in such profusion. The ceilings of the rooms were quite breath-taking in their colours and designs.

We finally arrived at the palace armoury which was a museum of weapons used by the Bikaners over the last three hundred years. Most impressive of all was a huge sword which must have been the better part of seven feet long. I could barely raise it in two hands but we were told that the Maharajah of Mogul days was himself a giant nearly seven feet tall with huge limbs to match and of ferocious strength, and he could heft that sword in one hand. There were ancient iron cannons with impressively wide mouths, although the accompanying ammunition, cannon-balls, left a lot to be desired with regard to a truly circular shape.

After this extensive tour we were released through a small wicket gate at the rear of the palace in order to explore the town. I suppose it said it all about India and its social system when you stepped from unimaginable wealth into streets teeming with people, some afflicted with diseases and malnutrition and most not knowing with any certainty where the next meal was to come from. Camels in this town were plentiful and formed the major mode of transport, indeed Bikaner was famous for its Mounted Camel Corps. The impression made by that visit stays with me even today.

After a trip north to Risalpur again, we did a special non-scheduled one taking in two other fascinating towns, Baroda and Maharajahpur. My principal recollection of the latter is the conversation I had with a hoary survivor from the Chindit expeditions. Maharajahpur had at one time been their base and after their first campaign in Burma they had returned there, weary and run down. Throughout the fighting campaign they had been having a daily dose of mepacrine to ward off malaria but on arrival back at their non-malaria infested base, they had one and all stopped taking the tablets with appalling results. High casualties ensued as two and three malarial attacks hitherto held in check, surfaced and with general health at a low level, many were struck down and not a few died as a result. It was a lesson that to a minor degree had some future application to myself.

November seemed to be our month for frontier trips, we did two more in quick succession. The second resulted in one of our rare aborted trips. After taking off from Chaklala on a northerly heading towards the mountains we came face to face with giant cumulo-nimbus clouds pushed up to enormous ceilings by their passage over the mountains. We flew hopefully on and tried to climb over the top. At 10,000 feet, maximum height without oxygen, it was obvious that the big black monsters ahead were soaring up to and probably above the 30,000 feet mark. Thus we began a descent, gingerly because there were a lot of stuffed clouds around. Up and down currents of the order of 130 m.p.h. were tossing the Dakota around like a feather and the wings were flexing visibly. It was just like the old battle with the weather in the wintry German skies. We had only an MF receiver which in these highly charged clouds received only static, we certainly could not hear Risalpur's beacon. We did of course have a drift recorder but it was useless in an airplane which was keeled over in a steep attitude and rushing up into the inky heavens at about 100 m.p.h. plus. So, after a very determined and quite perilous attempt to get through, we gave up, turned round and emerged from the black clouds into the sunlight with Chaklala visible nearly ahead.

For the rest of November I put in the hours flying south instead of north and this gave a good mix of meteorology! In the north the evenings were getting chilly, often back at base the temperature by day would be in the seventies and after sunset would plunge quite rapidly to the low forties so that at this time of the year at Palam we wore our blues. Going west and then southwards down the west coast the weather was largely clear until one got to the very south of India and over Ceylon, where the extremities of the north-east monsoons were encountered, mainly wet, woolly cloud. However as one flew north up the east coast the cloud and rain increased until it was quite common to land in blindingly heavy rain at Dum Dum in Calcutta.

In December my flying hours took a dip from the seventy to one hundred hours a month I had been doing. Demobilization had taken its toll and I was now the only war substantive Flight Lieutenant navigator left on the squadron. Thus pretty much by default I became Squadron Navigation Officer, which meant more paper work and less flying. It also meant that my demob which was coming up was delayed for six months. Air Ministry had no available Flight Lieutenant to send out and replace me so I was extended to May/June 1946.

December was noteworthy for another weird episode in my varied career. On arrival at Colombo we found that a new airfield well north of the town had been opened, this was Negombo so that I had already said goodbye, without knowing it, to my old favourite Ratmalana down south of Mount Lavinia. Negombo was all new roads and buildings, the latter being of a type of adobe construction. I stayed on camp that night as Colombo was now a long way away and was better visited on the following day, our rest day. During the course of the evening at the bar I had heard the Station Commander mention that there were a lot of 'loose wallahs' plaguing the camp. These characters were the thieves of Ceylon, very expert, very quiet and if disturbed, very violent.

I repaired to bed and in the rather airless room was having trouble getting to sleep. I had stowed my service .38 under the pillow — we had to carry them about in these days of mounting unrest in India and was always frightened of losing the revolver with the certainty of an ensuing court martial. It was my habit to have only five rounds in it, with the trigger on an empty chamber of the revolver. At some time after midnight there was a gritty noise of a footfall close to the bed, I grabbed the gun and just made out the forms of two men in dhotis moving towards the bed. In sheer panic I shouted and fired over their heads and the result was sensational. They leaped for the window and went through it, frame and all. Having pressed the trigger my itchy finger would not come off it until all five rounds had fired. These bullets taking an upward trajectory over the heads of the thieves clattered into the dividing wall and went through the adobe like a knife through cheese. I was told by my neighbours that their subsequent ricochets sounded like a swarm of angry bees.

So — no trip to Colombo next day — instead up before the 'Old Man' for a right royal rollicking. When I next saw him on the 4th January, he did say that the number of 'loose wallah' incidents had dropped considerably, so some good came out of my stupidity.

I mentioned Ratmalana, the old airfield south of Colombo, it evokes several happy memories and two rather unpleasant ones. I'll get the latter out of the way first. At the end of the war in August, I arrived there one night to find the place jammed with RAF and American squadrons in transit to various places. This placed a severe strain on accommodation and having arrived late in the evening, I was awarded a basha hut which had been closed and disused for months. The basha is constructed of straw and bamboo and is a very fragile building, but none the less it keeps you dry and sheltered from the weather. After a few drinks, I drifted over to my room in the basha, lit the lamp, quickly undressed and leapt into bed intending to read for a while. Shortly after opening the book, I heard a rustling noise above my head. I looked up into the beady eyes of a Tic Palonga as the natives called it (Russell's viper to the rest of us). The only thing between me and the snake was my mosquito net so slowly but very surely I tucked it securely under the mattress and then spent a nearly sleepless night with the lamp burning. The snake had withdrawn into the straw roof after that first confrontation so I never saw it again — but I KNEW THAT HE WAS THERE!!

The other rather nasty incident occurred one evening in July 1945 when I had spent the day with my brother, Ernie, and was looking for a taxi in order to return to camp. Ernie had always said that it was wise never to get into a taxi if it contained more than a driver. However, this night it was late, I had an early start in the morning and there were simply no other taxis about so clasping my ashplant swagger stick firmly, I climbed in and directed the driver to take me to Ratmalana. We drove off to the south at about 10.30 p.m. and some fifteen minutes later arrived at that part of the road which ran through the thick coconut plantations of Mount Lavinia. It was extremely dark when the car stopped and the driver said, "She broken down, sah." I hoped that this was not true and when the two in front descended and instead of making for the bonnet, headed for the passenger door, I guessed that it was not. As Matey opened the door, I struck him smartly with the ashplant and pointing to the front seat promised the driver the same if he did not get going. After some further argument and with some further threats of physical violence from me, I 'persuaded' them to drive up to the guardroom at Ratmalana where I immediately had the guard turned out and arrested them both. I departed to bed somewhat shaken.

Back in 1940-41 at RAF Cottesmore, that popular band leader, Jack Nathan had formed a station dance band and had often given us great pleasure in the concert hall. I had seen the boys on and off over the years around Bomber Command stations. One evening I had just landed at Ratmalana when to my pleased amazement I saw them arriving for a flight carrying their instruments. It was a very brief reunion but I knew that SEAC was in for some good entertainment as I saw Jack and his drummer, Jock McVey off to their aircraft.

Earlier I mentioned a friend of mine, Brian Woolston, who had been shot down in a Hampden over the North Sea in 1941. After his rescue he swore that he would never fly over water again — not even to cross the Wash!! One evening after we had landed at Ratmalana we decided to visit the hotel high on the cliffs at Mount Lavinia. Upon entering the lounge, it was obvious that a hell of a party was going on and to my delight, well towards the centre of it, I found Brian. The irony of it all was that it transpired that his squadron was being transferred from north-east Bengal to Australia. From where he sat to the next landing place on the Cocos Islands there were fifteen hundred miles of water and beyond that place to Perth, another fifteen hundred — and all of it was shark-infested. Brian was feeling no pain at the time and appeared completely unworried at the prospect. I murmured something about water under the bridge and concluded he had made a complete recovery from his ditching experience.

January was noteworthy for the introduction of the squadron beer run. With the war now truly over, we could now think about some creature comforts for the Mess, so on 23rd January the inaugural beer run was made by the Squadron Commander, 'Timber' Wood, the Squadron Signals Officer, Tim Pullinger and the Squadron Navigation Officer, me. We flew up to Chaklala and borrowed a transport to drive into Rawalpindi, and there we found a contractor prepared to supply us with wonderful Murree beer. This stuff was brewed beside the Murree river and used that cold clear mountain water and it was easily the best in the entire Far East. We loaded up a week's supply for each of the three Messes, airmen's, sergeants' and officers', and returned in triumph. The run was being made weekly when I left in June.

At the end of the month, we did another special non-scheduled flight to Cawnpore. I mention it because I well remember that as we swooped in over the near-side fence, a group of Indians hurled boulders at us and one succeeded in knocking a sizeable lump out of one blade of a propeller which induces instant and unpleasant vibration. It was a pipe opener for all the violence and fighting of the month to come. We arrived back at Palam from this trip to make our last landing at Palam for a couple of weeks or so. They were building a new runway and it was done in the time honoured way of the East, with hundreds of labourers (including women and children) employing hundreds of pairs of feet to flatten ground. We moved our aeroplanes to Gurgaon, a strip out in the country away from the cantonment.

February opened with trouble all over India and we kept catching passing glimpses of the battles between mutinous Indian Services and British troops and airmen trying to disarm them. For instance, we started on a westbound circular from Gurgaon to Jodhpur and Karachi. On arrival at Karachi, we discovered that the Royal Indian Navy had mutinied and taken over the destroyer *Hindustan* in Karachi harbour. It was rumoured that her guns were threatening the town, certainly British troops were very busy preparing for an attack to recapture the ship. A quick lunch stop was sufficient in such a loaded situation, so that one hour after landing we were airborne again and flying over the flat salt marshes of the Kutch on our way to Bombay.

In Bombay a full scale mutiny had taken place in the Indian Navy — some British officers were hostages in the ships which formed a little flotilla off the mouth of Bombay harbour. At Santa Cruz there was a grim reminder of my life of eighteen months before — the sight of Lancasters from 9 and 617 Squadrons loading bombs. As far as I know they were not used against the mutinous Indian ships, but they certainly presented a threat to the mutineers.

The following day we left for Bangalore, Cochin and Colombo. We never made Colombo that day, they diverted us to Trichinopoly, an oasis of calm in a very troubled continent. Colombo was the scene of a vicious transport strike and street battles were the order of the day. The police eventually got the upper hand and we flew into Colombo on the following day. Driving through the town on the way to visit my brother, signs of riot were all about. Many windows were smashed, broken paving stones lay about and one old tram was on its side. A strike in Colombo obviously had two meanings.

Next morning we flew back over the same route and still strife was observed in all the major towns. Back in Delhi inflammatory speeches were being made in front of the gates of the Red Fort and personal side-arms were now a must. The pressure on the British was rising and continuous and I believe that most of us felt that the end of the Raj was in sight. As February passed into March, the assaults on British servicemen increased and mobs roamed the streets of most of the major cities.

On 1st March I renewed my acquaintance with the Lancaster when I persuaded an old mate, Ernie Nye, to let me fly in one of 617 Squadron's aircraft on a rehearsal for a display that was to take place. I believe that the numerous air displays being put on all over India at this time had a political motive as well as being entertaining. Few of the Indian public had ever seen such large aeroplanes — nor such demonstrably large bomb doors. Air displays gave many a malcontent the chance to do both.

Early in March we flew a schedule Delhi-Allahabad-Calcutta (Night Stop) — Vishakhapatnam-Madras-Bangalore and back to Vizag. Here we were halted for twenty-four hours as there was no question of flying back into Calcutta which was apparently buzzing like a large disturbed wasps' nest. When we did arrive there and boarded the squadron coach to take us into town to our Mess, we found that all the windows had been covered with a kind of chain-mail. Our progress through Barrackpur and Outer Circular Road showed the necessity, stones flew in large numbers and sizes! In Calcutta the police and army were out in full force clearing barricades of bedding and old lorries from the streets. Large, sullen crowds stood at street corners watching them do the job.

We did not leave the Mess at all that night and early in the morning were woken by that strangest of all human sounds, the ululation of a yelling, screaming mob. This one was invading the flats of all the British residents in Middleton Street, throwing furniture out in the street where it was destroyed by fire and setting light to the curtains left in the flats. Then they came to our block. There were two crews in residence, one southbound and ourselves going north. Thus six chaps lined the head of the stairs, we were on the top floor of a three floor block, and presented .38 revolvers down them. The huge droning noise of the excited mob increased until with a crash, the door on the ground floor was hurled off its hinges and up the stairs came a mob hundreds strong. Roy, skipper of the southbound crew, shouted down to them in Urdu — "Stop or we fire." The leading files wavered but were pushed upwards by the hundreds of people behind them. Six shots scored the plaster above their heads and all was over. The crowd melted away at a fast rate of knots.

Somewhat shaken, we boarded our 'armoured' coach and departed to Dum Dum, again running the gauntlet of angry brown faces and a fusillade of stones as we passed through Barrackpur. Airborne and on the way to Delhi with a fairly distinguished passenger list, our day was not to improve. Shortly after overflying Fatehpur, we were ordered to return to Allahabad as there was a strong cross wind and rising sand back at base. Upon landing at Allahabad, a Royal Navy captain furiously cornered us and demanded that we fly to Delhi immediately. I was flying with a Warrant Officer pilot on this trip and poor Dobby was out of his depth with this raging Olympian figure. With a wink to my pilot, I took over the conversation and explained the situation to the good captain which drew the totally unwarranted remark that the RAF only chose to fly when the weather was good. I was more than somewhat aggrieved at this rejoinder and asked why there was a life and death hurry. It then appeared that the captain was the bearer of personal messages from Lord Louis Mountbatten to the GOC. I then telephoned base, explained that we had an urgent messenger aboard and demanded that we be allowed to try our luck at Delhi. After some argument, Tommy Thomas, the Wing Commander Flying came on the telephone and gave a hard and fast order, "Stay where you are until I tell you bloody different." There was no doubting the unambiguity of this order so obeying the old service adage, always obey the last order, I once again attempted to make peace with the captain. Again I was treated to a stormy interview which terminated with a request for my name, rank and number. These were carefully noted down and with a muttered, "You will hear more of this," I was left standing.

Later on in the day when it was quite dark and the wind had slackened, we were allowed to fly on. We made Palam without further incident, landed smoothly, and as we pulled to a stop, a large staff car bore our ill-tempered passenger away to GHQ. Forty-eight hours later we were predictably on the mat in front of our CO, 'Timber' Wood, who held an official letter of complaint in his hand, presumably from Lord Louis' office. I explained what had occurred and, still smarting, repeated the naval officer's remark about the RAF's reluctance to fly in bad weather. Timber bristled and with a, "Leave this to me," from him, the interview terminated. We, of course, heard nothing further.

A few days later, I was in Connaught Circus in Delhi and came face to face with a school friend from twelve years or so before. Reg Smallwood was now a captain in the 2/6th Rajpatana Rifles and their Depot Mess was only two miles from Palam. We made exchange visits on Dining-In nights but I believe he enjoyed ours more than I did his — it was a lot less formal when Mess Rugby,

Married v Singles started.

In the middle of March I flew another 'circular' and whilst having two nights in Colombo, stayed in the same bungalow as my brother and experienced a curious incident. I was given a very small bedroom on the ground floor which had one window looking out on to the alley running down from the Bambalpitya road to the sea-shore. The window was set with heavy iron bars only two inches apart and of course as it was very warm, the window was wide open. I had hung my bush jacket on a hook at the back of the door and retired to bed, but just could not sleep and so was lying atop the bed. The hook on which reposed my jacket was directly opposite the open window and I suppose this opportunity was just too good for one of the neighbouring 'loose wallahs'. I heard a slight grating noise and sat up on the bed to witness a long pole with a big hook on the end, being manoeuvred through the bars and in the general direction of my bush jacket. I leaped out of bed, grabbed the shaft of the pole and jerked it as hard as I could backwards through the window. There was a sort of screamed curse outside as the butt end connected with a breast bone and then the pole was seized, withdrawn and disappeared. I thought of how I would have been so puzzled waking up to find the jacket gone and the door still locked!

March melted into April as the temperatures began to increase fiercely again and here I was only a few weeks away from repatriation. As Squadron Navigation officer I was not flying as often as I wanted to now and in April I only managed to accrete just over thirty-one flying hours. At the end of the month my replacement arrived so that I was definitely to go home at the end of May. I had achieved one improvement in the navigation office — after weeks of spasmodic endeavours by the Station Works Dept. they had removed the floor and dug down deep enough to trace and kill the queen ant who was responsible for the long files of soldier ants marching across the office and eating all our records. On laying the floor back again, a thick bitumastic seal was laid all around the bottom of the walls and peace descended, as no more ants were seen.

With my replacement arrived, I was free to fly and promptly put myself on the schedules as often as possible and so much more than doubled April's hours in the air. The month produced sorties in the opposite extremes of weather. Down south the monsoon was approaching again bringing sudden outbursts of rain that blackened the skies and cut down visibility. I still have a mental picture of the wind-bent, rain-lashed palm trees on the approach to land on the island strip at Cochin. At the opposite end of the weather kaleidoscope, we arrived back at Palam on the 19th May having flown in a sandstorm for nearly two hundred miles and having to make a landing in winds gusting horribly and with a sand fog giving visibility of less than five hundred yards.

CHAPTER ELEVEN
Homeward Bound

Finally on the morning of the 30th, having made a very noisy and drunken exit the night before, I left in one of our Dakotas, heading for Bombay. At the end of two hours we just made Jodhpur with one engine on the blink. It seems that India was not going to let me go easily for it was five hours before the repair was made, so that instead of making Bombay that day, we only got as far as Karachi for the night. However, all went well next day and I arrived in Bombay to report to No. 3 BRD at Worli on the last day of May.

I had thought that arrival at Worli constituted setting off for Blighty, but as I said, India seemed reluctant to let me go. I slept on a pallet in a warehouse at Worli for eleven days and damned hot and uncomfortable it was too. Those days were spent exploring Bombay, there was absolutely nothing else to do. Finally early on the morning of the 12th June, transport collected us and off we went to Ballard's Pier, there to board the old SS *Georgic*, a passenger liner converted to a troopship, mainly by stripping out any amenity that made for comfort.

The day was a blinder, south-west monsoon gales, great outbursts of heavy rain, occasional thunder and lightning. I believe the *Georgic* was of the order of 26,000 tons, but even this monster was tossing uneasily on her anchor ropes at the end of Ballard's Pier. Eighty officers were given hammocks on 'D' deck, me among them, four decks down, hot and airless. This promised to be a lousy way to go home, there were 1,600 married families aboard and quite rightly, they had the best of the accommodation. I could not look forward to long nights well below the boat deck in the June temperatures of the Indian Ocean and the Red Sea.

As we cast off in blinding rain, the nose of the ship buried itself in the rollers whipped up by the south-westerly gales. As I had never been any real distance to sea before, I wondered whether I would be seasick. To test it, I stood at the bows and watched the green waves surging towards us. This did nothing for me so I turned to watch the yards pitching and circling against the storm clouds. Ten minutes of looking at them failed to produce any queasy symptoms, so I went below for lunch. Our table sat thirty people but that meal was the only time I saw a full house until we reached the Suez Canal well over a week later! This had its advantages as I used to feel quite hungry at breakfast and there were always second helpings going spare.

Two days after leaving Bombay, bored out of my skull, I volunteered to be Entertainments Officer. This occupied our time considerably, first unearthing the talent and then rehearsing it. All went very well although I was not entirely happy with the very over-confident young airman who was to be the compère. Days passed and eventually we pulled into Port Tewfiq at the southern end of the Suez Canal and anchored off the harbour entrance until the southbound traffic had cleared the narrow canal.

A few hours later we were on our way north through the canal and as the temperature was so high that it was sizzling, we had been allowed to sleep on the boat deck. Thus it was that we sailed between villages, steam trains and even camel trains and it was a weird feeling to see sandy deserts extending into the blurred horizon on each side from a SHIP! We halted for a few hours in the Great Bitter Lake which was a much more apt description than that of the nearby Sweetwater Canal. As the southbound traffic cleared the canal, we were off again and in the course of time arrived in Port Said. This town was a bit weird because from the ship, the warehouses and official residences appeared to float on tongues of land in the water. Oddest of all was the arrival of a grinning Egyptian rose seller who appeared suddenly sitting on the boat deck rails with his basket of flowers at his feet. The ship had not yet touched dry land, yet here he was, dry as a bone and ready for business. It was such a lousy climb up from one of the circling bum-boats, particularly with a basket, that it is a mystery to me to this day.

After entering the Mediterranean we had our final dress rehearsal and then embarked on the first of the two concerts we were to give. The turns were very good in effort if some were lacking in technique, but the compère!! We had all the VIPs seated in the front row, ship's captain, OC Troops, senior officers and so on, and the married ladies behind them. The first three jokes from our brash compère were so blue they made *me* cringe. There was total silence from the front of the house and I hastily arranged for a more mature and experienced man to take over the job. After that the concert was a fair success and putting on another one on the following evening helped to pass the time so much so that we seemed to be passing south of Malta in no time.

It was a great disappointment that we did not dock at Gibraltar but sailed on past the great rock into the narrows and out into the Atlantic. At this point, as the old service song says 'We threw all our khaki away' and became a blue Air Force again. Three days later we were at the entrance to the Mersey and although it was the 28th June, the weather was cool and cloudy. It actually rained as we debarked and piled into the coaches which were to take us to the demobilization centre at 101 PDC Hednesford. Once having left Liverpool the one thing that had struck me forcibly over and over again was how GREEN England is.

We spent three nights at Hednesford and, of course, the attached three days. The days were occupied in filling in forms, handing in kit and being fitted out with a civvy suit, shirt, tie and hat. The nights were so cold that even with layers of blankets on the bed, it was difficult to get warm enough to get to sleep. However, on the fourth morning, numbers of us were transported to Stafford to catch the train to London and home. I was a civilian again but the strange thing was that I did not really like the sensation.

Hours later I presented my gaunt (nine stones) frame and yellow features at the front door of the house that my clever wife had purchased in my absence and made the reacquaintance of my two-and-a-half-year-old son. It seemed that my flying days were over at last.

The author and Johnny Johnson at Palam, New Delhi,
in March 1946 — an 8½-stone weakling after
malarial dysentry!

CHAPTER TWELVE
Re-airborne and More Training!

This is a history concerned with my flying life so we will pass over the sticky two years when a job was hard to come by and money was very short. In fact my beloved made the suggestion of returning to some flying when I mentioned that the RAFVR were about to reform, we could certainly do with the extra few bob available from Thursday evening and weekend attendances. So it came about that I joined 84 Reserve Centre at Chessington, Surrey, with its flying unit at Fairoaks. I believe I was in the first ten to rejoin and on 9th May, 1948 set off on a very satisfying trip navigating an Anson from Fairoaks to Flamborough Head and back, a nice little three hours of reintroduction. In August of that year I reported in for my fourteen days' annual training and our old Anson covered the whole of southern and south-west England in that period. I even managed to scrounge a trip in the famous Tiger Moth and what joy that was sitting in an open cockpit with nothing but air around one on a beautiful summer's day. That trip was from Fairoaks to Hamble, near Southampton, where we landed for refuelling. Then we flew all along the south coast at 1,000 feet, or less on occasions, passing over Portsmouth, Bognor, Worthing, Brighton and then back to base via Horsham and Guildford. I have covered that area many times since in a car, but you can't beat flying over it at a few hundred feet. Throughout 1948, 1949 and 1950, I flew on an average once or twice a month and visited a number of well-known RAF airfields like Lyneham, Waddington, St. Eval and even made one flight over to Guernsey and back.

In August 1950, I was attached to Lyneham for my fourteen days' annual training and once again lived on an RAF station in the style of five or six years before. 511 Squadron made me very welcome and I spent a pleasant fortnight doing odd trips in their aircraft, Handley Page Hastings, the highlight of which was a double trip to Coulommiers near Paris, ferrying troops and equipment over for a NATO exercise. We went unserviceable over there on the second trip and so got a night at the hotel in Coulommiers.

Towards the end of the year, my wife brought up the subject of possibly rejoining the service. There were several reasons for considering the subject seriously. I had passed the entrance examination to the Clerical Grade of the Civil Service in early 1947 and had been a Clerical Officer, as they termed it, in the Ministry of Civil Aviation, but had had only about twelve months of the last three years with any real contact with aviation. Money was still tight, the job was not very exciting, and once I was sure that my better half was not too averse to the idea, I applied for a Short Service Commission. Within a month I was reporting into the Reception Centre at Biggin Hill and the following cold December morning was on the way to No. 2 Air Navigation School at Thorney Island for a refresher course.

There followed weeks of ground school, hours of cross-country navigation and monthly progress examinations, which all resulted in a good pass and, no, not a squadron, another course. This time on a Staff Navigator's course at the Empire Air Navigation School at Shawbury, deep in the wilds of Shropshire. It is true to say that I worked very hard on that course but it is also true that when I failed it, not by much, I was not unduly unhappy. A pass of that course meant a posting as an instructor at one of the Navigation Schools and I wanted to go to a front line squadron. Still it had one compensation, the last trip was a pressure pattern flying exercise to Gibraltar via Istres near Marseilles.

Pressure pattern navigation was in the forefront of new navigation techniques in 1951 — the theory was that one studied the weather pattern carefully before take-off and then elected to fly in a curve around a depression or high pressure centre so that you were always flying with the wind behind you. It was believed that although you flew in a curve from Point A to Point B, the wind assistance more than compensated for the extra miles from the point of view of fuel consumption. Thus:

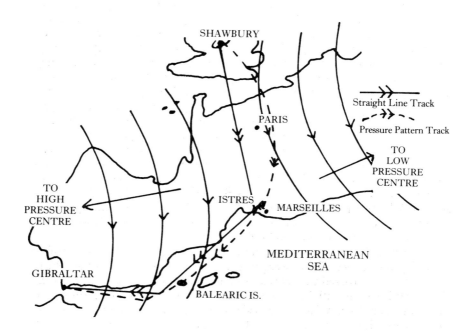

The navigation was much more difficult, constant checks on the wind were needed and air pressure measurement was all important. It was also somewhat alarming to one's basic navigation instincts to find oneself seventy or eighty miles to one side of the straight line track. However, the course spread over a number of Wellingtons, set out to prove the point. The idea was to depart Shawbury and fly pressure pattern to Istres which is about ten miles west of Marseilles and also incidentally on the edge of the trackless Camargue.

The straight line from Shawbury to Istres takes one down well west of Paris, imagine the uneasy feeling to find oneself east of Paris flying at a set height (the height band giving the strongest tail wind) and still apparently moving south-easterly on the heading. We did make Istres eventually but I did have to cheat a bit as we came up to ETA some miles to the east and therefore altered almost 90° to starboard to make the airfield after a flight lasting four hours and twenty minutes.

We had a very nice lunch at Istres but were very short of one commodity — water! At that time the water supply locally was undrinkable, tinged with salt from the flats at the rim of the Camargue and terribly cloudy looking. In its place we got local rough red wine and I can visualize even now the very thick glass goblets it was served in. Nevertheless we downed it on the assumption that if the French Air Force consumed it three times a day and operated after doing so, so could we.

A further attempt at the new navigation technique saw us swing into the Spanish coastline and actually pass over Ibiza and then at last that absolutely unique chunk of rock came into view. I was to visit it many times later but the first arrival was a bit of a shaker because a levanter (the local easterly wind) was blowing. The circuit at Gibraltar was round the Mediterranean side of the rock round Europa Point and back over the harbour towards the end of the runway which extends from dry land outwards into the harbour. On this circuit it is smooth flying down the east face of the Rock and bloody rough coming down across the harbour. The reason, see over:

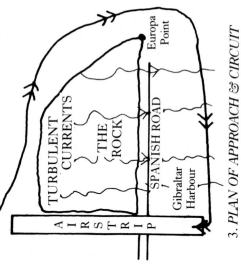

MEDITERRANEAN SEA

TURBULENT CURRENTS

THE ROCK

Europa Point

SPANISH ROAD

Gibraltar Harbour

A I R S T R I P

3. PLAN OF APPROACH & CIRCUIT

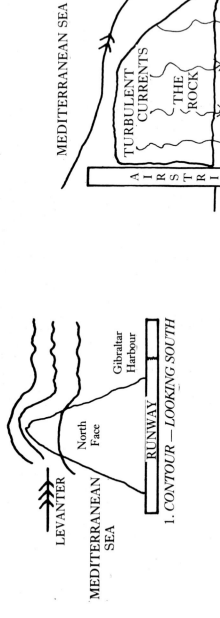

LEVANTER

MEDITERRANEAN SEA

North Face

Gibraltar Harbour

RUNWAY

1. CONTOUR — LOOKING SOUTH

LEVANTER

North Face

AIRSTRIP

EUROPA PT.

2. CONTOUR — LOOKING EAST

When the wind strikes the sheer 1,200 foot high rock it is broken up into currents and flying at right angles to it on the cross wind leg can be a very bumpy experience. The runway projects several hundred yards out into the waters of the harbour and the threshold rounds down into a curve into the water. It is one of the more unusual strips in the world because even after landing the wind can play tricks as after you cross the Spanish Road you run into the shelter of the huge north face of the Rock and the wind either drops or swirls according to which direction it comes from.

A very pleasant and cheap night's drinking in La Linea, just across the Spanish border, followed whilst on the next day, a Sunday, we had all day to explore the town on the Rock. I found it a fascinating place and as I got to know it better in the future, discovered the cemetery with all the tombstones recording the names of those who were buried there after the Battle of Trafalgar, and then the museum with its huge model of the Rock, depicting the days of the long eighteenth century Spanish siege.

On the Monday morning we left again for Shawbury and on arrival there discovered a small army of Customs officers awaiting us. They spent a very long time searching through every aircraft and to the amazement of most of us, unearthed a haul of cigarettes, bottles and nylons. Scuttlebutt insisted that the reception was the result of a tip-off from Gibraltar where someone had spotted one of Macropoli's vans backed up to a Wellington. The Station Commander was extremely annoyed understandably, and the whole course lost its end-of-course forty-eight hours' pass, which was how I came to be on the way to St. Mawgan in Cornwall without benefit of a weekend at home.

My next posting was to St. Mawgan, some three or four miles from Newquay and it was yet another course. This time though it looked more promising since graduation from this course was to a coastal squadron and that was just what I wanted, a flying job. The Maritime Training School at St. Mawgan had Lancasters on the strength so I was reuniting with my favourite flying vehicle. So far so good, but the living conditions were something else again. The camp had provided shelter to Polish refugees after the war and had then lapsed into disuse. We were only the third course to arrive and found ourselves sleeping in sparsely furnished Nissen huts, eating and relaxing in a Nissen hut Mess, operating from a squadron Nissen hut and the technicians were servicing our aircraft in hangars without walls!

The course was a good and interesting one, giving a thorough mix of navigation with maritime specialist subjects like ship recognition, maritime armament, submarine tactics, fleet co-operation and so on. It was on this course that I renewed acquaintance with practical astronavigation, got to practise it assiduously, and once having mastered it, enjoyed it tremendously. There was on the course one other wartime veteran, Len Hoxey, 6ft 5 inches of very fit and athletic humanity. Somewhat naturally we joined forces, flew the exercises together and did our 'dry swims' together. A 'dry swim' was a two hours or so navigation exercise on paper; it took place in a large class-room where you sat at navigation tables and were given a chart to work on together with pages of instructions unfolding your route, flight plan and all the nasty little incidents to upset your navigation — the ones you hoped would never happen in real life.

Len and I received a shellacking from the Station Navigation Officer, 'Pop' Pavitt, because we worked so fast and accurately that we were finishing an exercise designed to last two to two and a half hours in somewhere around one and a half hours. It had been, apparently, somewhat galling for the rest of the toiling course to see us push off so early whilst they had so much to do still! The course demonstrated to me that I had really found my niche at last. If I could join a coastal squadron and spend all day, every day, navigating, dropping torpedoes and depth charges, keeping a sono-buoy plot on a submarine, then I would be in the job of a lifetime. It was fun rather than work although it had a deadly serious purpose. We homed in on radar to buoys anchored way out to sea, then we plastered them with 7lb practice bombs. We dropped sono-buoys in the water, hopefully close to submarines allowed by the Royal Navy to help our training. We listened for bearings and attempted to plot the sub's course and speed and then dropped a dummy depth charge on it. We navigated for hours on drifts and winds picked up off the sea surface from the wind lanes. This was great fun — you left for this exercise from Bishop's Rock and then attempted to come back over it three or five hours later without once obtaining a navigational fix. The only time the radar was used for fixing was fifteen minutes before ETA Bishop's Rock when you looked ahead of the aircraft on radar for a sign of the Scillies.

The course finished on the 19th October 1951, I had notched up over seventy-seven hours flying in my dear old Lancasters and having achieved a good report, Len and I were posted — as instructors on the same unit.

The author, second from right, at RAF Thorney Island, December 1950

CHAPTER THIRTEEN
Instructor and Staff Officer

I took stock of things. Although disappointed in not going to a squadron, I remained on a unit using Lancasters. I had many good friends on the staff of the unit and I was based in what became my favourite county, Cornwall. Things could be the devil of a lot worse.

We went into the winter with thick mud everywhere, freezing Nissen huts heated by the old-fashioned barracks boilers, and condensation running down the walls. It chanced that in November the Secretary of State for Air paid us a visit, no less than Mr Arthur Greenwood. Who put him up to it, I do not know but within a very short while things began to happen at St. Mawgan. First the officers were moved into a hotel in Newquay, whilst proper prefabricated (and properly heated) huts were built for our quarters. The draughty old Nissen hut Mess was given a face lift and the rest of the residential areas were properly rehabilitated. Other improvements were rather slower to arrive — the hangars were still without walls and the technical sections were still in draughty Nissen huts.

The situation led (in aftermath) to an amusing incident which was ever after referred to as Basil Knightley's oil well. In the spring of 1952, it was announced that there would be an inspection by the Air Officer Commanding No. 19 Group. This of course was the signal for frantic preparations of all kinds based largely on the old Service precept for these occasions of 'If it moves, salute it, if it doesn't, paint it'. Now our station sprawled down a slope from the airfield which was on a tableland and nice and flat, to the guardroom in a valley probably the better part of 100 feet lower. Oil changes in Lancasters were messy businesses involving the collection of large quantities of dirty old oil. The problem at St. Mawgan was, amongst many other scarcities, a shortage of dumping space. Thus on the run up to the inspection oil was scoured off the hangar hard standings and, with surplus dirty oil, dumped into a ditch running down the side of the hangars. It mixed with and was blocked by various other rubbish in the ditch which, as it happened, led by the front of the station armoury. Basil Knightley, Station Armoury officer, inspecting his surrounding area, decided that the ditch contained too much rubbish and was unsightly. Having completed a marvellous sprucing up of the station armoury itself, he thought that the ditch rather let it down. Hence one fine morning a posse of his lads attacked the ditch with shovels to clear out the rubbish and succeeded in releasing the blocked up oil, which duly flowed in at the front door of the armoury and over Basil's nice clean floor. I am told that his language was a credit to the force.

The inspection went off rather well, having due regard to the scarcities and subsequent 'lash-ups' required. I had my own small trauma that day as Flight Commander of the course then in residence. Best blue was the order of the day but one of my merry men had seen fit to appear in pipe clayed gaiters and belt over battledress, and appeared at a time when it was far too late to do anything about it. 'Cocky' Spencer our AOC passed along the ranks until faced with the odd man out. "I don't bloody believe it," said he and passed on. At the end of the file, he turned, gazed back at the offender and said "Never seen anything like that in my bloody life," and true enough, you don't see much battledress on AOC's day usually.

1952 wheeled on, I was occasionally a course commander, always a lecturer, and sometimes an airman. The best deal came when as commander, I accompanied my course on their final 'passing out' exercise to Gibraltar. We set them a patrol exercise on the way down and so took over eight hours to reach the Rock in the late afternoon of Friday 23rd May. It was a gorgeous evening in Gibraltar and I could think of no better job I could have than sitting half-way up the Rock watching the sunset over Spain. We allowed the course navigators to come back as directly and quickly as they could to St. Mawgan at cruise speed, and we thus made it in five and three-quarter hours.

In June, almost midsummer's day, the 20th, I did the first Air-Sea Rescue scramble of my career, acting as back up to the regular squadron crews on the job. We flew out on a heading of 095° from Berry Head, almost to the French coast, searching for a small boat in distress, but it did not fall to our lot to locate it.

I paid a further visit to Gibraltar in November, whilst standing in as course commander for Len who had injured his leg in a sports meeting at Uxbridge, where he had been representing Coastal Command. It was around this time that I once again began to suffer appalling stomach pains. This saga had started in July and had resulted in my stay of a month in the RN Hospital at Plymouth. My station MO had sent me there for an X-ray which became a barium meal, and at the end of that intended one day visit, I was detained in bed. For a week under the influence of, I was told, belladonna, I just slept and ate hardly anything at all. It seemed that they were trying to cure a stomach ulcer and true enough after three weeks there was no more pain. After a further week recuperating, playing bowls, in Plymouth yet! I was released back to St. Mawgan. I well remember the parting interview with the Surgeon Rear Admiral, a man with very highly coloured cheeks incidentally, who said to me, "I see you have abnormally low blood pressure. You are probably a little better off than me, my blood pressure is very high." He went on, "I shall die of a stroke probably some time before you die of thrombosis. Oh well, we've all got to go some way, some time."

The result I suppose of a lot of work, I was running two courses together during November, was a breakdown in the ulcer once again. So, just before

Christmas, I was shipped off to Wroughton RAF hospital where, after a stay of three weeks and more dieting, I left for home for the Christmas holiday.

Upon my return to St. Mawgan in the New Year, the whole cycle started again, running yet another course of Coastal hopefuls. I was now somewhat of an expense to our Messing funds, being permitted only bland foods like milk, fish, chicken, ice-cream and the like. However this phase lasted until the beginning of February, when after a game of badminton in the hangars, I returned to my living quarters for a shower and promptly collapsed. A bumpy ride to the Royal Cornwall Infirmary at Truro ensued, and less than two days later the ulcer burst and surgery became necessary. Through a series of complications, I was forced to stay in bed from early February until final recovery and release on the Queen's Coronation Day in June.

The RAF looked after me well. I had an ambulance from Truro to my bed at St. Mawgan. A day or so later I had another ambulance from St. Mawgan to Padstow where, still unable to use my wasted leg muscles, I was loaded into the Atlantic Coast express bound for Waterloo. I was met by ambulance at Epsom and taken under the wing of the Rehabilitation Unit at Headley. The one place they had overlooked was Waterloo! I detrained at Platform 11 I think it was, and had to reach the Epsom train on Platform 2. In between was a couple of hundred yards of concrete to be walked and I could barely stand up. However, kind people assisted me across and, as I say, on arrival at Headley, the RAF took over once more.

Headley was a bit painful, but fun. On 'Early Legs' I learnt to walk and march again, we spent hours marching back and forth in front of the Mess. As I progressed, the Corporal PT of 'Middle Legs' took us into a squash court with a hard ball and a baseball bat. We pitched to him and he smashed it back to us, if you did not move quick enough you picked up a bruise. We became very limber in short order! On 'Late Legs' we were allowed to draw bicycles and go riding out and to play croquet on the lawns. The latter game was I thought rather savage, it certainly did not, as played by airmen, resemble any Vicar's tea-party I knew. Cycling was great fun, we covered miles of very attractive countryside. Best of all, only half a mile away on Headley Heath was a mock prisoner of war camp where they were making *Albert RN* and we thoroughly enjoyed watching the snail's progress they made in getting the takes into the can. Many famous faces were to be seen in The Cock at Headley during lunch breaks.

After a convalescence leave break I was attached to Coastal Command Headquarters at Northwood and my last association with the Lancaster was finally broken. Nevertheless I had added a further 223 hours in them to the 359 I had 'enjoyed' during the late war.

In the two months of my attachment to Command HQ I was asked to gather the material and put together a handbook for Navigators, which would cover everything (both technical and instrument handling) a navigator would require in actual practising of his art. Needing to know more about the equipment of front line Coastal squadron aircraft, I flew up to Kinloss on one day and Topcliffe on another, spending hours in the navigation compartments of Shackletons and Neptunes. I enjoyed the task and assembled the material just before departing to 1 Group HQ at Bomber Command in Yorkshire. Unfortunately a change in policy saw the Neptune replaced and newer equipment brought in, so that my masterpiece never saw the light of day. In October I reported to No. 1 Group HQ at Bawtry to find I was assigned as assistant to the Group's Intelligence officer.

If one has to be grounded for a spell, an interesting staff job is not too bad a way to pass the time. I got airborne in a Chipmunk once or twice a month when my boss 'Tug' Wilson decided to inspect the Intelligence sections of our various 1 Group airfields and on the odd occasion we took up a Chipmunk to keep in flying and map reading practice. In the December of 1953, the AOC himself took the controls of our Group Flight Anson and I served as his navigator for the trip to Scampton, one place I could always find!

Time passed pleasantly enough, I had enough to spare to compete for and win the Bomber Command Essay competition. This, I am sure, assisted me in my attempt to land a Permanent Commission, as my AOC being quite pleased with the fact that a member of his staff had topped the competition, put in a word for me at Bomber Command Headquarters, and six weeks later I was a permanently commissioned Flight Lieutenant on Flying Duties as opposed to General Duties. This was how the Service had divided at the time. Career officers, mostly Cranwell Graduates were General Duties and would have flying tours but more often staff tours. Squadrons would largely be manned by types like myself from other sources of entry. Thus the flying units were guaranteed experienced aviators and we in the Flying Duties category were guaranteed far more flying tours than staff tours. I believe it suited both sides very well.

In August of 1954, I was declared medically fit for full flying duties again and underlined this by taking a high altitude decompression test in the decompression chamber at Lindholme. Here I spent an hour at 25,000 feet and a further hour at 37,000 feet and, as may be appreciated, with outside air pressure vastly reduced at these altitudes, one's stomach does distend slightly. I emerged after the test none the worse and with all my operation scars in place.

Having achieved a full flying category again, I received permission to make occasional trips with the 1 Group squadrons and so made a trip in a Canberra and began to get some navigational practice again in Lincolns. These trips were quite extensive and of a special nature involving the practice of various radar and noise gadgets and they gave me a very contented day now and again, driving myself in an RAF Standard saloon through the Lincolnshire countryside, flying most of the day and returning home in the evening.

'Tug' Wilson was succeeded by Wally Bibby, and the only real change that this made was on the station inspection trips we made together. Whereas I used to give Tug a heading and we would proceed to fly it steadily, Wally, an ex-fighter pilot, would proceed to our destination in a series of slow rolls, loops, barrel rolls and the like. He always arrived glowing and in good form whilst a somewhat breathless navigator stepped out to establish which way was up.

CHAPTER FOURTEEN
Return to Coastal Command

In due course, two years had elapsed and it was time for me and my young family to change quarters and schools. I went off to Kinloss at the end of October 1955 for a two month course to reacquaint myself with newer Coastal Command tactics and get in the vital practice needed on submarine tracking and the various patrols in use and so on. By this time the Avro Shackleton had become the standard aircraft for the whole Command and what a reliable old beauty she turned out to be.

Kinloss in winter was very cold but beautiful, although some days the weather was foul in the extreme. Many of our exercises were flown through intermittent snow and hail showers with the turbulence rough enough and continuous enough to guarantee not one minute on an even keel in two hours. It was good though to work up one's bombing accuracy, tactical target selection, and submarine plotting and attacking skills. Most of the exercises had the mountains of Ross and Cromarty and the Dornoch Firth as a backcloth. The day of the CFI's final check arrived and we, by now a reasonably knitted crew, welcomed him aboard for an eleven hour trip which would see numerous practices of every situation imaginable.

We took off at ten minutes to ten, four days before Christmas 1955, into squally showers with intermittent but not very lasting, fine periods. We progressed through a largely grey and snowy atmosphere up to the Pentland Skerries. As a navigator one has to be careful here because in this narrow strait between the mountains of the northern tip of Scotland and the hills of the Orkneys, the wind seems to channel itself and produce a local but very strong upsurge in speed. The effect can be experienced up to fifty miles east of the Skerries out in the open sea. In cold winter-time the rocky coastline of the Orkneys seems more ironbound than ever. Massive waves thrash against the rock and spume flies high in the air. We flew westward through the Skerries and over the now abandoned isle of Rona (what a penal settlement that would make!) At the northernmost point of 62°N, we turned south-westerly to that lonely rock in the Atlantic known as Rockall. To find it is a reasonable navigation/radar achievement. I believe it is less than 100 feet high and is only a pin-point of rock sticking up from the sea bed. Arriving over it in due course we were required by the CFI to carry out various patrols and simulated attacks using the rock as a base. Hours later when darkness had well and truly arrived, we set course for the Pentland Skerries once more and with the advantage of a tail wind through the Skerries, finally reached Kinloss at 9.05 p.m. after eleven and a quarter hours continuous flying. It was a pointer to the kind of sorties we would have to make after reaching a squadron and an indication of the Shackleton's capabilities.

We were successful in our passing out flight and obtained the posting all of us most wanted — 42 Squadron, the oldest in the Command, at St. Eval in Cornwall.

After leave over Christmas and the New Year, we left our Bawtry Married Quarters in freezing fog and set out for London where my wife and children were to spend a day or so with her sister whilst I found new quarters in Cornwall. After a day long drive in icy conditions on the Sunday, I reported in to the CO on the Monday morning when I am bound to say that neither took to the other. I was allowed the Monday afternoon to find lodgings for my young family and after several hours' search at ever increasing distances, finally leased a flat in St. Austell, twenty miles away over the other side of the Cornish Alps.

Upon reporting back the following day, I was appointed Squadron Navigation officer and told to organize a trip out to Cyprus via Malta for the following day. This kind of event in fact set the pattern for what was to happen on 42 Squadron over the next fifteen months. I was reacquainted with Phil Carlisle whom I had worked with and liked in my instructor days at St. Mawgan. He was to be my pilot on the morrow and I found that he had as little liking for our Boss as I did. We decided to get off first and therefore bag first place in the queue at Blackbushe Airport where we were to emplane a Parachute Brigade from Aldershot. The CO, who had not yet qualified as an aircraft captain, was flying with another crew and arrived long after Phil and the rest of us had departed to the barracks for our night's kip. It proved to be the wrong move though, the old man simply shifted his flag to our aircraft which was going to have to be the first off!

On the following morning, 12th January, we emplaned our passengers and being at the head of the line we found we were carrying the Brigade HQ personnel, including the Brigadier himself, his second in command and staff, not to mention the Regimental Sergeant Major, a total of thirty-three bodies to be spread through the Shackleton which normally accommodated eleven crew members. By reducing the crew from eleven to seven, we managed to find a few square inches for everyone. As it was the most comfortable spare seat, the Brigadier sat in my second navigator's empty seat and was thus an interested spectator of my navigational efforts. We took off at 8 a.m. to the minute and were routed to overfly Marseilles and the south of Sardinia and thence to Malta Control Corridor. I was amazed to see that within minutes the soldiers had made themselves as comfortable as possible within the very narrow confines of their positions and were off to sleep!

Seven hours and twenty minutes later we had landed at Luqa and were taxiing towards the control tower. We had to pass the area of the resident fighter squadron who must have somehow discovered our mission because they were exhibiting large blackboards on which were chalked 'It's quicker by B.O.A.T.'

The lads were unloaded and we were all told that we would spend the night at Luqa and, as I remember it, I believe the parachute lads met some incoming King's Own Yorkshire Light Infantrymen (KOYLIS) returning from duty in Libya, which ensured a fair old dust-up. Be that as it may, we were fully loaded and off again the next day at 1 p.m. Malta time, and set off eastwards to Cyprus.

I obtained splendid pin-points from Pantelleria and Crete, but as it was deep mid-winter and we were traversing into yet another time zone it became quite dark after three hours flying, and the last two and a half hours were true night flying. A small argument developed over the intercom when we were flying at 10,000 feet when the Boss said he could see Nicosia ahead. I was doubtful about this, we were still approaching the west coast and Mount Trudos (some 9,000 feet high) stood in the way. Phil and I got our way and we maintained height until we contacted Nicosia Area Control who gave us a let down, and we finally landed five and a half hours after leaving Luqa.

The Brigade deplaned rapidly and disappeared into the darkness to find their bivouacs and prepare for the invasion of Egypt. We refuelled both the aircraft and ourselves and took off two hours later bound for Malta. After another five and a half hours flight we were back at Luqa in the wee small hours, only to find that we must now remain at Luqa to shuttle further troop loads to Cyprus as they arrived from the UK. All around us was great activity, fighters and bombers were steadily arriving from home and the Canberras were being armed with bombs landed from transports. Despite all this activity, our squadron was an island of inactivity such that when some army staff officers wished to visit Tripoli in Libya, there was a rush of volunteers for the trip. Phil knew the Force Commander quite well and got the job, so we made a quick overnight shuttle to Idris (this was Tripoli airport — it had been Castel Benito under the Italians and was renamed for the King of Libya). The flight was only one and a half hours each way, but a walk round the attractive bay in Tripoli and a drink in the Mocambo Club was a welcome break from standing around in Luqa. I advisedly said a drink because a round of drinks even at this uninflated period cost an average of 10/- per drink.

On our return to Luqa we hung around for some days. I was conscious of the fact that my family were still stranded in London and I wanted to get back to telephone and say come down. We pressurized the Force Commander and Control as much as we dare and after five days we got permission to return, but in trickles and to be replaced by other crews. Thus it was that I was one of the first to leave via a Transport Command Hastings which took us back to St. Eval directly on the 24th January. My poor wife who had been waiting for my telephone call for two weeks was soon on the train and installed at St. Austell. I suppose it was just our luck that she was greeted by a snowfall several inches thick, which Cornwall had not seen for years past.

Towards the end of the month, I had shaken down in the navigation office, made the acquaintance of all the navigators on the squadron and started to fly again myself. There were duties which kept me ground borne on many days. I had to examine and analyse the logs and charts of the squadron navigators, make the odd reports, run inventories on equipment and so on and, of course, there were always the Monday morning Prayer Meetings when all the Section Heads attended the Boss's office for an exchange of views. It seemed to me that much of what went on at these meetings was trivial in the extreme, but it did air the odd problem. Over the next two months or so, I got in about sixty flying hours and began the process of honing up attack procedures.

I participated in 'Dawn Breeze' on the 24th March, a NATO exercise carried out with ships from Belgium and Holland, as well as the Royal Navy. We were airborne for eight hours fifty minutes, more than half of it night flying, and concluded a fairly successful communications exercise with the ships involved. Then early in April the first 'buzz' was heard about the squadron converting to high level bombing for some kind of overseas detachment. Indeed on the 6th I flew up to Lindholme in Bomber Command with Phil and our CO to see what was involved and how we should do it. It was decided that we would operate with a Mark XIV sighting head without its connection to the huge computator box which had been the bomber's equipment at the end of the war.

We now commenced to use Chesil Beach Range near Portland to brush up the medium/high level bombing technique. This was necessary since we were all trained on the low level bombsight and seldom, if ever, bombed above 500 feet. We therefore decided on a bombing height, calculated a setting of the sight for this height and the aircraft's normal bombing speed, and then it was all down to the pilot to fly as rigidly as humanly possible at the predetermined height and speed. This came easy to some pilots and very hard for others. As Navigation officer for the Squadron I was called upon to fly with my CO as often as not and I regret to say that he was one pilot who simply could not fly the Shackleton firmly enough to ensure bombing within limits. After one or two practices with dismal results I rather wondered whether I was a bad bomb aimer so I changed pilots to some of the good ones and got equally good results, but I never did convince the Boss that it was down to him.

I was paying a number of visits to Lindholme to obtain technical assistance, supervising the arrival and installation of MK14 sights in a couple of aircraft and still endeavouring to improve my Coastal tactics, so it was a busy period. Then in mid-May, we learned that Coastal Command was to provide the aircraft for the Queen's Birthday Fly Past on the 31st of the month and this gave us roughly two weeks to achieve the necessary expertise in flying the monster Shackletons in tight vee formation. If memory serves me correctly, Cornish bases were to provide eighteen aircraft and Ulster bases nine. The fly past was to be in tight vees of nine in three flights with very little spacing between flights.

We began by operating three aircraft at a time in one vic formation and early attempts were pathetic because it simply did not seem sensible to put a 40-45 ton aeroplane right close to another. Eventually the pilots lost their inhibitions and we began achieving credible results. Next we flew the nine aircraft in a squadron vic and eventually all the Cornish Wing flew together. After this we began what might be termed the dress rehearsals when we left Cornwall in two flights of nine and picked up the Northern Ireland Wing of a further nine aircraft who fell in behind us at a prearranged time over St. Catherine's Point, Isle of Wight. Having settled in, we then proceeded up-Channel around the Thanet coast and tracked over Clacton before proceeding down the Thames to Fairlop, just east of London where we broke off the rehearsal.

By now we were quite adept at St. Eval in taking off in a stream, each aircraft staggered to the extreme left of the runway and then the extreme right side alternately, so that one avoided the worst of the slipstream of the one ahead. We also managed stream landings in much the same way. The advantage of this of course is that aircraft spend less time circling over the airfield waiting for the formation units to get airborne and join up.

Thus it was that at 9.35 a.m. on a beautifully clear and sunny 31st May our Shackleton left the ground at St. Mawgan as the lead aircraft of the second vic and within a very short time, eight other aircraft were gathered round us in what looked like touching distance. We fell in behind the leading formation and the parade moved off eastwards and the fruits of our training were seen when the Wing from Northern Ireland tucked in behind us, with the minimum of difficulty, over St. Catherine's Point. The fleet headed up-Channel and my only task as lead navigator of the second formation was to observe the shadow of the fleet leader pass over an object and click my stopwatch to start off. Ideally, ten seconds later we should pass directly over the same object. If we did not, a small course alteration had to be made; if we were more than ten seconds behind, a slight increase in speed had to be made or conversely a very small reduction in speed. These alterations were all very delicate ones and did not follow until the executive order was given by my pilot, Flight Lieutenant Jones, followed by the word "Go".

In this fashion we made a perfect approach to the City, spotted the sodium flares placed on various ground points and roof tops to give us a straight line to Buckingham Palace by lining one up after the other. The weather was absolutely perfect — in fact incredible for London — unlimited visibility being the order of the day. I give full marks to the Fleet Navigation Leader, being on track and bang on time. The lead flight crossed Buckingham Palace at 1 p.m. at 1,000 feet, we followed ten seconds later at 800 feet, and the last Wing ten seconds after us at 600 feet. Every camera in the Shackletons had been clicking away since Trafalgar Square, rear-facing, downward and hand held, and the photographs developed as a result were among the very best ever taken in the Command. I hope that they are still somewhere in the archives.

For myself it was a great thrill to take part in this majestic event and from the astrodome I had had a fleeting glance of the Royal Family on the veranda of the palace and too I'd seen the town of my birth as I had never seen it before. Strangely the formations peeled off over Barnes Bridge close to where my wife and family had lived. The aircraft proceeded back to their bases individually, all strain and stress now over, and this one-off formation exercise was over. We landed at five past three and enjoyed the rest of the day off.

June saw an interesting development in the new role we were assuming. I and a few others flew up to Abingdon in Oxfordshire to be given a demonstration on supply dropping. We boarded a Hastings and observed practice drops at Watchfield and then we each had a go. The results were distinctly encouraging but I still thought that if we were to do it in Shackletons it would best be done by eye, in a freefall from about fifty feet above the terrain.

Early in June I was offered a flight in a Fairey Gannett by a visiting Royal Navy pilot. Always keen to try a new experience I accepted smartly and we spent half an hour beating up the north Cornish coast at ten feet or so above the ground. To demonstrate its extreme manoeuvrability, Lieutenant Hallam flew towards Trevose Head lighthouse and then pulled the stick back in a vertical climb. I caught a quick glimpse of a somewhat alarmed lighthouse keeper and seconds later we were at 1,500 feet and heading for St. Eval's circuit and a nice landing.

On the 10th July I flew a sortie on a NATO Exercise entitled 'Ratrap' in which we had to fly at very low levels in to the Dutch coast at Oudoorp and then fly over Holland very low as far as IJmuiden before departing seawards back to base. I presume this six and a half hours trip was to give the Dutch radar some custom and exercise in detecting low flying aircraft.

In the next ten days we made our preparations for the squadron's annual detachment to the Mediterranean in order to practise submarine detection in warm waters. It is a fact of life that a submarine operating under a layer of warm water is ten times harder to detect — the warm thermal current acts almost as a shield. Our base was to be Luqa, Malta, for a period of three weeks and hence the detachment bore the code name of 'Fair Isle'. On the 20th July we set off for Malta leaving St. Mawgan at 09.25 a.m. and arriving in Malta nearly seven hours later. I was very unfortunate on this trip. I had finally parted company with all my often decayed teeth recently and had just acquired dentures. The top plate was a perfectly comfortable fit, but half an hour after we were airborne, I had taken the very uncomfortable bottom set out and wrapped them in a clean handkerchief which I placed in my pocket. Some considerable time later between Marseilles and Sardinia, I pulled out the handkerchief to blow my nose, the teeth dropped to the floor and it was just my luck that they fell right in the path of the heaviest Flight Sergeant in the Command. Nearly seventeen stones crushed them into small pieces, which condemned me to a very peculiar diet in Malta for that three weeks stay — if it was not soft, I couldn't eat it!

Our crew put in fifty-three flying hours in that three weeks, tracking (or attempting to track) and sometimes attacking HM Submarine *Totem* all over the Mediterranean. There was an exercise with the *Totem* which involved two frigates HMS *Chaplet* and *Undine* and this lasted all day — we flew for over ten hours continuously.

Immediately on the following day we took off at 12.45 p.m. and flew to Cyprus and this was the high spot of the detachment as it was an operation for real. Known as a 'Marzo' it involved flying right round the coast of Cyprus on continuous patrol and investigating every suspicious radar contact we got. The reason of course was to intercept if possible the caiques gun-running for the Enosis lads who were then causing the army a lot of trouble in Cyprus. We investigated numerous contacts and dropped a number of flares during darkness. Three such ships revealed looked very suspicious so they were reported in to the Cyprus control station who arranged for a sea interception.

Flying at 500 feet or less around the mountainous areas of Cyprus, particularly in the west, one found oneself in the 'wind shadow' of the mountains when the breeze dropped suddenly as the great hills shielded it. This had a tricky effect on the courses in and out of every bay and inlet.

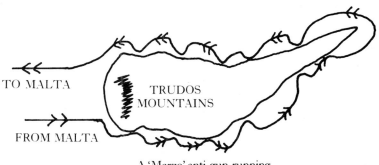

A 'Marzo' anti-gun-running patrol — plan shows how each inlet is investigated.

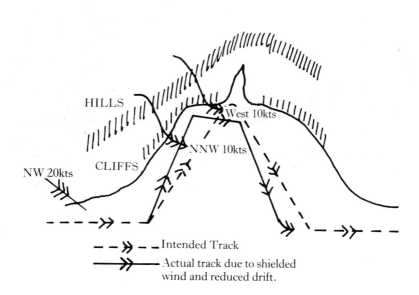

—— >> — — Intended Track
——————>>——— Actual track due to shielded wind and reduced drift.

We finally arrived back at Luqa at 04.20 a.m., having been continuously airborne for fifteen hours and thirty-five minutes. With the naval exercise of the day before, we had been in the air for twenty-five and two-third hours out of the last forty-five hours. No wonder we got a whole day off after the 'Marzo'.

On the 9th August we set off for home and having taken only six and a half hours to do the trip, we caught the HM Customs from Falmouth on the hop — they had not left Falmouth for St. Mawgan. The entire squadron flew up and down Cornwall until the customs lads had taken up their position on the squadron's hard standings in order to see what came out of the aircraft. Nothing unduly untoward was landed, but of course some charges were incurred by some of the chaps — after all we had to cover the expense of fetching them up from Falmouth!

In October we paid another visit to Abingdon, loaded up with training stores and dropped eleven packs of stores at Watchfield with fair success. Next we went up to the Luce Bay Live Bombing Range in Wigtownshire in the south- west of Scotland and dropped twenty 25lb flash bombs and four live 500lb medium casing bombs. I was thrilled with the low error rate obtained, all four 500lb bombs were within twenty-five to thirty yards of the target, but Doug Borland was flying the Shackleton and he was one of the chaps who could fly to tight limits.

On the 12th and 15th October, still with Doug Borland, we were on Air-Sea Rescue standby when we got the call to go. On the first alert time was of course of the essence as the Mayday call had only just been received from a United States Air Force Liftmaster ditching into the Atlantic about one hundred miles north of Cape Finisterre. We rushed off into the air at 6.15 a.m. and travelled out as fast as possible to a position 47°N 8°W in the Atlantic and then commenced a patrol known as a Creeping Line Ahead on a bearing of 060°, its limits in width two hundred miles, and each step was twenty nautical miles. The distance of the step is determined by the visibility available weatherwise and the type and size of object you are searching for. Fortunately, whilst the weather was not particularly good, visibility was to the horizon and as we were searching for ten men dinghies, Group HQ Rescue Centre decided that we would spot it through a binocular search up to ten miles. The shape of the patrol is as follows:

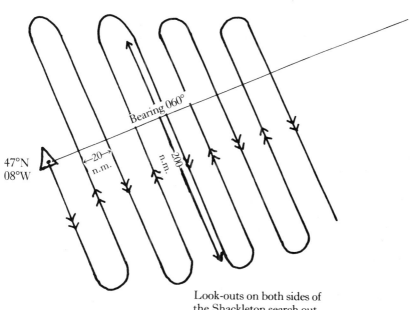

Look-outs on both sides of the Shackleton search out to 10 a.m.

Continued until maximum patrol time arrives.

From this illustration one could see why it is called a Creeping Line Ahead. As the first on ASR standby you carried only 2,400 gallons of fuel, the theory being that it was your primary job to get out to the area as fast as possible, try and find the wreck and/or survivors and commence to mark the spot with smoke markers which would burn for two hours. This did tend to limit the time you could stay in the area but it gave back-up crews time to assemble the facts transmitted by the first aircraft at the scene, thus making for less time wasted in searching and to fuel the aircraft fully. We spent nine hours on patrol but failed to locate anybody and after handing over to the relief aircraft on the search, we departed for St. Eval, landing at 7.20 p.m., just over thirteen hours after take-off.

Unhappily few survivors were located so that three days later, on the 15th we again flew out at 6.15 a.m. to relieve an aircraft and continue the search. This time we ranged far out into the Atlantic and conducted a box search of fifty nautical miles east/west by sixty nautical miles north/south, but again with no success so that we finally returned to base after sixteen hours in the air, only to be diverted in very foggy weather to the neighbouring base at St. Mawgan.

CHAPTER FIFTEEN
Air Policing in the Aden Protectorate

On the 29th October, fifteen minutes before midnight, a crew largely composed of the CO and all the squadron section heads took off with destination Aden. The big secret had come out earlier that our conversion to medium level bombing and supply dropping was to enable our squadron to replace the existing heavy bomber squadron at Aden with its ageing Lincolns now about to be returned to maintenance units for break up. 42 Squadron was to commence this tour of duty in the New Year, but because of our NATO commitments at home, we were obliged to retain half the squadron at St. Eval, whilst the other half was stationed in Aden. Rotation of crews was to take place every three months so that nobody was away from their true role in Coastal Command for too long. This trip was necessary for all us leaders to ensure that we had what we needed out there and to arrange for the transport out of anything we had not got.

We flew all through the night via Bordeaux, the Toulouse/Carcasson Gap and were over the Mediterranean when dawn broke at 6 a.m. Then flying over Lampedusa, we landed at Idris airport in Libya at 8 a.m. (10 a.m. their time). We had the rest of the day off and went sightseeing in town. After a good night's sleep and a fairly warm but restful day, we left Idris at 6 p.m. their time and commenced the long flight to Aden. The first leg was mainly southerly to a point some forty miles outside the Egyptian borders where the western and southern meet. This flight of some twelve hundred to fifteen hundred miles was navigated entirely on astro-navigation, we two navigators took it in turns to run the navigation plot on the table and to take hourly three star fixes. Astro-navigation under these conditions is fun and very interesting. The stars seem nearer when the latitudes are in the twenties, the night was very clear and as it was night-time, there was practically no turbulence. So with a steady platform and a clear night our fixing was accurate and that made for excellent wind finding by air plot and track and ground speed checks.

As dawn broke we were flying east towards Port Sudan and when the sun began to appear above the earth's rim, the colours of the desert were beyond description. Grey turned into gold, shot with green and orange, until as the sun climbed higher the colour of the day, hot yellow, asserted itself. At Port Sudan we turned south down the Red Sea, flying in the middle of it with Eritrea to starboard and Saudi Arabia to port. Since you could see both, navigation could not be easier and on arrival at Perim Island at the bottom of the Red Sea, we simply turned left for Aden just up the coast.

The first impression of Aden was very bleak, rocky hills, sandy coastal strips, apart from the little town clinging to the hollow in the hills on the coast. The harbour was somewhat more impressive, opening out into a considerable anchorage. Overall the sun beat down out of a cloudless sky even at 9.45 a.m. (Aden time). We landed and stepped on to the ground for the first time in fifteen hours and it was like stepping into an oven.

On Saturday, the 3rd November, we were emplaned into a Pembroke of the Khormaksar Station Flight and taken up country for a look around the operational area. The flight lasted for two and three-quarter hours and in that time we over flew the army post at Wadi Beyhan, looked at the area around the Dhala Pass and looked down on the tiny but troublesome village of Al Quasab. My overall impression was that we were overflying a lunar landscape — all sharp toothed rocks, very dry and bare of vegetation and not a living soul to be seen.

A couple of days later we made a longer sortie in one of the Aden based Lincolns when the pilot displayed to us his considerable local knowledge. This flight was in fact an anti-gun-running patrol around the northern towns of the Protectorate which faced the Rubh-El-Kali, the Empty Quarter. It was an apt description, the stony desert on a high plateau stretched off into the hazy distance with not a sign of human habitation in sight. The route took us over villages with rolling Arabic names — Nisab, Aiyadh, Shabiwa, Husn Al Abr, Zamakh, Minwakh, Thaniya, Aryam, Arain and back to Nisab and Khormaksar. They represented the 'frontier' villages at the edge of the Empty Quarter in a crescent round north-west and north of the Aden Protectorate and of them all Hasn Al Abr seemed to see more of the camel caravans out of the desert than the others. We flew round this village for a spell as there were camel trains entering its northern gate. On this occasion there appeared to be no hanky-panky out in the desert and the trains were being checked as they came in so we reckoned there were no guns coming in on this occasion.

On the following day we were to depart for the United Kingdom, so after arriving back from the patrol I got down to route planning, for this time there was a snag. The Egyptians and the Israelis were at war with each other and this made the Middle East a no go area for non-combatants. There were two alternatives, one to fly round the coast of Arabia into Iran and refuel at Teheran, then to fly north-westwards to Turkey crossing the border close to the USSR, and so on to Cyprus. This route proposal favoured by the Boss gave me the shivers, aside from being too close to the war zone, in my opinion there was also the question of proximity to the Russian border. Not too long before a Tudor aircraft of Transport Command had strayed over the border using a beacon signal from Russia on the same frequency as, but stronger than, the one in Turkey.

The alternative was a long trip but a relatively safe one, southwards to Nairobi in Kenya and then across the Congo to Kano and thence across the

Sahara to Algiers and Gibraltar. This route was the one accepted by 19 Group HQ and at 9 a.m. on the 6th November we left Khormaksar for Nairobi, via Hargeisa and Garissa, the trip lasting five hours forty minutes. Nairobi was in the middle of its 'Short Rains' season when small but frequent showers occurred. The runway, which was 5,500 feet above sea level, was long enough for the Shackleton but only the first four hundred yards were tarmac, the rest was red murram, and after rain this became very muddy and slippery for weighty aircraft. The Boss was flying the first leg and in his attempt to get the wheels firmly down on the concrete before reaching the murram, set the aircraft down rather heavily, resulting in a radiator cracking in one engine. Subsequent enquiries revealed that there were no spare radiators for a Shackleton anywhere in Africa. This meant that our base at St. Eval would have to despatch one from London Airport via the civil air lines. The whole process of receiving, fitting and testing was going to take a week.

Tony Talbot-Williams had the bright and right idea of hiring a Volkswagen mini-bus for the week and to travel about Kenya seeing the sights. We visited Brackenhurst and Thompson's Falls, where there were stalls selling the products of the local crafts. We visited the Kenya National Park outside Nairobi and were very lucky in catching a family of lion cubs and all at feeding time. We also went up to Njbini on the edge of the Aberdares, had a marvellous lunch in The Brown Trout and met many of the local planters who had recently been in action against the Mau Mau. Both parties in this conflict were reported to have done some daft things. We imported 49 Bomber Squadron whose Lincolns spent some time blowing up trees in the Aberdares. The Mau Mau had a cook in the RAF Officers' Mess at Nairobi and instead of poisoning them all, which he could have done easily, he set fire to the Mess which was more difficult and not very successful.

The war against the Mau Mau caused a considerable development in helicopter flying. The parameters of its performance were powerfully extended. An old acquaintance of mine, Frankie Bernard, was regularly landing and taking off choppers in the high Aberdares in the remarkably thin air around 10,000 feet above sea level. This was thought, heretofore, to be courting disaster but Frankie had been landing and picking up Mr Henderson of the Kenya Police, in small clearings close to 10,000 ft. above sea level.

We had a final day driving up to the very top of the Ngong Hills for a picnic lunch and then on the 13th left Nairobi at 4 p.m. lightly laden with petrol so that we would not stick in the wet murram. An hour and a half later we set down at Entebbe in Uganda which was operated by BOAC and East African airways. We spent a night in the luxurious Lake Hotel, overlooking Lake Victoria and took off at 4 a.m. next morning with a maximum fuel load.

It took over eight and a half hours to fly from Entebbe to Kano, and the route was virtually down the line of the river Congo. The weather was mainly cloudy with many showers and the navigation was largely accomplished by recognizing pin-points and calculating track and ground speed winds. We flew fairly low, mostly under the clouds, and I was astonished to see how really thick a rain forest can be. At times the trees grew into an interlaced roof and blotted out the river entirely. At other times the river widened hugely and large numbers of diverse types of craft could be seen on its surface.

After an early night in Kano, which included a quick visit to a mosque and the muezzin's tower, we were airborne at 5 a.m. to fulfil one of my two life's navigational ambitions — a trans-Sahara trip. I was in for a few surprises for I had imagined the Sahara to be a great flat sand sea. True, as we overflew Timbuctoo on the approach to the desert it was flat and sandy. However, two hours into the trip great sand ridges appeared and an hour later approaching Tamanrasset, the ground began to rise higher and higher until it very nearly reached our flight level at 10,000 a.m.s.l. It was also extraordinary to see so much colour high in the hills surrounded by hot sandy desert. There were flowers, bushes and fruits of all sorts and many tracks out of the area showed where camel trains arrived and departed. After this surprise the desert rolled monotonously on but its dunes and valleys were surprisingly high and deep. We passed over the romantic (at least in books) forts of the Foreign Legion, Zindeneuf and Lamy and by constant use of that basic but very important instrument, the drift sight, eventually we arrived over Algiers and turned west for Gibraltar where we landed after a flight of eleven hours and thirty-five minutes with one lifetime's ambition in the bag. This chance had come out of the blue but there was no foreseeable chance that I would ever get to navigate across the Atlantic, or so I thought.

There followed eight weeks of preparation so that the first four crews and aeroplanes could be in position to take over from the Lincolns in Aden by the third week in January 1957. A week before our scheduled departure, I flew an Air-Sea Rescue mission in Flight Lieutenant Hobday's crew which put up my own personal record for the number of hours in the air on one flight. We were detailed to search a box ninety nautical miles north/south, sixty nautical miles east/west out at 31°W in the Atlantic. We were to look for the SS *Nordic Star* which was overdue and had been caught up in violent storms in the Atlantic in early January. I regret to say that despite spending eighteen and a quarter hours continuously in the air we found no trace of her. The take-off for this flight was at 8.35 a.m. and the landing was made at 2.50 a.m. on the following day, the 10th January.

Six days later after much flight planning, four Shackletons left St. Eval for Aden and I was navigating for Doug Borland AFM. On the 16th we flew to Idris in North Africa, leaving at 9 a.m. and arriving eight hours later. On the 17th we made my second crossing of the Sahara on a route from Idris via Ghat — Posn 2330N 0940E — Zinder to Kano in seven hours forty minutes. On the following day we once again traversed the major part of Africa, this time from west to east along the Congo to Lake Victoria, over Entebbe and in to Nairobi, a flight of ten hours and forty minutes. We then enjoyed a rest day in Nairobi since we had risen in Kano at 3 a.m. and had left the ground there at 4.20 a.m.

which made for a long and tiring day. However on the 20th the trip was completed via Garissa and Hargeisa in British Somaliland and we landed in Aden at Khormaksar at just after 3.30 p.m.

The next two days were fully employed in shaking down in our quarters, flight area and sorting out our technical back-up. On the third day our crew with Doug as Captain were detailed for operations. The task was to make a reconnaissance and escort a motor convoy over a stretch of desert between strange sounding named villages on the route, Nisab, Wadi Beyhan, Al Qsab, Mannawa and back. For the first time we played our three routine roles in the Protectorate, first to reconnoitre, second to warn our ground forces of impending attacks, and lastly to act as an airborne telephone exchange. This latter role was supremely important because the terrain in Aden is so mountainous that it breaks up ground-to-ground communications and confines them to short ranges of perhaps ten or twenty miles. With the advent of the sophisiticated communication channels available in the Shackleton, our ground forces could be in contact with their Headquarters in Aden by relay through us and this was to become essential as time wore on.

Two days later we were scheduled to repeat the operation but heavy cloud over the mountains up country made it impossible to get further north than Wadi Beyhan. This cloud incidentally brought rain to Aden for the first time in over three years I was told.

Khormaksar was north of the town of Aden and they both stood on the coastal plain at the southern tip of the Protectorate. There was just one village north of the airfield, also on the plain, and then the terrain rose to nearly 10,000 feet in a series of bare, rocky hills. This was known to us as the escarpment and it was said that one dissident Arab sat up there with a .455 elephant gun and fired each time an aircraft passed low overhead in its climb over the 'moon country'. God it was desolate up there, I do not know how even the native Arabs put up with it. By day it baked in temperatures well over 100° whilst by night the temperature fell by some 60°. There were of course routes into and through this wilderness but only one of them was a road running from Aden up to Dahla in the north of the country.

Which leads into our next trip on the 29th when we were sent up to Dahla airstrip, through Queriba Pass to fly over several other airstrips at Mukeiras, Lodar, Malifid and Attaq. We visited each in turn and came to the conclusion that they would make emergency landing strips only for us, we'd never get off again. They accommodated relatively short run take-off aircraft like the Pembroke and were used mainly for that sort of aircraft to fly in with supplies. These were co-ordinated by officers on the ground and information obtained by contacts living among the tribes was often passed out this way too. I remember seeing two of these mysterious beings on separate occasions at Khormaksar. Both were very taciturn men and both were tanned as deeply as any Arab I met.

I met and immediately liked Willie Wells, the Squadron Leader who was

156

Station Armament officer and on one occasion I accompanied him to the Armoury on a Saturday morning. He had told me that by a clause in our Treaty with the Protectorate tribes, they were allowed to bring in their personal arms for servicing in our Armoury. He had also mentioned that some of the guns were home-made, some incredibly old and most downright dangerous to the owner. I thought at the time that perhaps he was pulling the long bow but I took it all back during a couple of hours of that Saturday. Most of the weapons properly belonged in a museum. I did not actually see a muzzle loader but everything else back to the early 1800s I should think. The story goes that one such rifle owner was warned that nothing further could be done to make it good and that it was dangerous to fire it as it would probably blow up and injure the man who pulled the trigger. "Good," said the wrinkled and bewhiskered old Arab, "I shall make my enemy in the tribe a present of it."

We were doing practice bombing exercises when possible, and on the last day of the month went up the Wadi Beyhan to a fort, called something like Nejdzr, and spent some time doing a mosaic of the area. This was in fact photographing the area by doing timed runs side by side which slightly overlapped. From the dozens of photographs so obtained, clever cartographers could draw up-to-date maps.

On the first day of February we were sent up on a patrol through the area of Haddinyah and Saudinyah where there had been quite severe fighting with some few casualties sustained on both sides. We patrolled busily for over six hours, reporting back to Base on anything that moved.

Three days later we carried out an anti-gun-running patrol over a number of villages at the southern end of the Rubh Al Kali (the Empty Quarter). Unlike the Sahara, desert winds did not blow very frequently and consequently the flattened paths made by the camels showed up as tracks slightly lighter in colour than the surrounding sand, and they seemed to endure for quite some time before the winds shifted the sand over them. This made for good navigation because once having assessed their bearing from one of the little villages mentioned above, they could be used as position lines, eventually leading to a fix, thus:

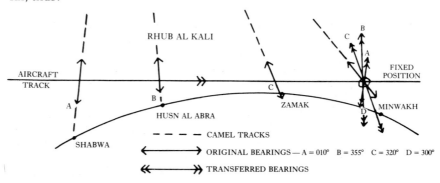

The first bearing was taken as you crossed the track, the second at the next time of crossing and the third similarly. You then transferred the first one along the aircraft track by the number of miles of ground speed elapsed between the time of the first and last. The second line position was transferred in the same way and you therefore established a position where the intersection of the lines took place. The same thing can, of course, be done by radio beams if you can receive and measure them and its original application was to landmarks on which you physically took compass bearings. Good basic navigation!

On our return we were able to say that there was no one out in the desert who was not expected. Our contacts with the Arabs on the ground knew the rough whereabouts and expected times of arrival of the various camel trains. Any other collection of men and animals out in the desert were immediately suspected as gun-runners from the north.

Early in February we were called to give air cover to a convoy of men and supplies travelling from Metaar to Makeiras through the troublesome area of Haddinayah. This place is in the west of the Protectorate and frequently saw the invasion of Egyptian troops with artillery which supported the Yemen forces hoping eventually to take over Aden. On this day circling west of Mukeiras we came under anti-aircraft fire from the ground. No damage was done to us, but it did demonstrate that we were in a shooting war even if it had not been declared and despite the fact that we could not retaliate.

In the meantime, training continued offering the occasional job of range safety officer on the bombing range to the north-east of Khormaksar on the coast. The range was a vast expanse of sand bordering the sea with a large metal triangle for a target in the middle. The range safety officer's hut with its small R/T set for communication with the bombing crew, was situated about 1,000 yards from the triangle and we observed the fall of bombs through binoculars from it. One fine morning in the middle of an exercise I had to have it stopped quickly as a motley collection of Arabs rode on to the range mounted on camels. They made towards the triangle and I assumed that they would traverse the length of the range and disappear from view. Not so, having arrived around the triangle, they proceeded to scour the area for the metal shards remaining from the hundreds of 25lb practice bombs dropped there. I jumped into a jeep with my interpreter, one of the Aden levies, and rushed across to the marauders. We eventually got them to understand that the big bird circling in the sky above them was about to drop more metal which would do them no good at all. They could come back late in the day if they wanted to when bombing was finished and scavenge to their hearts' content for all I cared. To my relief the camels padded off and the exercise was resumed.

On the 10th February we were warned for an operation the following day in which we were ordered to destroy an Arab village, Ad Danaba, deep in the dissident area. The Squadron CO had arrived at the beginning of the month and he it was who flew the aircraft over the range on the 10th whilst we calibrated the bomb sight during the exercise. Our Station Commander at St.

Eval, Group Captain Innes, had also flown out for a visit and decided to accompany us on the operation on the 11th. The background to it all was the death of six Cameronian soldiers ambushed as the Regiment proceeded up the Dahla road to take over the Dahla Fort from the RAF Regiment. It had been established which tribe was responsible and they had come from Ad Danaba. Accordingly on the 10th, Meteors from Khormaksar flew up country and dropped leaflets advising them that we were coming on the following day to destroy their village. This exercise was repeated one hour before we were due to arrive and it was anticipated, correctly as it turned out, that they would evacuate the village.

Accordingly at the civilized hour of 9 a.m. our four squadron aircraft got airborne, each carrying twenty-four 500lb M.C. bombs. At the briefing prior to take off, Air Vice-Marshal Donaldson had made it clear that we must ensure that there were no stray bombs off the target. When the target situation was seen, we realized what a tall order this was. The village was on a ledge half-way up a mountain and for preference I would have opted for bombing it along a line parallel to the mountains. Thereby hangs the snag — about a half-mile before Ad Danaba and roughly half a mile past it were two other villages and it was absolutely verboten to put either of them at risk. This inevitably called for a bombing run into the side of the mountain, deliver a bomb — for there wasn't time for more than one or two releases before the Shackleton had to be hauled round in a tight rate four turn. With four aircraft in the queue and given the restriction we had, it is not surprising that the job took over three hours.

However the village was finally levelled although the stone of which the buildings were constructed was so tough that they were often rather displaced than demolished. It was somewhat ironic to have its inhabitants demonstrating extreme faith in our bombing accuracy by being seated all round the surrounding hills watching the show. It was a difficult job and in my view was performed extremely well by the squadron. Whether it achieved whatever the political men desired is another matter. Certainly a Major in the REs of my acquaintance in Aden reckoned that he and eight men could have done the job in half the time at a tithe of the cost. He, of course, was missing the political men's point which was that these large flying birds are for ever watching you naughty Arabs on the ground and if you don't behave they will come and lay explosive eggs on you! Anyway, we were in the air for five and a quarter hours and I had dropped my first high explosives for twelve and a quarter years — for practically all the other chaps it was their first attack in anger.

Some days later our crew spent over twelve hours in the air doing one of the most boring operations available, escorting an army convoy out of Aden and up to Dahla. The column was picked up at first light, just after 6 a.m., when it was just clearing the northernmost village on the plain and starting the climb through the hills. The route was through the Queriba Pass to such exotic sounding (but not looking) places as Nobat Dakim and Al Milah. The scenery surrounding the road is 'Moon Country', rolling ridges of solid rock up which crawl the figures of Arab riflemen to get into position to ambush the convoy below. Our job was to spot it, warn the flank forces who would then winkle the buggers out before the convoy passed by below. Our secondary job was to act as an airborne telephone exchange and pass messages to and from Base for the convoy. Flying in a cloudless sky in blinding heat it required the utmost concentration for all of us to do our twenty minute stint with binoculars about every hundred minutes or so and make sure no insurgents got into a position to threaten the convoy. On arrival back at Khormaksar at sunset, twelve and a quarter hours after taking off, we all felt absolutely whacked out.

An unusual trip came our way on the 19th at a place called Sanau. It seemed that the Resident Political Officers in this area were calling all the tribes together to settle a border dispute. We flew up through Nisab, Husn Al Abr, Minwakh Thamed and on arrival at Sanau encountered a truly amazing sight. There must have been a thousand Arabs mounted on spirited horses milling around. We were supposed to arrive on the scene, as we did, flying very low to impress on these argumentative tribes that the big bird in the sky was here to settle their hash if they did not iron out their dispute. As it was, they nearly settled ours! We came in very low over their heads and with one accord they gave a fusillade of gun shots by way of a welcome. We survived with just one bullet-hole in the tail but I shudder to think what sort of impression the big bird would have made on those Arabs if the bullet had entered two inches higher and severed the elevator wire!

Four days later the training we had received at Watchfield was put to the test when we were ordered up to Wadi Beyhan and Wadi Nahr to do a garrison supply drop. Among the supplies was a month's beer ration so the onus was heavily on us to get the drop right. In the event, we flew up the two wadis (one after another of course) at a very low level with towering hills on either side at a distance of about three or four wing spans away. The drops went extremely well, all supplies dropping on the DZ and the cases of heavily protected beer got into the right hands. It was a shit or bust effort as once having flown low into the wadi, there was no turning around for another go. If we had not been able to release, it would have meant flying up to the top of the valley, climbing over mountains and coming all the way back to the entrance to the wadi and starting again.

On the 27th February we flew off to the Ain-Mergib area to search for some stranded paratroopers. We searched along a route from Wadi Beyhan to Attaq for over three hours, located them and then could not tell anyone because our W/T set had gone unserviceable. We returned to base and relayed the good news from there about an hour later.

On the 7th March, whilst flying with Flight Sergeant Dicky Worthing, I encountered an old enemy — a major sandstorm. We had been on a bombing and gunnery exercise on the ranges just north of Khormaksar for about three hours when the sky to the west took on a black and threatening hue. We spoke over R/T to our base and were informed of the approach of a sandstorm.

Quickly breaking off the exercise we returned to the airfield to find the storm was just arriving. All the old familiar effects, static, rough house flying and low visibility were present. We carried out a controlled landing and made it on to the ground before the storm centre arrived.

The following week we were ordered back to St. Eval, after having spent ninety-two hours in the air on the Aden detachment over a period of just over seven weeks and taken part in a number of new experiences over some of the most hostile country in the world and even been shot at into the bargain. We came back by the most direct route as the Middle East war was now well over, up the Red Sea to Port Sudan, across to the south-west corner of Egypt at Jebel Uweinat and then up to El Adem on the Libyan coast. Since this flight took a shade under twelve hours, we had a night stop at El Adem and flew home the following day, 13th March, and made St. Eval via Malta, Cape Teulada in Sardinia, through The Carcassone, Toulouse Gap to Bordeaux in eleven hours and twenty minutes.

On arrival back at St. Eval we landed and were followed down the runway by a familiar looking Austin Lichfield saloon — my wife had arrived to welcome us in a little too enthusiastic manner for the peace of mind of the control tower staff!!

To my utter horror I discovered that someone had been too busy for my good, I was posted off to Fighter Command to train as a Fighter Controller.

CHAPTER SIXTEEN
Grounded Again

Between arrival back from Aden to posting to Eastern Sector in Fighter Command, I spent only four and three-quarters hours in the air, all of it sitting in a Balliol acting as a target for my fellow course members on the ground. From arrival at Coltishall in Norfolk, our base for the Sector, until the end of my Fighter Controller tour two and a half years later, I managed to scrounge two detachments back to Coastal Command at St. Mawgan and this together with other odd scrounged rides gave me a total of eighty-two flying hours. On the other hand I did sit in a hole in the ground for nearly 5,000 hours before radar interception screens and conducted hundreds of intercepts. I must also I suppose thank this unwanted interlude for making it possible to do a bit of flying in the Meteor and Javelin, an experience not to be missed. In these aircraft I rose to heights never before experienced, 40,000 feet in a bowl of dark blue where aircraft only a thousand yards away were well nigh invisible. Nobby Armstrong on 23 Squadron treated me to two totally new experiences. One was flying in a tight formation practising for AOC's inspection day. Sitting at respectable heights with these quite large delta winged aircraft all round one was quite a thrill — after all it was being carried out at nearly Mach One. The second treat was to experience what happened when the wing boundary fences were extended. It was akin to hitting a brick wall at about fifty miles per hour when the speed suddenly decreased by two hundred miles per hour from over five hundred miles per hour.

The two visits in 1958 and 1959 to St. Mawgan were bare-faced wangles. I convinced Fighter Command that I needed a couple of weeks each year to refresh my Coastal techniques as, I said, I will undoubtedly be returning there. I pulled strings with old pals at Coastal Command HQ and got the connivance of my old mate, Jack Dingley on 220 Squadron. In the end it worked and I flew with Jack's crew (he was navigator/captain) in Shackleton Mark IIIs which were slightly larger, and had a nose wheel instead of a tail wheel.

On the first detachment from 23rd June to 7th July, 1958, I put in just over sixty hours very satisfying flying carrying out all the usual Coastal exercises, an airways exercise (always difficult for Coastal aircraft with mostly the wrong type of navigation equipment for it) and two sorties on a NATO exercise 'Freshwind'. These involved intercepting and working with a Task Force well out into the Atlantic and on the second one, flying up to the north-west of

Scotland between Stornoway and the Orkneys to co-operate with another Task Force. I enjoyed that detachment thoroughly.

The following year from 27th September to the 11th October, I got myself attached to 42 Squadron and having established a precedent the previous year, it was easier to get the break laid on. I did not fare so well for flying hours but did at least get in a flight to Ocean Weather ship *Kilo* upon whom we dropped mail and newspapers. I achieved a total of twenty-two flying hours in this two weeks on a mixture of Shackleton IIs and IIIs and a Varsity.

Towards the end of October I had the agreement of Fighter Command to my return to flying. This was the first hurdle over and I handed over my job as Mess Secretary at Coltishall which I had enjoyed doing for the best part of two years, stopped supervising fighter interceptions on radar and presented myself at 72 Navigation Refresher Course at RAF Topcliffe in North Yorkshire on the 22nd October 1959. After a week's ground school, flying started and I began beavering away in Valettas and Varsitys to get all round navigation up to scratch again. I completed thirty-seven hours flying on the course which included night astro trips and a passing out flight to Takali in Malta via Orange in the south of France. A very pleasant weekend was spent in Malta since the weather was a whole lot warmer than North Yorkshire at the time. I left Topcliffe on the 2nd December and having got a posting back to Coastal Command made my way much further north to the maritime operations course at Kinloss.

This was my third stay at Kinloss and it was still as bitingly cold and breathtakingly beautiful as before. I flew most of the course with Flight Sergeant Terry and crew and we pursued all the usual Coastal training exercises plus an airways exercise in which we groped our way around the invisible sky corridors from Dean Cross to Chepstow and on to St. Mawgan. On the following day we flew out to the Finisterre area, carried out an exercise patrol and proceeded to Gibraltar, flight time seven hours and twenty minutes. Three days later we returned from Gibraltar to Kinloss via Ocean Weather ship *Kilo* a hell of a long way out in the Atlantic, on this occasion flight time was over thirteen hours and nearly six hours of it in darkness.

On 22nd March 1960, we got to drop four 250lb depth charges live and the resultant fountain of water was something to see. After the usual CFI's test we were passed out as fit again for Coastal operations and to my great joy I was posted back to 42 Squadron now based a few miles down the coast from St. Eval — at St. Mawgan.

CHAPTER SEVENTEEN
How Lucky Can You Get? 42 Squadron Again

I reported in to St. Mawgan on the 5th April 1960 and then arrived at 42 Squadron. The Squadron CO was now Wing Commander Jack Ramsden AFC and I took to him at once. The atmosphere on the squadron was good, happy but efficient and totally different from my last arrival just over four years before. My introductory trip on the 26th April was with Flight Lieutenants 'Dicky' Dixon and George Middleton and I enjoyed every minute of the twelve hours we were airborne on this mixed bag of a training exercise, day/night bombing, navigation route flying at sea and Sarah homings at base.

May was a busy month with bombing and photography practice, exercises with two submarines, *Undaunted* and *Undine*, and practice Air-Sea Rescue Scramble on AOC's inspection day and sono buoy exercises. At the end of it I was well settled back in the squadron and had spent over forty-seven hours airborne.

After a mail drop out at Ocean Weather ship *Juliet* at 20°W in the Atlantic, I crewed up with Squadron Leader Ted Willey of 'B' Flight for a flight to Aden to deliver a Shackleton to the resident squadron there which had finally taken over from 42, a year or so previously. We flew the usual route out via the Toulouse Gap, Cape Tenlada, Sardinia and overflew Malta *en route* to El Adem. Half-way across the section between Malta and El Adem we ran into a storm, suffered a lightning strike and lost an engine. As maintenance facilities were very much better at Luqa, we turned back to Malta and spent the night there while the chaps worked on the aeroplane. It was not serviceable again until 1 p.m. the following day so that we finally got airborne to El Adem at twenty minutes to two and arrived in North Africa at half-past four, in time for tea.

We left again at 7.30 p.m. that evening and flew the long leg down to the Jebel Uweinat and Asmara on the Red Sea, by using astro fixes every fifty minutes. It was a perfect night for it and the results were magnificent, steady checks on a following wind by comparing astro fix with the air plot and bang on track at daylight. The whole trip took only ten and a half hours and we delivered Shackleton II WL 753 in good shape at Khormaksar at 9 a.m. local time on 26th June. We were flown back as passengers in a civil airline Brittania via Benina and then through the European airways from Naples via Milan, Geneva and Dijon to Stanstead airport. The remainder of the journey was completed by railway!

July and August passed busily and exercises were carried out with the destroyer HMS *Gambia* and later with the submarine HMS *Urchin*. We also carried out a mail drop to Ocean Weather ship *Kilo* and then made for Gibraltar. It took us ten hours and fifty minutes to do this trip but only five and a half hours to come back. This was fairly typical of ordinary flying life on the squadron and I was averaging over forty hours a month in the air. I was also fully occupied in two other directions so that there was definitely no time to ever get bored. I had been elected Messing Officer and had taken over at a time when messing was not paying its way and the varieties of foods were not that good. It took quite a lot of work on the books to get straight and then I spent time around Newquay getting to know our suppliers and over a period we managed to improve things to a satisfactory standard.

The other job arose in a typically Jack Ramsden fashion. One lunch-time he invited me to travel back to the squadron (some mile and a half from the Mess) with him in his car. On the way he proposed that I became his squadron training officer. Mindful of the not too happy experience I'd had as squadron navigation officer three or four years before, I hedged. He persisted and I reluctantly agreed and thereupon Jack said, "What is your objection to doing the job?" I told him that the last time I had held a squadron appointment I had been subject to considerable, in my view, unwarranted interference. The forth-right reply went something like: "You do it, I won't interfere unless the training standards slip and then I'll kick your arse." Who could refuse that offer? In addition to becoming training officer I was also boarded by the Coastal Command Categorization Unit and made the squadron categorizing officer on the subject of meteorology. I was now not only interested in but also quite learned about this subject and used to spend time with Owen Shortt and Peter Drinkwater, our station Met. Office forecasters of the time. This was always worth doing for two reasons, first St. Mawgan was almost the first place in Britain at which Atlantic weather arrived so it was sensible to have an idea of what you were going to encounter out at sea. Secondly, I made a point of sending back hourly weather reports which these chaps were keen enough to plot on the charts and by encouraging other squadron navigators to do likewise, we helped to keep their weather forecasting up to date.

In the space of five days in late September, we flew three long distance exercises in Exercise Fallex, Swordthrust I on 23rd, shadowing a refuelling group over thirteen hours, First Watch, shadowing a forming convoy for over fourteen hours and Swordthrust II back to shadowing the refuelling group for a further fourteen hours. Thus between 6.15 a.m. on the 23rd September and 6 p.m. on the 28th September, we spent forty-two hours in the air out of one hundred and thirty-two hours elapsed from our temporary base at Aldegrove, Belfast.

In early october we did exercise Squarebash VIII and spent six hours with the 'Black Ranger', two frigates and a destroyer in close contact. We then set off on the 10th October for twelve hours to search for Francis Chichester who was somewhere out in the Atlantic between Cornwall and Ocean Weather ship *Kilo*. On the 22nd October we shadowed HM ships *Victorious*, the aircraft carrier, *Camperdown*, *Saintes* and *Solway* out in south-west Biscay, and after ten hours flew on into Gibraltar again. After a short weekend in Gibraltar we came back to Cornwall doing a series of exercises including day and night bombing. The return trip, including exercises, took up twenty-four hours flying time.

On the night of the 1st/2nd November we were out on Exercise Squarebash IX in close and distant support of a Task Force. It was a night of force nine gales and a sea stirred up into totally white foam. The aircraft bumped around in very turbulent air for nearly eight hours right through the night and, of course, we saw nothing! Why should we? Any submariner with a grain of sense was riding out the storm a hundred feet below the surface.

On the last day of November I navigated the Varsity from our Communications Flight up the airways to Northolt where we were returning the Argentine Air Attaché, Air Commodore Claret. This trip was memorable for the fact that London radar had us stacked on the Watford Range at 8,000 feet and with no VOR but only an MF radio compass, I was having trouble navigating the racecourse shaped holding pattern in a very high wind. London radar twice requested our position in the pattern, a sure sign that they themselves were nervous, on the third go they gave us immediate clearance to Northolt and obliged with a heading which was very tactful but acceptable guidance.

On the 6th January 1961 it was 42 Squadron's turn to attend the yearly JASS(Joint Anti-Submarine) Course at Londonderry. The course was always interesting, it brought us up to date with the doings of our friends in the Royal Navy, and it enabled us to solve difficult problems on the tactical floor, and from our base at Ballykelly we flew many sorties on anti-submarine chases in close co-operation with naval surface forces, on this occasion totalling thirty and a half hours.

On the 15th January, we flew out to the Bay of Biscay on Operation Eclipse. This trip was laid on so that we could transport a covey of Press representatives, BBC and ITV cameramen to the area in order to witness and photograph the eclipse of the sun. As the eclipse was scheduled for 07.15 hours, the Press men had to rise very early for we left St. Mawgan at 04.30 a.m. and I navigated out to position 4630N 0430W where we all saw a splendid eclipse. We were airborne for six hours and twenty minutes, landed just before 11 a.m. and the first pictures were on TV's 1 p.m. news.

I was out on an exercise with Ted Willey, Frank Hercliffe and the Boss, Jack Ramsden on the 11th April when we were diverted away to escort a 22 Squadron helicopter to SS *Upshur* which had a severely injured man aboard. It was necessary for us to be there to guide the chopper because the position of *Upshur* was way out to sea, 4939N 0653W, many miles south-west of the Scillies, and visibility was down to two hundred to three hundred yards, which left us to do the navigation for the chopper. That crew did a marvellous job, winching the stretcher up from a wildly undulating stern deck and then under our guidance, landing the man outside Penzance hospital and thereby undoubtedly saving his life.

On the 17th we were selected to represent 42 Squadron in the famous Command Aird Whyte Cup Competition. We flew up to Ballykelly for the occasion but despite doing everything very well, lost out because our radar operators failed to locate the target submarine. So it was not our year in 1961 — there were to be compensations to come however.

In May, we flew out to Ocean Weather ship *Juliet*, dropped the mail and newspapers and spent some hours following the exhaust trails of various ships. We then went into Lajes in the Azores for the night. After paying for our night's kip and the meal from our two dollar allocation we had one dollar cash to spend. Tommy Samuels, the popular squadron Air Electronics Officer — an Australian what else? — suggested we pool our one US dollar each, change it into quarters and go and feed one particular one-armed bandit in the Officers' Club with the proceeds. His theory bore fruit when I was taking the fourth stint of feeding coins and pulling levers — we hit the jackpot. The club secretary paid us twenty-five US dollars and the whole crew was subsidized for Budweiser for the rest of the evening. On the following day we flew across the Atlantic to Gibraltar, still with a little in hand!

On the 26th May the town council of Bodmin paid the squadron a visit and in the interest of public relations we took them up in a Shackleton and flew them all over Cornwall and the Scillies which seemed to give them a lot of pleasure.

Life wended its pleasant way through the summer of 1961, I was always busy with my two other jobs and the many hours spent in the air. Live torpedo drops came our way together with many exercises with units of the Royal Navy. Then around the end of August we heard that we had been picked to go to Norfolk, Virginia to take part in a NATO Exercise — Fishplay. I could not believe it, all my life I had had two ambitions as a navigator — to cross the Sahara and the Atlantic. One had been achieved in 1956/7 and now here was the chance to do the other. We got kitted out in London with the special RAF uniforms for North America and took off at 9 a.m. on the 14th September for Lajes in the Azores. On arrival we found that Hurricane Debbie had not yet cleared the area and a force eight gale was blowing *across* the single runway at Lajes so we were accordingly diverted to the civil international airport at Santa Maria, where we landed at 6.15 p.m. after a nine and a quarter hours flight.

The following day at ten to two, just after lunch, we launched ourselves off westwards across the vast expanse of the Atlantic at 1,500 feet. The American Air Force officer who gave me the clearance for the squadron aircraft could not believe it — 1,500 feet? Mad Limeys! Twelve hours later came big decision time and it came about this way. We had been trialling the new Doppler equipment which measured drift and ground speed automatically but it relied on a bit of a popple on the sea surface to throw back the signal sent down to it and therefore register the required measurements. For over two hours in the middle of the Atlantic the sea had gone mirror smooth with not a ripple and this had unlocked the Doppler equipment which was not then registering any measurements at all. Furthermore, with a flat calm surface it was not possible to measure drift, but I knew that there was a bit of drift in these light airs.

Twelve hours out from the Azores it had been dark for five hours and we were now flying at 3,000 feet. In the past four hours I had taken four astro fixes, the last with some difficulty an hour before as heavy cloud was encountered. It was now thundercloud we were in with lightning forking about all over the place, heavy static on radio and, worse still, cloud shadow all over our 10cm radarscope so that nothing showed through it. We could hear Kindley Tower transmitting from Bermuda but in the pitch blackness under the storm clouds could see no gleam of light. I was now, according to my reckoning, some fifteen minutes away from the island which meant that it ought to be about thirty-five miles ahead, but nothing could be seen. The Boss was with us and I could sense that he was getting a little twitchy due to the fact that we had about enough fuel for a further two hours whilst the nearest American coastline was over three and a half hours away.

I re-examined my plot and looked again at the last astro fix. Position had been calculated on this one by bisecting the angles made by all three positions because they had resulted in a large 'cocked hat' instead of a neat intersection. Very obviously one of those position lines was inaccurate, probably due to the intermittent cloud and turbulence we had been experiencing when the shots were taken. The following diagram illustrates the position and the dilemma:

My 'Bermuda Triangle' Problem

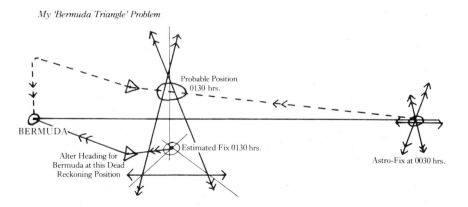

Reviewing all the factors, I came to the conclusion that we were probably some miles north of track and so requested a 90° turn to port on to a southerly heading. I'll never understand 10cm radar, but the act of banking the Shackleton for the turn, displaced the aerials and swept the radar screen clear of cloud for the half minute or so we were in the turn. Tommy Samuels said, "You are right, Eddie boy, the island is straight ahead," and then added as we straightened up, "about forty-five miles, but the screen is swamped with cloud again." Twenty minutes later we were in Kindley Field's circuit and landed in blinding rain in a thunderstorm.

As we did not hit the hay until 2 a.m. local time, we slept in until about 8.30 a.m. and then proceeded downstairs to the dining-room in the American Officers' Club and demolished a gargantuan breakfast. By noon we were ready to go again and so we took off on the final leg. This was accomplished without incident although we were made aware of American preparedness as we entered their Air Space and were challenged, checked and passed on. We crossed the coast of the United States north of Cape Hatteras and landed at Norfolk, Virginia after a flight of four hours. This was at 3 p.m. local time on 16th September, and we had only just unpacked in our quarters at Elia Hall on the base when a hurricane warning was received. Truly enough throughout an otherwise quiet Sunday, the wind rose gradually and the sky darkened. By Monday morning, the 18th, the Base Commander had received a more accurate forecast for the time the hurricane would hit and decided that every aircraft on the field which could not be protected below ground should fly off inland to a series of preselected airfields.

On the Monday morning there were hundreds of aeroplanes in the queue for take-off. It took us two hours to get to the end of the runway, ahead of us the Boss, Jack Ramsden, flying with another crew failed to get off as oiled up engines refused to develop full power. They, poor chaps, spent the next four days marooned on the base with a shrieking wind and tropical rainstorms for company. We were luckier, we did get off but an aircraft and crew less equipped to fly high in American air lanes did not exist within hundreds of miles. By the time we had queued up and got airborne it was getting dark and the American Controller sent us up to 9,000 feet with instructions to report in over Gwynn beacon. The problem was to receive that beacon on our simple MF receiver when all the American beacons were geared to VOR, (VHF Omnidirectional Range). Having had quite a time getting this clear to the ground area control, they then did us proud. We indentified ourselves on the area screen by doing a procedural turn on request and they took us over. We were then passed from Richmond to Pittsburgh controls as we flew up the air lane over Richmond-Gordonsville-Elkins-Zanesville, where we were transferred to Colombus Control. These kind gentlemen stepped us down gradually to 2,000 feet over Colombus, Ohio and then said, "Switch to Port Colombus Tower frequency, the airfield is to starboard of you." There was only one snag, we could not see it and could not find it. Believe it or not, the reason was that like many towns in the USA, Colombus is built with streets running in straight lines east and west, north and south, and every damned one of them looked like a flare-path. However, with a little further help from our friends, we were positioned in the funnel, 1,000 feet up and proceeded to land straight ahead.

If I remember correctly, there were five crews sent to Colombus and we were accommodated at the Seneca Hotel and became a source of great curiosity to the Colombusians. They treated us with considerable kindness and friendliness and even invited a couple of the chaps on to a TV quiz show. However, before this could be accomplished, we got the recall signal and returned to Norfolk on the 21st in daylight so that the flight, whilst still controlled, was navigated off a map. Why we left Colombus at ten to five in the morning I really do not know, but we were back at Norfolk by 7 a.m. and began preparing for the NATO Exercise Fishplay, which is why we had come in the first place.

On the 24th/25th September we were airborne for fourteen hours and thirty-five minutes and made no submarine contacts in all that time out in the exercise area a hundred miles or so east of Chesapeake Bay. We did make one contact on our radar screen, with Hurricane Esther, which had only just recently cleared the Virginian coast.

Two days later we spent a further ten and a half hours airborne searching the exercise area which was now considerably nearer the coast. Flight Lieutenant Tom Wood on our squadron reported at the general debriefing on the tactical floor at Norfolk, in front of the Admiral, that he had a definite strike on the submarine HMS *Alliance*, I think it was, because he had seen Commander Todd's ginger beard clearing the conning tower with all speed!

On the 28th we gave our Shackleton, WL 754, a thorough air test in the region of Chesapeake Lighthouse and left her prepared and ready for the flight home. We were then given three days' leave over a long weekend and four of us hired a car which George Ogden, our Squadron Navigation Officer, drove to Washington DC. On the way we visited Jamestown and inspected the monuments to the defeat and surrender of 'Gentleman' Johnny Burgoyne. We spent an enthralling few hours in the small colonial town of Williamsburg in which buildings and residents were exactly as they were in the eighteenth century. Finally we reached Washington late on a Friday evening and had the nerve to book in for a couple of nights at the USAF base at Andrews Field. Over the weekend we explored Washington and saw all the usual tourist sights and some not so usual. I simply could not comprehend how a town so beautifully planned from the Lincoln Memorial to the Washington Monument could become a teeming black area of densely packed houses in so short a distance.

On Wednesday, 4th October, we left Norfolk and its fabulous porterhouse and delmonte steaks behind and flew off to Bermuda, landing on the island at a little before 1 p.m. We had the rest of the day off and so went swimming in the afternoon and the local RAFA branch were kind enough to invite us to an evening's barbecue at the house of one of their members. On the next day we left Kindley at 8 a.m. and with a good stiff following wind (the petered out remains of Hurricane Esther) we crossed the middle of the Atlantic in just less than ten and a half hours to land at Lajes with no dramas this time. The last leg was completed in five and three-quarter hours on the following day and we touched down at St. Mawgan just before 4 p.m. I was thrilled to have accomplished my particular ambition and reviewing the trip in my mind wondered whether my experience in the 'Bermuda Triangle' might not contain some of the reasons for other people's weird disappearances.

The rest of the month was a busy one for me, catching up on the backlog of my two ground jobs and highlighted by a sudden diversion from some circuits and bumps we were doing as part of our two pilot's mandatory monthly training. We were sent out to the southern approaches of the Irish Sea to search for survivors of a sunken trawler, in consequence our hour's circuits spread into darkness and a five hour trip. I regret to report that although we succeeded in locating a life raft, its occupant was dead. We directed HMS *Centaur* to the spot where she took the raft and body aboard.

Having waited nearly twenty years to navigate across the Atlantic it is ironic that the second opportunity arrived within seven weeks of the first. I was lying on my bed in my quarters after a hard game of squash, relaxing before dressing for dinner, when the Tannoy spoke: "All 42 Squadron crews to report to the Control Tower immediately." Being a living-in member of the Mess I was one of the first to arrive and before the chaps who were in dispersed Married Quarters could be collected in. Then I learned about 'Operation Hattie' and what a high degree of urgency there was. We got the ground crews to work immediately and four aircraft were made ready for immediate detachment for an unspecified time. When we were all gathered it emerged that Hurricane Hattie had proved to be one of the most disastrous of the season for the tiny colony of British Honduras. It had curved in south of Cuba, Haiti and Jamaica and struck the coast of Central America with vicious force. Belize, the capital of British Honduras had been flooded and the area, being so isolated, was devoid of immediate surrounding assistance. Thus it was planned to send in units of the Royal Navy's Caribbean Squadron, one of them would act as our locating beacon just off shore since all communications with the one and only airfield at Stanley had been wrecked. The urgency of the situation lay in the inability of those countries close enough to help significantly and it was therefore up to us and the USAF from Cuba and Florida to do as much as we could as soon as possible.

Commendably, the four aircraft were airborne at 10.30 p.m. and driving directly on through the night arrived at Lajes in the Azores six hours and twenty minutes later, 4.50 a.m. (2.50 a.m. local time). We snatched an early breakfast and were in bed by 4 a.m. (local) and having lunched, arranged rations and obtained a clearance, we got airborne again at 3 p.m. (local). This was the fastest dash we could safely make at the higher end of the cruising range and we made Kindley Field, Bermuda in ten and a quarter hours, 10.15 p.m. (local time). We were off again at 7.30 a.m. and turned south-south-west in the direction of the Southern Bahamas where the sun was high and hot and the sea lightly transparent seemingly since around the islands the rocks and sandy bottoms were clearly discernible under the water. I guided us through the Windward Passage between Haiti and Cuba and entered the Caribbean for the first time. Shortly afterwards we turned to the west with the mountains of Jamaica closing in on our right hand and finally landed at the oddly shaped Palisadoes Airport at the south end of Kingston Harbour, five and a half hours after leaving Bermuda at 1 p.m. (local time). Three and a half hours later, after loading an additional 5,000lbs of freight, adding to the medical supplies and blankets we were already carrying and totalling 9,000lbs in all and with twelve soldiers aboard, we were off on the first run to Stanley Airport in British Honduras. We took back bearings on Jamaica, drifts all the way across the Caribbean, a running fix off the Swan Island Radio beacon and pin-points on islands off the Central American coast, finally homing in on the Royal Navy's portable beacon before queuing up to land at Stanley. In the queue were the large Hercules of the USAF and since conditions at Stanley were appalling, space on the tiny airfield very limited, it took longer than was originally anticipated to unload large aircraft and get them off again. There was no question of refuelling at Stanley, there was neither the time nor the space, if indeed they had the necessary amount of fuel. We always fuelled up at Kingston and were fully prepared for a return trip plus diversions whilst at the same time reducing the normal fuel load so that we could add men and freight as compensating weight.

We left Stanley at 10 p.m. and my two very tired pilots, Frank Hercliffe and Fin Blake, were spelling themselves during the nearly four hours of the flight back to Kingston. On arrival at Kingston at ten minutes to two in the early hours we found ourselves sliding into a thunderstorm over the airport. After landing we and our kit were taken to Up-Park Camp in Kingston, home of the Royal Hampshire Regiment at the time, where we literally fell into bed. From leaving St. Mawgan at 10.30 p.m. Wednesday 1st November, fifty-six hours had passed and we had been flying for a shade over twenty-nine of them — it was, I think, the most sustained chunk of airborne time I ever put in.

We slept through Saturday, rose very early on the Sunday, 5th November, and took off at 7 a.m. for Stanley with twenty-six Jamaican policemen aboard and 8,000lbs of freight. The flight was just under three and a half hours each way and with time on the ground over there for unloading, we put in a ten to eleven hours day.

I was highly impressed by one fact about the hurricane which I discovered at Stanley — its wind speed. God knows what it had been but the anemometer (wind measuring machine) on the roof of the Control Tower had stuck fast registering 105 m.p.h.

Sunday, 5th November set the pattern of our detachment, relief supplies, soldiers and police flown in and refugees and returning exhausted aid workers flown out. As the rescue services got the upper hand and less freight was needed, so the frequency of our flights lessened. Our crew did eight return trips in two weeks which meant that I navigated the Caribbean west/east sixteen times in the first fortnight and was getting to be a dab hand at not wasting a minute of flying time *en route*, but thank heavens for Swan Island and its beacon situated almost plum in the middle of the trip. After a few days of heavy use, as might be expected, the concrete runways and taxiways at Stanley began to crack up — they were never designed to sustain the weights and frequencies of aircraft that were now arriving and departing. This was when the old wartime PSP (Pierced Steel Planks) proved their usefulness once again. Originally used as emergency surfaces on swampy land, they supported us and the Americans for as long as it was necessary. The other point of heavy wear and tear was of course the aircraft themselves and twice towards the end of the operation we had to return to Kingston on three engines, but both times we completed our schedule because they did not go unserviceable until the return trip.

Our ground crews were doing a magnificent job during all this time. Working in cramped conditions in a corner of Palisadoes airport, accommodated in unused airport buildings with beds crowded in here and there, and with food supplied mainly from airport resources they lived a very far from comfortable life. They worked like Trojans, spares were hard to come by and usually a signal to Coastal Command Headquarters would result in the arrival of the required spare part by a Civil air line two or three days later. Somehow they contrived to keep all four aircraft in the air and remained cheerful all the time.

On the 20th November we ferried the late Hugh Fraser, MP over to Stanley where he was a visitor in his capacity as Colonial Under-Secretary of State. He wisely arrived in civvies and delayed changing into the stiff, gold brocaded formal uniform until the last possible minute. We were all tactfully facing forward as he wrestled with the exchange of clothes in the confined space at the rear of the Shackleton.

As the frequency of the sorties began to tail off, everyone had more time to spare and I give my ungrudging admiration to the Royal Air Force Association in Kingston who contacted people all over the island and arranged for them to entertain us. We were taken to dinner on two occasions at people's houses and the highlight for me was an offer by a traveller to accompany him in his car on a visit to the north coast. We left Kingston on a lovely sunny morning, this time of the year was the best in Jamaica, fairly dry air with a temperature of 80°F, and drove through the 'cockpit' in the centre of the country which is true Rastafarian territory. We toured a Canadian bauxite factory with whom he had some business. We went down a sunken road entirely hedged in by large bamboo trees — it was like entering a tunnel, the sun's rays did not penetrate the thick foliage. The fields and gently rolling country of the interior would not have been too unlike those of England were it not for the more exotic plants and vegetables growing there. Banana trees seemed favourite followed by plantains, pineapples and sweet potatoes and, of course, corn.

Towards lunch-time we struck the north coast at Ocho Rios and visited the Arakan Hotel where I believe my host had more business to do. This hotel was extremely luxurious and at that time was a favourite spot for the thousands of Americans spending their winter holidays in a warmer climate. This meant, of course, that prices matched the rich clientele and one drink in the bar for experience was as much as an RAF type could afford. I was then taken to lunch at the Plantation Inn and thoroughly enjoyed the good food and conversation taken in good company at the hotel owner's table. It was a fabulous day out and I have always been grateful to that kind man who enabled me to see quite a bit of a very attractive island.

There was, of course, a seamier side which was very visible in Kingston. There were tens of thousands of people unemployed in the town and they could be seen clustered at every street corner. The morning paper there, the *Daily Gleaner*, used to record almost a murder every night and each one was the result of an argument or fracas between very volatile people who carried knives. At the end of our detachment I went into Kingston market to buy a stand of bananas for the family. You bought them green and saw that they were entirely free of spiders, etc. before taking them away. The market was an enchanting sight, all colour and bustle and the air was filled with the music of the oil drums.

On the 26th November we did our eleventh and last return trip to Stanley which brought my flying hours for that month up to one hundred and three and a half! Hugh Mansell had succeeded Jack Ramsden as the Squadron's Commanding Officer and he it was who organized a farewell fly past for the benefit of the people who had been so kind and friendly to us. We took off at ten minutes past eight on the morning of the 2nd December and the four squadron Shackletons flew in a creditably tight formation over the route Palisadoes-Wreck Reef-Old Harbour-Spanish Town-Caymanas-Ferry Hill-Half Way Tree-Kingston and back to Palisadoes at 9 a.m. Two and a half hours later we were airborne for home via Bermuda and Lajes. We flew home rather more leisurely than we had come out and with strong following winds from the west had to fly less hours to do it. It took six and a half hours to Kindley Field, only just over nine hours to cross mid-Atlantic to Lajes (this leg we did by astro-navigation all night) and a further five and three-quarter hours to St. Mawgan, which we reached on the 5th December. All in all it had been a very satisfying five weeks because we had flown a lot and helped to achieve something very positive, the rehabilitation of a town.

Throughout 1962 I continued to fly often and to hone my capabilities as a Coastal Command Navigator. In this role you were more than a mere navigator from A to B. One must be capable of locating vessels hundreds of miles out to sea, bearing in mind that both they and you are moving. It was also necessary to be able to maintain a tactical plot when either co-operating with HM surface ships or hunting a submarine. Correct weapons selection was vital and so was the ability to drop them where they could do the most good. Then one must also be able to operate a battery of various cameras when occasion demands and know something of their operation in case of failures. Above all, one has to be weather wise because weather rules so much of what can or cannot be possible to do way out at sea.

On the 22nd January, 1962 it was our Londonderry time again, we stayed there for the next four weeks, flew five exercises with HM ships *Walrus*, *Scorpion*, *Trafalgar*, *Broadside*, and *Jutland* from Ballykelly and 'enjoyed' the worst of the winter weather again.

On 20th March we left St. Mawgan at 7 a.m. on 'Operation Cold Road', and this trip called on practically every facet of our acquired capabilities. To begin with we flew up the airways under area radar control. Always a difficult task for a Shackleton navigator. Having left the air corridors at Ottringham near Hull, we set off in a northerly direction up the North Sea and searched a block of sea between 62°N and 64°N and 2½°E to 7½°E for a sight of any Russian ships, particularly their Elint trawlers which were very well equipped spy ships. Our Intelligence people had got the area right, there were two large fleets of Russian fishing vessels in residence and among them the odd Elint at work intercepting naval and air force communications in order to 'place' units, break codes and the like. We arrived at Andoya in the Lofoten Islands at 6.30 p.m. during one of their frequent snow showers. Up here it was still very much winter-time with a couple of feet of snow about everywhere and snow/hail showers about every half an hour. Having held off for a few minutes, we landed in the near darkness in the next clearance.

We were given the following day off to rest between two long trips and we occupied the morning by walking into Andesles, a small fishing town and port. It proved to be quite a hard exercise; the surrounding countryside was completely snow covered, the only road in was covered in hard packed snow which was frozen and slippery on top and the weather itself was not very pleasant. About every twenty minutes or so, the weather would go dark with heavy clouds blotting out the sunlight and down would come a heavy snow-storm and through it all, it was really freezing cold. The Norwegian Air Force was very welcoming but I was, and am, one human being who functions much better in warmer and indeed hot climates. I witnessed a novel arrival for lunch at Andoya. I was standing outside the snow encrusted portals of the Officers' Mess just after I had finished lunch. Looming over the Mess was a hill, typical of the area, about 2,000 feet high with a radar hut perched on the top. A small figure appeared outside the hut and then very suddenly began to get nearer at an alarming speed. He was skiing down the slopes for all he was worth in order to make lunch at the Mess. He suddenly appeared high over the hedgerows bordering the road and landed in front of the Mess with a great hiss of skis as he twirled to a stop. It was really well and athletically done — but what about that 2,000 ft. snow-covered climb to be done after lunch!

We left Andoya at 8 a.m. sharp on the 22nd March and flew towards Bear

Island where we did another large patrol, but this time without picking up any significant Russian units. The patrol was between 73N and 70N and 20E to 23E and it was fairly close to the Norwegian/Russian border at the far north of Norway. Thirteen hours after leaving Andoya, we landed at St. Mawgan at almost 9 p.m., but the weather whilst cloudy was a whole lot warmer.

The rest of the year up to October passed with the training mixture as before with one or two highlights when mass exercises were participated in. In July we released two live torpedoes on the Fowey Sea Range and followed that up by finding *Britannia* at sea which was gleefully photographed from all angles. On 1st August we flew a surveillance exercise off the north-west tip of Spain out to sea and then continued on to Gibraltar for NATO 'Exercise Riptide'. We carried out an offensive sweep on the 11th and on the 12/13th maintained close and distant support to a convoy as requested. Somewhat surprisingly, Gibraltar, North Front, misted over during the evening of the 12th and we were forced to divert to Montijo, just outside Lisbon landing there at five past one in the early morning hours. We returned to Gibraltar the following afternoon, spent two days working our exercises through on the tactical floor at Group Headquarters and then enjoyed a complete day off when everyone went in swimming and came out again three minutes later blue with cold! A cold current from the Atlantic had passed through the narrows and made the water off Eastern beach untypically very cold for the time of the year. We returned in good shape on the 16th August arriving back at St. Mawgan at 4 p.m. to a 'Customs' welcome. The Customs chief at Falmouth had deployed almost his entire force to search our luggage and the aeroplane. Fortunately no one was seeking to avoid duty and we were all given a clean bill of health.

The hours and exercises continued to pile up and then on the 27th September we flew up to Kinloss to position ourselves for Exercise Matador which took place on the following day. We spent most of that day on a line patrol in the area of the Faroes Islands without seeing a thing. After nearly fifteen hours in the air we returned to Kinloss and on the morrow to St. Mawgan. Those three days clocked up twenty hours and twenty minutes flying time.

October arrived and after doing one ten and a half hour trip, I never flew in a Shackleton again. The Cuba missile crisis developed and for days the squadron was on emergency standby. I was due for posting at the end of the month but Hugh Mansell was not about to break up an experienced crew until we could all breathe again as Kruschev backed off.

CHAPTER EIGHTEEN
Last Fling

The RAF was kind to me for my last posting, I was due to retire in August 1965. I had asked to go to the Command Communication Squadron at Bovingdon, Hertfordshire, as my family were established at our house in East Sheen and I hoped to be allowed to live out, thirty miles from the base. As I say, everyone was very kind, I got the posting I wanted and on reporting in on the 6th November 1962, the Station Commander agreed to my request. Having swapped our large 25 HP Rover for a very small Austin A30, I now motored from home to work and back every day, just over sixty miles. At work I found myself navigating Ansons from the front seat in order to allow passengers to occupy the rear. Our job was to ferry Command Staff Officers on their necessary visits to Coastal Command airfields. The wheel had really turned full circle because I was virtually back to 'seat of the pants' navigating again with the assistance of maps, working out track and ground speed winds on the CSC as I went. It was a great job — a new place every day and most days returning home for the night.

There were days when we wrestled with the weather for hours on end, culminating in a flight through thick cloud over the Scottish Highlands to do a GCA landing at Kinloss and sometimes never seeing the ground until popping out of the cloud on the final approach. I thoroughly approved of GCA (Ground Controlled Approach) since, given a good controller, you arrived over the airfield with no further worries. He could see you on his radar screen and was able to keep you clear of hills and obstacles as he lined you up with the best approach to be made.

Early in December 1962, Flight Lieutenant Yates and myself took passengers up to Kinloss arriving there at 12.30 p.m. We left again at ten past three to pick up some officers from Leuchars on the south bank of the Tay, and after leaving there at twenty past four, climbed into a dark winter's sky through a layer of stratus and set course for Bovingdon at 3,000 feet. It was quite weird in its way, we had absolutely no cloud above us and a thick blanket of stratus beneath us totally covering the ground. Not once in the flight did we see a hole or any opening in the cloud and so happily navigating on Gee Fixes and Track/Ground Speed winds we approached Bovingdon. Here we had a surprise, the cloud and visibility were below blind landing limits and we were diverted to the only airfield in southern England in the clear — Thorney Island, a hundred miles away. We were taken out towards Reading beacon by London radar and at Woodley turned south for the Sussex/Hampshire borders and Thorney Island. There was a queue of aircraft waiting to land but as we had been in the air for over three hours, our fuel was getting low so they took us in almost at once and we landed at half-past seven. Under the stratus cloud it was a very dark night indeed and it then struck me that the whole of England and southern Scotland was under a single sheet of stratus cloud, a fairly rare situation I should imagine.

By the end of the year I had paid visits to Scotland, Northern Ireland and Germany — no one could say that we lacked variety in life. The trip to Wildenrath in Germany was controlled by ground radar controllers over the entire route. Crossing Belgium via Ghent and Brussels we were told to fly at 10,000 feet and this brought the additional hazard of icing on the wing or ice building up in the carburettor — shades of the early 1940s. By the end of the year, after two months on the Communications Flight, I had built up a total of forty-eight flying hours which in aeroplanes like the Anson and Devon was not bad going in winter weather.

January 1963 was a month of heavy snowfalls in which I got airborne only three times and in which our poor little Austin A30 was biffed twice, once in a shunt and once in Chipperfield Woods when I stopped on ice before a bend and received a slowly revolving car coming round the bend into my right wing. Thank goodness for the motor club at Bovingdon who rebuilt the bonnet and wings with Isopon! One of the three trips in the month was a VIP flight to Aldergrove, near Belfast. We had to go to Lyneham in our VIP Devon to pick up our passenger, General Sir Richard Anderson, and Flight Lieutenant Tony Joy and myself took off at around 11 a.m. and delivered our distinguished passenger to the army at Aldergrove at 12.45 p.m. The return, through some pretty bad weather, took nearly two and a half hours. The other flights in the month were both on the short side seized during temporary weather clearances.

On the 5th March I paid my first visit to Holland with Master Pilot Mann. We delivered some Command Staff Officers to Soesterberg in central Holland. Having delivered them by 10.45 a.m. and with orders to be available first thing the following day, the rest of the day was ours. We filled it with quite a long walk into Amersfoort which as we entered I thought was a village, but as we proceeded further on, became a fair sized town. The walk had been enough — we got a bus back and being a bit higher up, one could see even further over the flat fields to the sky line.

Late in April I flew with Flight Lieutenant Dicky Colbourne GM, our unit commander to RAF Boscombe Down and saw the VC 10 at close quarters on the ground and in the air for the first time. It was being trialled for Transport Command and I thought she was a beauty, with the high set jets in the rear and the big uncluttered swept wing.

In May, with Master Pilot Regan, I flew out to Brest to take some Royal Navy officers out to the French Naval HQ there. We cleared Customs through

Thorney Island and then left on a route which took us over Fawley, Alderney and Guernsey, arriving at Brest at ten past twelve. They returned with us at twenty past six and on arrival at Thorney Island we had an unserviceable engine, so after landing at half-past eight in the evening, we had to spend all next day there whilst they fixed the engine.

Another interesting trip in May with my same friend, Mr Regan, took us off first to Jurby in the Isle of Man, where we stayed for lunch. Here I ran into Jack Goodman who had been with me at Hastings in 1939 and it was my first sight of him for over twenty-three years, how we must both have changed from those unblooded nineteen-and twenty-year-olds. After lunch we took off across the sea to Mull of Kintyre and Machrihanish. This airfield was just north of Kintyre on a flat piece of land with water east and west of it. Then we got airborne again and this time managed to fly the length of Loch Lomond on our way to Edinburgh (Turnhouse) Airport and for the experience we flew down the side of the Forth Bridge. After a night at Turnhouse we returned to Bovingdon having collected a total of five and a half hours flying on a crowded two day trip.

In July it was decided to merge the two communications squadrons of Coastal and Fighter Commands into one to be titled 'Southern Communications Squadron'. This opened up a number of new routes to us as we would now be flying to Fighter Command airfields as well as our own Coastal Command ones. Dick Colbourne became a flight commander and the new Squadron Commanding Officer was Squadron Leader D. H. Ward. The effect on our flights was immediate as we now also served Bomber Command as well and it was nice to return to places like Waddington and Coltishall. I had amassed a total of two hundred and sixty-nine flying hours in the eight months on the Coastal Command Flight and I figured that if I could keep this up on the new squadron, I would have nothing to complain of.

In July Dick Colbourne and I reaped one of the benefits of the merger, we got a trip to a French Fighter airfield at Melun, south of Paris. Of necessity most of the trip was under Ground Radar Control, Paris is, like London, a very congested area. The most interesting part of this trip was to stand on the steps of the Mess overlooking the old N1 (now the Autoroute du Soleil) and watch the traffic going south on holidays to the Mediterranean. The drivers with the usual French insouciance were driving side by side and nose to tail at 60-70 m.p.h. One shuddered to think what would have happened if one blew a tyre!

In September by coincidence I navigated out to Brest again with Master Pilot Regan and this time we experienced the loss of oil in one engine, which inevitably means you lose it, which we duly did about forty miles off the French coast. We made a splendid one engined landing at Brest at 11.20 a.m. and then had to wait for repairs. In the event it took all day so that we were left with an unexpected night stop-over. We were guided around Brest by a French Naval Commander who was a pre-war regular and in the course of conversation I learnt that as a pre-war entrant who had stayed with the French Navy during the war, he was now *persona non grata* with the De Gaullist officers who ran the fleet, and he could expect no further promotion. It showed the deep divisions that still existed in French life as late as 1963!

By the end of that year I had flown four hundred and seventy-eight hours at Bovingdon on the Command Flight and Squadron and had made dozens of visits to Wildenrath, Ballykelly, Kinloss and every other point in Britain including the Channel Isles. After landing at more than a hundred and twenty airfields in about fourteen months I now believed that I could pin-point myself at any time almost anywhere in Great Britain. On the penultimate day of the year this was put to the test. We were required to fly over to Wattisham, pick up a group of Fighter Command officers and study at low level a route into London which would yield distinctive landmarks for jets to pick up easily. This reconnaissance was to be flown so that the best route could be plotted for fighters which were to do a fly past Buckingham Palace in celebration of the birth of another baby prince. With Master Pilot Tatum we set off from Wattisham at 11.15 a.m. with permission to fly at 500 feet or lower if required. We flew to Hoddesdon in Hertfordshire and tracked into London over Barnet and Southgate to Trafalgar Square and then broke off over Waterloo Station returning via Highgate, Barnet and Hertford.

The principal impression I obtained out of this flight was the enormous acreage that was devoted to cemeteries in North London. This added to my determination to be cremated when my time comes — what a waste of land which could be used for the benefit of children and the homeless.

At the end of January 1964, Dick Colbourne and I paid a return visit to Soesterberg in Holland with a group of Fighter Command staff setting up a NATO exercise. We had to stop over the night and so hitched into Utrecht and sampled an Indo-Chinese meal, for the first time as far as I was concerned. The following day we had to fly to Brussels National Airport (Melsbroeck) and this was interesting because we were instructed to fly from Soesterberg to Rotterdam and then enter the airways system for Brussels. My log book tells me that we flew via a series of beacons known as Woensdrecht, Nicky and Bruno. Again we had a night stop-over and having arrived at Melsbroeck at 11 a.m., we had time to spend the rest of the day sight-seeing in Brussels, and who would miss such a chance to see the Grande Place and Manikin-Pis!

In August of 1963, Squadron Leader P. A. Lewis had taken over command of our squadron and a popular CO he turned out to be. I flew with him on a number of occasions, including Saturday, 11th April 1964, when we flew to White Waltham to pick up Air Vice-Marshal Holder and took him to Shawbury for an Air Display. One thing about being crew to high ranking officers, you do get a good seat at the show.

On the 30th April, Dick Colbourne and I were off on a real one-off trip to a place called Leck in Germany, which I had never heard of. We left Bovingdon at 9.15 a.m. and flew via Brookmans Park Beacon, Clacton, IJmuiden (an old friend!) Spijkerboor and Enkhuizen to Eelde airfield just outside the town of

Groningen in North Holland. After a refuelling stop, we were off again just before noon to Heligoland off the German coast and thence to Leck, quite near the Danish border. Fortunately, it was a fine day and I am not ashamed to say that the only way we found it, snuggled away in a thick growth of pine trees, was by pure map reading.

We had lunch there with the German Air Force, a somewhat weird feeling, and left just after 2 p.m. for a flight back over the north of Holland and then back into Germany to RAF Wildenrath, returning to Bovingdon the following day.

Another trip to Soesterberg came up early in May and in the meantime now conscious for the first time that my flying career had a finite limit — fifteen more months before retirement — I was volunteering for every trip in sight so that I was often airborne for more days in the month than I was on the ground. The monthly totals tell their own story, fifty-seven in April, twenty-four in two weeks in May (the other two weeks were leave) thirty-six in June, and so on.

A rather hairy incident occurred towards the end of May. On the 25th I took off with Flight Lieutenant Kelly, an Australian, and we had a party of Fighter Command officers aboard whom we duly delivered at Leuchars, just south of the Tay. We had to stay here overnight and fly them to Stornoway the following day. On the 26th we had left Leuchars at 10.35 a.m. and were cleared to Stornoway through the Glasgow Control Area. We were in thick cumolo-nimbus storm clouds over the west coast of Scotland when I received a tap on the shoulder, turned and saw one of our passengers pointing out of the starboard window. Glancing out of my window in the front I could see nothing special happening and wondered what was worrying our passengers. I walked back to the passenger window which looked out on to the wing and engine and then saw the reason for their unease, oil was pouring out of the engine at an enormous rate. I walked forward again to Jack Kelly who was wrestling the aircraft through the heavy up and down currents in the thundercloud and gave him the glad news. Minutes later the oil pressure gauge showed a dramatic drop and the engine temperature showed a sensational rise, the combination that says you have just lost one engine. We closed down the faulty engine and then contacted Glasgow Area Control for an alternate. Given that our destination was Stornoway, that we were high (about 8,000 feet) over the west coast of Scotland and that the Western Isles would lie dead ahead, we were told to go to Benbecula.

Descending gingerly through the thick muck, under constant check from my gee fixes, we came out the bottom at about 1,000 feet and made for a straight in approach at Benbecula. We arrived as an emergency landing about five minutes or so before BEA's Island Hopping Service. I have never seen a sinking ship deserted so quickly. As soon as we had rolled to a stop our passengers with their baggage were rushing down the steps and across the tarmac to the Handley Page Dart Herald of BEA whose next port of call was Stornaway. We were left with our Anson with a busted oil cooler and oiled up engine on an island used only by the personnel of the Rocket Range and a few sheep farmers.

The message was passed back to the squadron and a new radiator and a couple of mechanics were sent up the next day. We spent the afternoon and the morning of the following day sunbathing on a very large beach on the west coast of Benbecular in the surprisingly warm sunshine considering the latitude. The aircraft was not, after all, ready on the following day so we spent one more night at the Rocket Range Army camp, witnessed a not very successful rocket launch and finally left there at 2 p.m. on the 28th May, but not back to base. We were instructed to cut across Tiree and Islay and go to Aldergrove in Northern Island to pick up some passengers for London. We arrived back at Bovingdon just before 7 p.m., three and a half days after leaving on a two-day trip. On the 16th June, flying with F/Sgt. Keay, we created something of a squadron record by making eight landings in nine hours at five different airfields — always something different every day.

On the 29th June I took off with the Boss, Peter Lewis, to go to Bentwaters fighter station and pick up some Belgian Air Force officers who had been on a liaison trip with the RAF. We were to return them to their home base at Liege, the airfield of Bierset-Awans. It was a very enjoyable trip across the North Sea from the Suffolk coast to Flushing on a fine summer's day and thence by map reading at a comfortable height to Liege. On landing I had gone through the Terminal Hall to file my return flight plan at Control when a booming voice behind me said, "Good-morning, I did not expect to see the RAF here." Turning I confronted the beaming, bewhiskered face of the late Sir Gerald Nabarro. I gave him a brief outline of the reason for our presence and after having replied to his question as to whether I had met his cousin in the Service, he wished me a good journey whilst he departed for the Ardennes.

I navigated a 'mercy flight' as it was called, which involved flying to St. Athan to pick up a doctor, then to St. Mawgan to pick up the patient, and then to a hospital in Kent to which the nearest airfield was Manston. This massive zigzag across the south of England was accomplished in just under four and a half hours.

By now I was thoroughly accustomed to go anywhere at the drop of a hat and to carrying Air Force officers of the highest rank, gentlemen all. As I have said, the fascination was a new place every day, different flying conditions each time and a degree of difficulty of achievement from very high to a piece of cake. It was a perfect last posting in the Air Force.

On the 8th June I had achieved another first — my first touchdown on the Shetland Islands. We had come up to Kinloss the day before and set off from there at just after 9.30 a.m. Flying off the east coast of Ross and Cromarty in the direction of the Orkneys, the weather got worse and worse. Cloud increased and its base lowered, the wind increased and the sea began to show whitecaps and worse it got very misty. I left Wick, picked up the Orkneys slightly to port and headed for Fair Isle. As we passed over this island we were forced down to about 200 feet by the lowering cloud base and were in contact with a murky looking white flecked heaving sea. Visibility was down to about a mile and with sea all round us it became very necessary to spot the towering rock of Sumburgh Head before we ran into it. Two pairs of eyes, mine and the pilot's, Master Pilot Nash, anxiously scanned the mist ahead and eventually of course we saw this black smudge ahead. I suppose the Anson was travelling at about 135 m.p.h. which meant that we covered 3.960 yards every minute and with visibility so poor, we did in fact have just under thirty seconds to turn right and avoid the huge rock rearing out of the sea. It also meant that within one minute we were off the end of the airfield which was located just to the north of the Head. With weather closing in, neither of us wanted to hang around so the pilot made a 90° split-arse turn and sat the old Annie down on the runway, a sort of bent straight in approach. We found that Sumburgh airport, which of course was a civil airfield, had no accommodation for an overnight stay and we were eventually driven some miles down wind-swept roads across a rocky treeless landscape to a private house. Here we enjoyed a good evening meal and a night's sleep in a huge feather bed. The lady of the house sat at a knitting machine for most of the evening knitting Shetland sweaters and pullovers. It was amazing to see how quickly the garment formed under her flying fingers and at the same time we were snug and warm in front of a peat fire whilst the wind howled around the house which was a considerable distance from any neighbours. The weather did not clear sufficiently until just before 2 p.m. but the trip was a little easier in the misty conditions because you spotted the fairly flat side of the Orkneys before crossing the Pentland Skerries and so got correctly positioned for the run down towards Dornoch Firth and Kinloss.

In the November of 1964, I again crewed up with our CO Peter Lewis and this time got to Stornoway. We had a call to make at Glasgow Airport (Renfrew) on the way, but we eventually made the airfield outside the little fishing port just before 3 p.m. At this time of the year it was dark soon after landing so that little of the countryside could be seen as we motored into the town. We stayed the night in a hotel opposite the harbour and having missed lunch during the day, enjoyed our evening meal. After dinner we went into the lounge for a beer, a Scottish ale, and were sitting there in deep discussion with some of the locals when at 9 p.m. the lights went out. I thought perhaps there had been a power failure but it was not so, five minutes later the lights went on and the local police force were in the act of departing. Apparently licensing hours extended only till 9 p.m. and then the bar officially shut during the black-out only to open again at the end of it for the benefit of residents of the hotel. I must say there seemed to be an awful lot of 'residents' for such a relatively small hotel.

The following day, owing to the requirements of our passengers, we described a very errant pattern across the skies of Great Britain. We took off from Stornoway just after 10 a.m., and it had not been light all that long, and flew straight across to the west coast of Scotland at Cape Wrath. Peter elected to enjoy some low flying so we flew across the steely grey heaving water at about thirty feet above it. Approaching Cape Wrath I thought how well it deserved its name. Great rocks climbed up sharply out of the sea forming cliffs 100 feet high. The sky was dark, the clouds low and the sea seemed to heave towards and threaten the coast, altogether a most unfriendly looking area. We proceeded just off shore, still low, off the north coast of Scotland to Thurso and then rounded the corner between Scotland and the Orkneys and headed due south for Kinloss, landing in time for a quick early lunch just before noon. At ten minutes past one we set off again and once more Peter elected to follow coastlines so along the Moray Firth we went to Kinnairds Head before turning south past Aberdeen, Montrose and on to North Berwick. Here we struck inland across Northumberland Durham and Yorkshire and finally landed at our next port of call, Cosford. It took half an hour for a change of passengers and a quick refuel before leaving in the dark just after 4.30 p.m. We next cut across to Wyton on a south-easterly heading, spent ten minutes on the ground there and then hastened back to Bovingdon, landing just before 6 p.m. Altogether we had been away from Bovingdon for thirty-three hours, had spent just over ten of them flying and visited five places between Hertfordshire and the Hebrides.

On the 25th February 1965 I got airborne with Master Pilot Croft to perform a fairly unusual service. One of our aircraft had lost the use of its Pitot tube in some way and the pilot had no indication of his air speed. Landing in this condition was always pretty fraught so we took off and flew out to Leighton Buzzard where we intercepted the Anson returning to base. We formated on him passing speeds by R/T and eventually took him round the circuit at Bovingdon paralleling his circuit outside of him. We came down side by side, the crippled Anson following Mr Croft's landing profile exactly. At about twenty feet we pulled up our wheels and overshot, leaving him to land nicely straight ahead. I felt for that guy — I had tried to land without air speed in a Hampden a quarter of a century earlier, with dire results.

So eventually came Friday 13th August 1965, my last day in the Air Force. The Boss gave me a parting present in the form of a flight to Jersey. It was arranged that I would screen a recently joined navigator on the way down by showing him the ropes as far as airways procedures were concerned and thus leaving me free to have a couple in Pat Patterson's wine bar in St. Helier. Pat was a great friend to Bovingdon crews and we in turn were always delighted to see him and his air cadets from Jersey during the summer when they came for a fortnight's training and flew all over the place. It is strange that my personal odyssey in the air ended rather with a whimper than a bang. I nestled down into a passenger seat in the back of the Anson and slept the very warm August afternoon away!

EPILOGUE

I had acquired nearly 1,100 hours flying in the Anson during my two and three-quarter years at Bovingdon and this brought my total airborne time as RAF crew of one sort or another to a few hours short of 6,000. Over the years I had obtained immense skill as an air navigator but even more important, I had enjoyed it all. The callow London youth of 1939 was now forty-five years of age and had come to the end of the flying road but by gum, he had seen and experienced much along the way.

I could not complain, the choice to retire was mine. I had been offered, about three years previously, an extension of ten years with the prospect of limited promotion to possibly Wing Commander at best. I had rejected it because at the age of fifty-five I would have been unemployable whereas now at forty-five I had been offered a post by Midland Bank. Here I could have a further career over the next twenty years provided I worked at it and settled for far less adventure. None the less when I reported for work at the bank at 9 a.m. on 6th September 1965, as I walked between the tall buildings of wind-swept Old Broad Street in the City the ghostly question echoed in my head — 'Oh God, what have I done?' In the event it all turned out rather well, but that is another story.

Since September 1965 I have flown in civil aircraft on holidays and visits on about twenty-four occasions. Despite all the efforts of the cabin staff, I find travel this way to be incredibly boring. The windows really give very little view of the ground from the immense heights at which we now fly, so that even rough and ready navigation on the company's route map is not possible. I generally eat, read and sometimes, if lucky, sleep and the trip to Brisbane in Australia which I did in 1981 was the worst ever. Twenty-seven hours in the back of a large aeroplane with over three hundred other passengers with very little idea of where you were at any given time. Now if only I were up in the sharp end . . . . . oh well!

APPENDIX 'A'
Summary of Flying Hours 1939 to 1965

AIRCRAFT TYPE	Single Engined Day	Twin-Engined		Multi-Engined		Total
		Day	Night	Day	Night	
Miles Magister	45.00	-	-	-	-	45.00
Blackburn B2.	62.35	-	-	-	-	62.35
Airspeed Oxford	-	126.15	5.05	-	-	131.20
N. American Harvard	1.00	-	-	-	-	1.00
Avro Anson	-	1564.40	62.25	-	-	1627.05
Handley Page Hampden	-	85.50	30.15	-	-	116.05
Vickers Wellington	-	91.10	12.05	-	-	103.15
Avro Manchester	-	9.35	7.30	-	-	17.05
Avro Lancaster	-	-	-	260.15	313.10	573.25
Short Stirling	-	-	-	26.10	11.00	37.10
Douglas DC3 Dakota	-	846.20	99.25	-	-	945.45
Lockheed Liberator	-	-	-	19.10	-	19.10
Douglas DC4 Skymaster	-	-	-	7.50	-	7.50
D.H.Tiger Moth	1.45	-	-	-	-	1.45
Handley Page Hastings	-	-	-	12.55	-	12.55
D.H. Chipmunk	17.10	-	-	-	-	10.15
Vickers Varsity	-	43.00	5.10	-	-	48.10
Avro Lincoln	-	-	-	44.00	-	44.00
Eng.Elect.Canberra	-	1.50	-	-	-	1.50
Avro Shackleton	-	-	-	1673.50	450.40	2124.30
Fairey Gannett	-	.25	-	-	-	.25
B.P.Balliol	4.45	-	-	-	-	4.45
Gloster Meteor	-	1.55	-	-	-	1.55
Gloster Javelin	-	.35	-	-	-	.35
Vickers Valetta	-	3.35	3.40	-	-	7.15
Handley Page Halifax	-	-	-	2.15	-	2.15
D.H.Comet II	-	-	-	-	.25	.25
D.H.Devon	-	7.45	-	-	-	7.45
Percival Pembroke	-	5.55	.40	-	-	6.35
Grand Totals	132.15	2788.25	226.15	2046.25	775.15	5968.35

Air speeds of aircraft flown range from 80 m.p.h. to 180 K.ts and in odd cases to Mach 1.
Taking an overall average of 170 m.p.h., the resulting air mileage of 5,968.35 hours in the air is
1,014,645. I therefore reckoned I joined the One Million Air Miles Club around the tail end
of 1964.

APPENDIX 'B'
Record of Unit Movements 1939 to 1965

From	To	Unit	Location
15 April 1939	1 September 1939	15 E & RFTS	Redhill, Surrey/Store St. WC1
13 September 1939	5 November 1939	3 ITW	St. Leonards, Hastings, Sussex
6 November 1939	6 March 1940	4 EFTS	Brough, Nr. Hull, Yorkshire
7 March 1940	28 April 1940	14 FTS	Kinloss, Morayshire, Scotland
29 April 1940	11 July 1940	14 FTS	Cranfield, Nr. Bedford, Beds
13 July 1940	26 August 1940	School of Air Navigation	St. Athan, Glamorgan, Wales
27 August 1940	25 January 1941	14 OTU	Cottesmore, Nr. Oakham, Rutland
25 January 1941	1 August 1941	14 OTU	Woolfox Lodge, Rutland
1 August 1941	18 July 1942	14 OTU	Cottesmore, Rutland
19 July 1942	4 September 1942	57 Squadron	Methwold, Norfolk
4 September 1942	28 September 1942	57 Squadron	Scampton, Nr. Lincoln, Lincs
29 September 1942	29 September 1942	106 Con. Flight	Coningsby, Nr. Horncastle, Lincs
29 September 1942	13 October 1942	106 Con. Flight	Skellingthorpe, Nr. Lincoln, Lincs
13 October 1942	18 October 1942	106 Squadron	Syerston, Nr. Newark, Notts
19 October 1942	1 November 1942	1064 Con. Flight	Wigsley, Lincs
2 November 1942	10 July 1943	57 Squadron	Scampton, Lincs
11 July 1943	4 August 1943	SHQ	Scampton, Lincs
5 August 1943	16 October 1943	83 OTU	Peplow, Shropshire
16 October 1943	27 October 1943	Group School of Navigation	Tilstock, Shropshire
27 October 1943	22 January 1944	83 OTU	Peplow, Shropshire
23 January 1944	23 June 1944	11 (NZ) OTU	Westcott, Nr. Aylesbury, Bucks
24 June 1944	9 July 1944	1657 Con. Flight	Shepherds Grove, Suffolk
10 July 1944	18 July 1944	Special H2S Co'se	Stradishall, Suffolk
19 July 1944	25 July 1944	1657 Con. Flight	Shepherds Grove, Suffolk
2 August 1944	7 August 1944	3 Lancaster Finishing School	Feltwell, Norfolk
7 August 1944	11 August 1944	3 Lancaster Finishing School	Woolfox Lodge, Rutland
12 August 1944	20 December 1944	75 (NZ) Squadron	Mepal, Nr. Chatteris, Cambs
21 December 1944	1 February 1945	238 Squadron	Merryfield, Nr. Illminster, Somerset
2 February 1945	28 February 1945	1315 (T) Flight	Merryfield, Somerset
28 February 1945	5 April 1945	SHQ	Merryfield, Somerset
5 April 1945	9 April 1945	Att. 525 Squadron	Flight outbound to India
9 April 1945	17 April 1945	9 Transit Camp	Mauripur, Karachi, India
19 April 1945	28 April 1945	CCTFTU	Gujrat, North-west India
29 April 1945	1 May 1945	229 Group HQ	New Delhi, India
1 May 1945	9 September 1945	353 Squadron	Palam, New Delhi, India
12 September 1945	30 September 1945	SHQ	Cocos Islands, Indian Ocean
1 October 1945	31 May 1946	353 Squadron	Palam, New Delhi, India
2 June 1946	12 June 1946	3 PDC	Worli, Bombay, India
12 June 1946	28 June 1946	SS *Georgic*	Inbound Troopship to UK
29 June 1946	1 July 1946	101 PDC	Hednesford, Staffs
19 March 1948	1 May 1950	84 Reserve Centre	Fairoaks/Chessington, Surrey
1 May 1950	18 August 1950	84 Reserve Centre	Fairoaks/Hallam Street WC1
19 August 1950	1 September 1950	Attd. 511 Squadron	Lyneham, Wiltshire
1 September 1950	10 December 1950	84 Reserve Centre	Fairoaks/Hallam Street WC1
10 December 1950	11 December 1950	Induction Centre	Biggin Hill, Kent
11 December 1950	6 April 1951	3 Air Navigation School	Thorney Island, Sussex
9 April 1951	23 July 1951	Central Navigation School	Shawbury, Shropshire
24 July 1951	21 November 1951	Maritime Recce School	St. Mawgan, Newquay, Cornwall
24 November 1951	4 December 1951	Joint Anti-Submarine School (JASS)	HMS *Sea Eagle*, Londonderry NI
5 December 1951	6 December 1951	HMS *Loch Farda*	At sea
10 December 1951	17 March 1952	Maritime Recce School	St. Mawgan, Cornwall
18 March 1952	24 April 1952	Intelligence Course	Air Ministry, London

25 April 1952	18 July 1952	Maritime Recce School	St. Mawgan, Cornwall
18 July 1952	19 July 1952	HMS *Osprey*	Portland, Dorset
19 July 1952	19 July 1952	HMS *Flint Castle*	At sea
20 July 1952	4 June 1953	Maritime Recce School	St. Mawgan, Cornwall
5 June 1953	5 July 1953	Medical Rehab Unit	Headley Court, Surrey
4 August 1953	10 October 1953	Coastal Command HQ	Northwood, Middlesex
12 October 1953	3 March 1955	Headquarters 1 Group	Bawtry Hall, Yorkshire
4 March 1955	17 March 1955	USAFE Survival Course	Bad Tolz, Bavaria, Germany
18 March 1955	31 October 1955	Headquarters 1 Group	Bawtry Hall, Yorkshire
1 November 1955	23 December 1955	236 OCU	Kinloss, Morayshire, Scotland
9 January 1956	19 July 1956	42 Squadron	St. Eval, Cornwall
20 July 1956	9 August 1956	42 Squadron	Luqa, Malta GC
9 August 1956	16 January 1957	42 Squadron	St. Eval, Cornwall
17 January 1957	20 January 1957	42 Squadron	In transit Europe/Africa/Asia
20 January 1957	12 March 1957	42 Squadron	Khormaksar, Aden Protectorate
14 March 1957	22 April 1957	42 Squadron	St. Eval, Cornwall
24 April 1957	21 June 1957	Fighter Controller Course	Middle Wallop, Hampshire
22 June 1957	21 June 1958	271 GSU	Neatishead, Norfolk
22 June 1958	4 July 1958	Attd 220 Squadron	St. Mawgan, Cornwall
5 July 1958	29 April 1959	271 GSU	Neatishead, Norfolk
29 April 1959	1 May 1959	RRE	Malvern, Worcestershire
1 May 1959	27 September 1959	271 GSU	Neatishead, Norfolk
28 September 1959	10 October 1959	Attd 42 Squadron	St. Mawgan, Cornwall
11 October 1959	2 December 1959	72 Navigation Refresher Co	Topcliffe, North Yorkshire
3 December 1959	4 April 1960	37 MOTU	Kinloss, Morayshire, Scotland
5 April 1960	16 September 1960	42 Squadron	St. Mawgan, Cornwall
16 September 1960	30 September 1960	42 Squadron	Aldergrove, Belfast, NI
30 September 1960	6 January 1961	42 Squadron	St. Mawgan, Cornwall
6 January 1961	27 January 1961	42 Squadron	JASS. Londonderry NI
27 January 1961	14 September 1961	42 Squadron	St. Mawgan, Cornwall
14 September 1961	16 September 1961	42 Squadron	In transit Atlantic Ocean
16 September 1961	4 October 1961	42 Squadron	Norfolk/Virginia, Colombus/Ohio
4 October 1961	6 October 1961	42 Squadron	In transit, Atlantic Ocean
6 October 1961	31 October 1961	42 Squadron	St. Mawgan, Cornwall
31 October 1961	3 November 1961	42 Squadron	In transit, Atlantic/Carribbean
3 November 1961	2 December 1961	42 Squadron	Kingston, Jamaica, West Indies
2 December 1961	5 December 1961	42 Squadron	In transit, Carribbean/Atlantic
5 December 1961	9 August 1962	42 Squadron	St. Mawgan, Cornwall
22 January 1962	23 February 1962	JASS	Londonderry, Northern Ireland
9 August 1962	17 August 1962	42 Squadron	North Front, Gibraltar
17 August 1962	2 November 1962	42 Squadron	St. Mawgan, Cornwall
3 November 1962	1 July 1963	Coastal Command Flight	Bovingdon, Hertfordshire
1 July 1963	24 September 1964	Southern Command Sqn.	Bovingdon, Hertfordshire
24 September 1964	2 October 1964	Southern Command Sqn.	St. Mawgan, Cornwall
2 October 1964	13 August 1965	Southern Command Sqn.	Bovingdon, Hertfordshire

APPENDIX 'C'
Airfields at which Landed 1939-1965

1 — UNITED KINGDOM

Bedfordshire	Cranfield, Henlow, Luton
Berkshire	Aldermaston, White Waltham, Woodley (Reading)
Buckinghamshire	Booker, Westcott
Cambridgeshire	Cambridge (Marshall's), Mepal, Oakington, Upwood, Waterbeach
Cheshire	Hawarden, Sealand
Cornwall	Culdrose, St. Eval, St. Mawgan
Derbyshire	Derby (Burnaston)
Devon	Chivenor, Exeter, Roborough (Plymouth)
Essex	Bradwell Bay, North Weald, Stansted
Gloucestershire	Aston Down, Bristol (Filton), Hullavington, Kemble, Little Rissington, South Cerney, Staverton
Hampshire	Andover, Hamble, Hurn, Lee-on-Solent, Middle Wallop, Odiham, Sandown (I.o.W) Thorney Island
Hertfordshire	Bassingbourne, Bovingdon, Hatfield
Huntingdonshire	Alconbury, Wyton
Isle of Man	Jurby, Ronaldsway
Kent	Biggin Hill, Lympne, Manston, West Malling
Lancashire	Blackpool (Squire's Gate), Burtonwood, Liverpool (Speke), Manchester (Ringway), Samlesbury, Warton, Woodford, Woodvale
Leicestershire	Bramcote, Braunston, Husbands Bosworth, Mkt. Harborough
Lincolnshire	Binbrook, Coningsby, Cranwell, Fulbeck, Grantham, Hemswell, Manby, Scampton, Skellingthorpe, Strubby, Swinderby, Waddington, Wigsley
Middlesex	Heston, Northolt
Norfolk	Coltishall, Feltwell, Marham, Methwold, Sculthorpe, Swanton Morley, Watton, West Raynham, Wratting Common
Northamptonshire	Chelveston, Peterborough, Wittering
Northumberland	Acklington, Ouston
Nottinghamshire	Hucknall, Langar, Newton, Syerston
Oxfordshire	Abingdon, Benson, Bicester, Upper Heyford
Rutland	Cottesmore, North Luffenham, North Witham, Saltby, Woolfox Lodge
Shropshire	Peplow (Child's Ercall), Prees Heath, Shawbury, Ternhill, Tilstock
Somerset	Colerne, Merryfield, Weston-super-Mare
Staffordshire	Stoke (Meir)
Suffolk	Bentwaters, Honington, Mildenhall, Shepherds Grove, Stradishall, Wattisham
Surrey	Blackbushe, Fairoaks, Gatwick, Kenley, Redhill, Forced Landing at Sandown Park Racecourse
Sussex	Shoreham, Tangmere
Teeside	Middleton St. George
Warwickshire	Cosford, Gaydon, Stratford-upon-Avon
Wiltshire	Boscombe Down, Lyneham, Old Sarum, Upavon, Wroughton
Worcestershire	Pershore

Yorkshire	Brough, Church Fenton, Dishforth, Finningley, Leconfield, Leeming, Lindholme, Linton-upon-Ouse, Skipton-on-Swale, Topcliffe
Channel Islands	Guernsey (St. Peter Port), Jersey (St. Helier)
Northern Ireland	Aldergrove, Ballykelly, Bishop's Court
Scotland	Abbotsinch (Renfrewshire), Aberdeen (Dyce), Benbecula (Western Isles), Edinburgh (Turnhouse), Evanton (Ross & Cromarty), Glasgow (Renfrew), Kinloss (Morayshire), Leuchars (Fife), Machrihanish (Argyllshire), Prestwick (Ayrshire), Stornaway (Western Isles), Sumburgh (Shetland Isles), West Freugh (Wigtownshire)
Wales	Aberporth, Brawdy, Pembrey, St. Athan, Swansea (Fairwood Common), Valley (Anglesey)

2 — EUROPE
Belgium	Brussels (Melsbroeck), Liege (Bierset-Awans)
Cyprus	Nicosia Airport
France	Brest (Guipavas), Cambrai (Neirgnies), Marseilles (Istres), Melun (Villaroche), Orange (Caritat), Paris (Coulommiers)
Germany	Bruggen, Leck, Wildenrath
Gibraltar	North Front
Holland	Groningen (Eelde), Soersterberg
Italy	Sardinia, Cagliari (Elmas)
Malta	Luqa, Taqali
Norway	Andlesnes (Andoya)
Portugal	Lisbon (Montijo)

3 — THE AMERICAS
Azores	Lajes, Santa Maria
Bermuda	Kindley Field
British Honduras	Belize (Stanley)
Jamaica	Kingston (Palisadoes)
United States	Norfolk (Virginia), Port Colombus (Ohio)

4 — THE MIDDLE EAST
Aden Protectorate	Khormaksar
Bahrain Island	Bahrain
Egypt	Cairo West
Iraq	Habbaniyah
Libya	Benina, El Adem, Tripoli (Castel Benito or Idris)

5 — THE FAR EAST
Ceylon	Colombo (Ratmalana), Kankesanturai, Minnerya, Negombo
Cocos Islands	West Island
India	Agra, Allahabad (Bamrauli), Bangalore (Yelahanka), Baroda, Bikaner (Nal), Bilaspur, Bombay (Santa Cruz), Calcutta (Dum Dum), Cawnpore (Chakeri), Cuttack, Delhi (Palam), Gujrat, Gurgaon, Hyderabad (Hakimpet), Jodhpur, Karachi (Mauripur), Lahore, Madras (St. Thomas's Mount), Maharajhpur, Nagpur, Raipur, Rawalpindi (Chaklala), Risalpur, Sulur, Trichinopoly, Vishakhapatnam

APPENDIX 'D'
WIND FINDING METHODS

1 — BY AIR PLOT

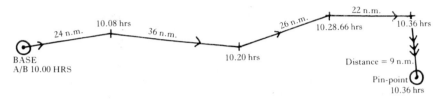

Scale = 1/8 inch to 2 miles. Speed (Airspeed) 180 knots. Elapsed time to pin-point 36 minutes. Wind found blows from southerly direction (175°) speed 9 n.m. in 36 minutes = 15 Knots.

2 — BY TRACK & GROUND SPEED

Scale still 1/8 inch to 2 miles. Airspeed say, 170 knots. Time between pin-points 1 & 2 is 20 minutes elapsed, therefore ground speed is 3 x distance of 64 n.miles between the points which is 192 knots. Drift is 3 degrees to port. On the Course Setting Calculator, the results would be set out as below;

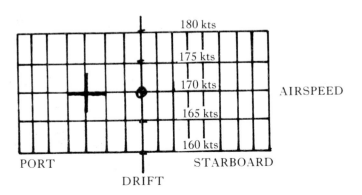

When the CSC is rotated so that the cross is immediately below the datum circle, the wind direction can be read off the top arrow on the CSC and the difference in nautical miles between the datum and the cross, read off against the speed lines, gives you the wind strength. The answer in this case is likely to be of the order of 175° at 12 knots.

3 — BY THREE DRIFT METHOD

a. Course steered is say, 090 degrees, Note drift of say 2 degrees port.
b. Course altered to 150 degrees, drift noted of 1 degree port.
c. Course altered to 030 degrees, drift noted of 3 degrees to starboard.
d. Each heading should be held for exactly two or three minutes, the same amount of time in all cases, and then the original course of 090 degrees can be resumed with no loss of accuracy in the main course heading required, 090, but simply a loss of two or three minutes in time on it as the case may be.
e. The resultant drifts are applied to the CSC and where the drifts intersect, a cross is made and the measurement made as in 2 above of the wind.

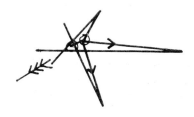